PETRA

ART, HISTORY AND ITINERARIES IN THE NABATEAN CAPITAL

To the Jordan People

PETRA
JORDAN'S EXTRAORDINARY ANCIENT CITY

Texts by
Fabio Bourbon

Translation
Barbara Fisher

Graphic Design
Paola Piacco
Clara Zanotti

Maps and drawings
Monica Falcone Bourbon
Fabio Bourbon

JEBEL AL DEIR

34   33

WADI SIYAGH

31

UMM EL BIYARA

WADI THUGHRA

N

CONTENTS

The publishers wish to thank:
Royal Jordanian,
Jordan Tourism Board of Amman,
Intercontinental Hotel of Amman, and
Petra Forum Rest House, for their invaluable
assistance with the preparation of this book.

© 1999 White Star S.r.l.
Via Candido Sassone, 22-24
13100 Vercelli, Italy.

Distributed in Jordan by
REDWAN BOOKSHOP
P.O. Box 61 - Aqaba - Jordan
Tel. 03/2013704 - Fax 03/2015588

ISBN 88-8095-341-9

Printed
by Grafedit, Italy

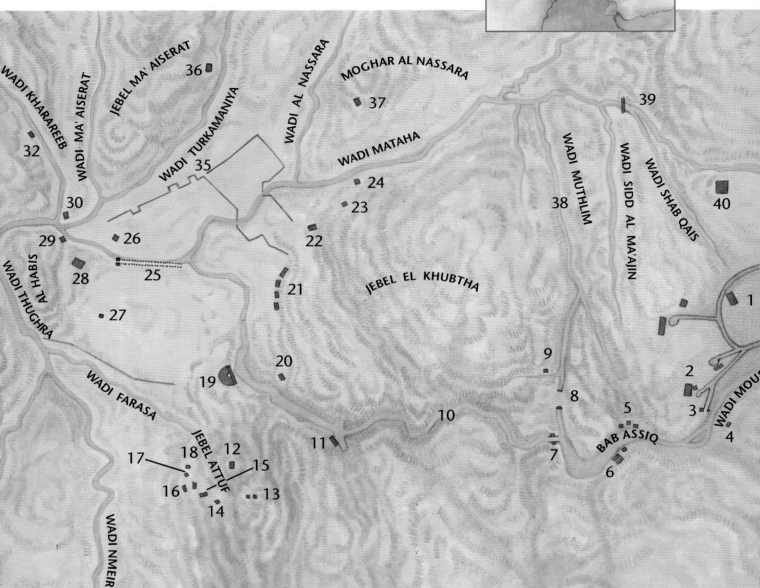

1 The Bab el Siq Triclinium and the Obelisk Tomb above it are two prime examples of Nabatean monumental rock architecture.

2-3 In this stunning photograph, the top of the Deir – or Monastery – emerges like part of a surreal stage set from behind the rocky ridges that surround Petra.

In the presence of such a spectacle it is easy to understand why, even in antiquity, the Rock City enjoyed an extraordinary reputation.

4 Mountains of multicolored sandstone, the most typical landscape in Petra and the surrounding region, were fashioned by the erosive action of the elements.

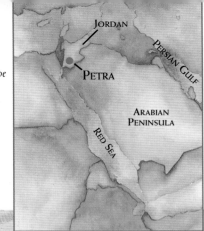

JORDAN

PETRA

PERSIAN GULF

ARABIAN PENINSULA

RED SEA

WADI KHARAREEB

JEBEL MA' AISERAT

WADI MA' AISERAT

WADI TURKAMANIYA

WADI AL NASSARA

MOGHAR AL NASSARA

WADI MATAHA

WADI MUTHLIM

WADI SIDD AL MA'AJIN

WADI SHAB QAIS

WADI HABIS

WADI THUGHRA

WADI FARASA

JEBEL EL KHUBTHA

JEBEL ATTUF

BAB ASSIQ

WADI MOUS

WADI NMEIR

LEGEND

1	Wadi Mousa	9	Eagle Monument	17	Renaissance Tomb
2	Petra Forum Rest House	10	Siq	18	Broken Pediment Tomb
3	Entrance Gate	11	Khasneh	19	Theatre
4	Brooke Hospital	12	High Place of Sacrifice	20	Tomb of Uneishu
5	Djin Blocks	13	Obelisks	21	Royal Tombs
6	Obelisk Tomb and Bab el SiqTriclinium	14	Lion Monument	22	Tomb of Sextius Florentinus
7	Triumphal Arch	15	Garden Tomb	23	Carmine Façade
8	Nabatean Tunnel	16	Roman Soldier Tomb and Triclinium	24	House of Dorotheus
				25	Colonnade Street

26	Temple of the Winged Lions	36	Turkamaniya Tomb
27	Pharaoh Column	37	Armor Tomb
28	Kasr el Bint	38	Little Siq
29	Old Museum	39	Aqueduct
30	New Museum	40	Crusader Castle of al Wu'aira
31	Quarry		
32	Lion Triclinium		
33	El Deir		
34	Monument 468		
35	City walls		

INTRODUCTION

The ruins of Petra constitute one of the most extraordinary and fascinating monumental complexes of the ancient world for the outstanding quality of the architecture and for the city's remarkable position among rugged hills and narrow gorges. Further charm is added by the color of the rock the buildings were built into. Petra is without doubt one of the marvels of the world, a place that will captivate even the most hardened traveller, one of those places that you never forget, not even years later. How strange that, in the era of the "global village", with distances cancelled by the Internet, mass media and millions of pictures of the farthest corners of the globe, there is still something that can astound technological man. Petra does this and without difficulty. Photographic reports on this

sensational part of Jordan appear regularly in magazines and specialist journals, dozens of documentaries have described its splendor, and even those least susceptible to the charms of archaeology have seen it thanks to film director Steven Spielberg, as some of the most spectacular scenes in the film "Indiana Jones and the Last Crusade" were set in Petra.

So, Petra ought to surprise no one, least of all the well-prepared tourist, who reads every available guidebook before setting off and thinks he knows all there is to know. But, once he or she is actually *there*, even the hardest materialist will be overwhelmed by emotion.

What really takes everyone by surprise is its *dimension*, not merely in terms of surface area occupied by the archaeological site. Petra is, indeed, far larger than can be imagined, but this is not the point. The rock structures are also colossal and, at the end of the day, visitors return to their hotels with stiff necks caused by looking up all the time; but not even this justifies the sense of wonder produced by the Rose-red City.

It is the *dimension* entered as soon as you pass through the gate, a perception of space and time that is different from what you are accustomed to. As well as being an actual location, Petra is a place of the mind. In Petra proportions seem inexplicably different, time flows at a different pace, the very air seems to take on a new consistency. Nothing is more agonizingly beautiful than that moment, at dusk, when the sunbeams flood the great carved rock façades with light and the rock itself creates a kaleidoscope of colors unequalled anywhere on the multicolored surface of the Earth.

In Petra, a sense of the fantastic is normal.

In Petra the word *impossible* has no meaning.

6 left The photograph shows the huge tholos of the Deir, one of the most stunning and best-preserved monuments in Petra.

6 top right Although the combined action of wind and water have undermined their original splendour, Petra's monuments preserve unequalled majesty. Here you can see a detail of the Palace Tomb.

6 bottom right The perfect symbiosis between the glowing colors of the stone and the structural fantasy of its ancient creators makes Petra a unique archaeological site.

7 The contrast between the delightfully shady Siq and the façade of the Khasneh, bathed in warm, golden light, is perhaps what most thrills visitors to the ancient Nabatean city.

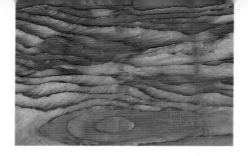

In Petra, Mother Nature has achieved one of its most original creations: improbable geometry, unbelievable colors, contrasts that would be unthinkable elsewhere.

However, all this fails to explain the magic of Petra, for Petra is one of the few places in the world where the work of man has completed the work of creation with complete harmony and grace. The Nabateans, who were responsible for this extraordinary miracle, did not violate nature, they conformed to it, adapting and indulging it with the utmost elegance. This is what makes Petra unique.

A Gothic cathedral, a mosque, a Hindu temple are constructions of man that often assert, even more than the glory of God, the conceit and power of their builders. They are *made* of stone taken *from* the ground, and rise *above* its surface, interfering with the earth's natural balance. Men, by their very nature, tend to alter the world around them. However, in Petra, all that has been built is one with, and inseparable from, the rock itself.

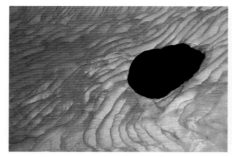

They built huge monuments to celebrate their civilization, but they did so with unequalled discretion and sensitivity. One could argue that the Nabateans also wanted to leave a proud mark of their passage on this planet, but there is a huge difference between what they did and what has been and still is the norm elsewhere. Although the centuries that will pass

The manmade structures extend and complete the natural formations, making sense of the lines of force that run beneath the crazily wrinkled surface of the stone and turn it into pure art. Two thousand years before Alvar Aalto, Frank Lloyd Wright and the appearance of the very concept of "organic architecture," the Nabateans succeeded in a matchless undertaking: They managed to create a total and successful balance between the needs of civilized life and the laws of nature.

before erosion eliminates all traces of Petra, may seem like an eternity, they are a mere blip in the flow of geological time.

When the concerted action of wind, water and sun has completed its task, not a trace of Petra will remain: not a ruin, not a carved block, the cavities will have turned into caves or been reduced to fissures, gorges will become openings indistinguishable from the surrounding delirium of natural form. The earth's surface will regain its pure

and primitive appearance. Even in death – in its long, sweet, inevitable death – Petra is an organic part of the mountains that surround it and of which it is made. This is what makes it so fascinating and this is why we ask anyone wishing to visit it to do so with respect. Nothing is more irritating or annoying than to hear the shouts and yells of insensitive people who come here and act as if at the stadium or on the streets of a modern metropolis.

8 and 9 Inside, the tombs of Petra usually consist of large totally unadorned rooms, with pits or wall niches of varying sizes, which contained the dead. Whether or not they were originally plastered and decorated remains open to debate; some underground rooms still frescoed in Wadi Siyagh and el Barid would suggest this, but many believe that the Nabatean builders usually preferred to exploit the natural veining of the sandstone, to surprising effect. Certainly, the color combinations of the rocks are of matchless beauty.

Leave no trace of your passage, leave no litter or cans and make no more noise than is necessary. Respect the mysterious sacredness of this place and do so in tribute to those who devotedly and lovingly keep vigil over this masterpiece. In return, Petra will give you its charm. Take your time, look for a quiet spot and listen to the poetry of silence, look around, observe the changing colors, corners created by shadows on rock walls and on sculpted stone façades. Take a deep breath of the dry air, feel intoxicated by such abounding splendor, fill your eyes with beauty, and be moved. If you do not believe in magic then you will have to change your mind. When you go home, a treasure will be stored deep down in your heart.

HISTORY

Frontiers of the Nabatean kingdom at the time of its greatest expansion.

Travelling from Amman along the modern but extremely monotonous Desert Road, or along the older and more spectacular King's Road, after a wide bend you will come across the first powerful vista of the stunning mountains that lovingly embrace and conceal the ancient Nabatean capital. You are at a height of approximately 3,280 feet, on the edge of a great depression, the lowest point of which (at approximately 1,312 feet below sea level is the lowest point on earth) is occupied by

that geological oddity known as the Dead Sea. On the horizon, hidden from view by a striking number of towers fashioned by the wind, opens the great fault called Wadi Arabah, along which the Jordan River used to flow into the Gulf of Aqaba. Extending as far as the eye can see is a phantasmagoric succession of fine sandstone rocks worn smooth by erosion. Some are reddish and pockmarked with thousands of irregular holes; others, round, polished and white, look like huge, surreal skulls. Opening between one mountain and the other are deep drops steeped in shadow, their darkness a striking contrast to the blinding sunlight reflecting off the limestone peaks. The spectacle is breathtaking.

Before us lies the spacious valley in which stands the modern village of Wadi Mousa, dotted with comfortable hotels. Nothing would suggest that hidden a few miles away is the hollow in which the legendary Petra once flourished. Yet, it was this very "invisibility" – combined with the hostile and barren region around it – that for centuries guaranteed the safety and prosperity of the Rose-red City.

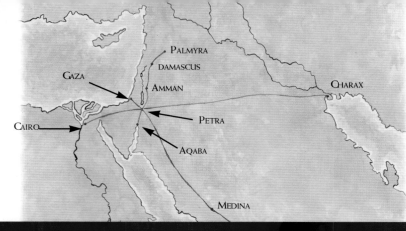

10 top The map shows the position of Petra and the other main settlements in the region.

10 bottom The Nabatean culture was initially aniconical: Sculptures, reliefs and other representations are therefore expressions of an imported art.

11 top As shown on this map, Petra was situated in a highly strategic position; quick connections via the Red Sea allowed profitable communications with Arabia and Mesopotamia, while the route through the Negev Desert to Gaza guaranteed an outlet on the Mediterranean and access to the ports of Syria.

10-11 Petra valley was permanently inhabited from approximately 1500 BC until the Arab conquest, and countless traces of this long occupation remain. This quern for grinding corn is just one example.

11 bottom The numerous rock inscriptions found in and around Petra prove that the language spoken by the Nabateans was of Aramaic origin.

Situated in southern Jordan, approximately 190 miles south of Amman, Petra is repeatedly mentioned in the Bible with the name of "Sela" (rock in Hebrew), whereas the Arabs called it Wadi Mousa, or "Valley of Moses;" the oldest local name for the city is still unknown. Petra is simply the Greek translation of the Biblical toponym. Although their name will always be bound to that of Petra, the Nabateans were not the first inhabitants of this place. During the Paleolithic period, the entire region was inhabited by groups of hunters and food gatherers who roamed endlessly in search of game and edible plants. Finds made by archaeologists prove that from 9000 BC on, during the Neolithic period, small communities given over to farming and the rearing of domestic animals settled here. A settlement that can be dated to this period in history has been found at el Beidha, situated slightly north of Petra.

During the Aeneolithic period and the subsequent Bronze Age (between 4000 and 2500 BC) in the region there were villages that lived off farming – therefore inhabited by stable populations – and camps of nomads, essentially devoted to sheep-rearing and thus ever on the move because of the constant need to find new land for grazing.

Later, at an as yet undetermined time, the villages of southern Jordan were abandoned for reasons linked perhaps with a worsening climate, and only the settlements of nomad tents survived and are known to have been present until the seventh century BC.

At a time fixed today at around 1500 BC – about the middle of the Bronze Age – the Bible states that the Orite people settled in the valley of Petra, inhabiting the numerous caves set in the sides of the mountains.

The Orites were subsequently

driven away by the Edomites, a people of Semitic stock, who came to occupy the lands between the Gulf of Aqaba and the Dead Sea around the 13th century BC. The Edomites claimed to be direct descendants of Esau, thus belonging to the same dynastic line as Moses. Despite this, when Moses, with the people of Israel, reached the borders of the kingdom of Edom, he was denied permission to cross the territory to reach the Promised Land. This story, however, was recorded in the Old Testament by the descendants of Moses and consequently, subsequent judgements regarding the Edomites (all negative) must be considered biased and not very reliable. Although the Bible is of questionable historic value, the relationships between the Israelites and Edomites are known to have been very bad for several centuries. After the fall of Jerusalem at the hands of the Babylonians in 587 BC, the inhabitants of Edom repeatedly attacked the kingdom of Judah. It must, however, be stressed that the Edomites themselves were under increasing pressure from a nomadic

people of Aramaic stock from the Arabian Peninsula who would soon oust them completely.

The Nabateans are first mentioned (with certainty as older evidence is considered controversial) in a historic document dating from the fourth century BC, although their arrival in the area had clearly started much earlier as they were driven north by Babylonian expansionism. Described as inhabitants of the desert, given over to sheep-rearing and ignorant of farming, "they built no houses nor drank any wine." Harsh, determined and resourceful, they managed to survive in the hostile climate of the Arabian desert thanks to the custom of digging large cisterns in the solid rock; the rare rainwater was channelled into the cisterns and conserved during the driest months. Their prosperity derived from

control of the caravan routes between Arabia and the Mediterranean, and those between Egypt and Mesopotamia and this control was maintained after they had settled in Petra.

In the early centuries of the Nabatean settlement, at least, Petra was very different from the splendid metropolis it was later to become; it consisted basically of a huge, disorganized camp of tents similar to those of present-day Bedouin families. Part of the population (still semi-nomadic) had to live in the numerous natural caves that opened in the uneven sides of the surrounding hills. The mountain of Umm al Biyara – called Petra, *the rock*, by the Greeks and which later gave the city its name – served as a stronghold in the event of enemy attack: Not surprisingly, numerous remains and some huge cisterns have been found on the top of it. Thanks to the strategic position in which the settlement had developed, the Nabateans made a living supplying water and food to the caravans, imposing a sort of levy and trading the most remunerative commodities themselves. Around the mid-fourth century BC, the Nabateans were becoming increasingly rich from the trade of spices, silver, frankincense and myrrh. Perched on the top of Umm al Biyara, in 321 BC, they managed to drive back an attack mounted by Antigonus I Monophtalmus (one of Alexander the Great's generals, who became king of a Hellenistic state), sanctioning their independence. Over the following 150 years, Petra succeeded in cheating the expansionist aims of Ptolemaic Egypt and Seleucid Syria, continuing to prosper. Because of the lack of written documents, this period remains rather obscure, although it is

clear that the Nabateans were growing increasingly sedentary. Little by little, tents were replaced with houses, built along the bed of the Wadi Mousa and the camp was turned into a proper town.

The decline of the Hellenistic kingdoms coincided with the rise of Nabatean power, now backed by a solid monarchy. The first sovereign known by name was Aretas and he is mentioned in the second book of the Maccabees in connection with an episode that occurred around 168 BC. His successors included Aretas II (115-96 BC) and Obodas I (96-86 BC) who continued his expansionistic policy at the expense, in particular, of the Seleucid kingdom. In 85 BC, Aretas III (86-62 BC) even occupied Damascus. By the first century BC the Nabatean trade network had grown to include a number of caravan stations spread over a vast

12 left The Nabateans lacked a figurative tradition of their own, so sculptures found in Petra, such as this eagle, were either imported from the Greek-Roman world or produced by local workshops but based on western iconography.

12 top This panel adorned with a male head (perhaps the god Ares) was found with others near the monumental three-vault gate; all depict deities of the Greek-Roman pantheon.

12-13 Some Latin inscriptions have been found in Petra. Having entered the sphere of Roman influence as early as the first century BC, the Nabatean kingdom was subjugated by Trajan in 106, apparently without bloodshed.

13 right This splendid relief, portraying a young woman with a veiled head and wearing a diadem (almost certainly the goddess Aphrodite) betrays the influence exercised by Hellenism on local artists.

area, from Hegra (today Madain Saleh, in Saudi Arabia) to the towns of Negev, Oboda, Mampsis and Sobata (today's Advat, Mamshit and Shivta, in Israel). Actually, the extensive area that constituted the Nabatean kingdom had no precise boundaries, as these depended mainly on the military supremacy that each sovereign managed to assert over bordering states. In general terms, it stretched from the south of modern Syria to the Gulf of Aqaba, including the Negev, Sinai, Trans-Jordan and part of Arabia, as far as Hegra. Communities of Nabatean merchants settled in major ports of the East (Sidon) and West (Pozzuoli, near Naples), and in Rome.

Although difficult, relations with the Jewish world were essentially marked by policies of non-aggression; during the same period, the

Nabateans managed for a long time to maintain total independence from the growing Roman power.

Petra – which the Nabateans called Reqem – had in the meanwhile expanded into the vast hollow between the mountains of Umm el Biyara and Jebel el Khubtha, where the Wadi Mousa, Wadi Mataha and Wadi Turkamaniya flow into a single seasonal river, Wadi Siyagh. The decision to make it the capital (perhaps made after the first friction with Rome) was motivated by safety requirements, as it was an ideal place of refuge hidden in the mountains with just a few easily controlled entrance routes.

Ongoing relations with the leading trading groups and increasing prosperity made it extremely cosmopolitan, which is particularly evident in the numerous monuments that the Nabatean kings had hewn into the rock walls around the city. Petra was enriched, in just a few decades, by artistic contributions from Syria, Egypt and the Hellenistic world and synthesized very different architectural and decorative canons into

14-15 Urban Petra consisted of raised constructions, but because of the earthquakes little more than the rock structures have survived.

14 bottom The Nabateans surrounded Petra with open-air sanctuaries where they venerated their gods. This is a detail of such a sanctuary on Jebel Attuf.

a unique formal language.

At the height of its splendor, the city must have numbered between 30 and 40 thousand inhabitants, most of them occupied in trade. For more than 200 years from the first century BC on, the public buildings became increasingly imposing in appearance. Great temples, markets and palaces were built along the city's main street, running from east to west. Of these, only Kasr el Bint has survived, and this tetrastyle temple is the only fairly well-preserved raised structure remaining in the whole of Petra. The reign of Aretas IV (8 BC - 40 AD) in particular constituted a golden era for monumental building; the construction of the so-called Great Temple and numerous other rearrangements of the urban fabric were designed to make Petra a worthy capital for the wealthy and famous Nabatean people.

Such prosperity, however, concealed a fundamental military weakness. The Roman civil wars had already posed a considerable danger to the stability of Petra. Aretas II, who had in 65 BC laid siege to Jerusalem, was forced to retreat before the legions of Pompey. Even worse, one of the Roman general's lieutenants then besieged Petra, although without managing to take it. In order to maintain their independence, the Nabateans agreed to pay tributes to Rome, thus becoming a client state.

The tax situation worsened considerably after Malchus I (59-30 BC) allied with the Parthians in their disastrous campaign against the Romans. In subsequent years it was again the Romans who further debilitated Nabatean power by tracing new trade routes through Arabia and relegating Petra to an ever-more-marginal position.

Therefore, the peaceful and prosperous reign of Aretas IV represented the culmination and, at the same time, the "swan song" of the Nabatean civilization. The last Nabatean king, Rabbel II (70-106 AD), perhaps having sensed what was about to happen, decided to transfer the capital to the north, to Bozrah. Despite the kingdom's continuing prosperity, the picture was changing rapidly. The Roman troops proceeded on their expansionist marches to conquer Syria, Judea and Egypt, tightening their grip on Petra. The end came suddenly and probably with no great shedding of blood. In 106 AD, the Emperor Trajan ordered his troops into the city and Petra was annexed to the province of Arabia.

Roman occupation was accomplished by sending an imperial legate to the city, which slowed down Petra's evolution, although without halting it entirely. Building continued, but as other caravan centers such as Jerash and Palmyra flourished its importance gradually diminished. For some centuries the Rock City resolutely lived on as a fairly active trading center; after the re-organization of the empire decided in 293 by Diocletian, it became the capital of the province of Palaestina Taertia. With the penetration of Christianity it rose to the status of an episcopal see and in the Byzantine period still enjoyed a certain prosperity; at the same time, numerous

15 top This altar, standing approximately six and a half feet high, is sculpted in the rock of Jebel al Deir. High places were particularly sacred to the Nabateans, whose most important deities were Dusares and Al Uzza.

Nabatean rock structures were turned into Christian churches. After the 551 earthquake and the Arab conquest of the region, which took place in 663, Petra declined completely, although for a brief period in the 12th century it was fortified and defended by the crusaders, who called it Li Vaux Moise, the "Valley of Moses."

15 center and bottom Originally nomads, the Nabateans probably first started work on the rock structures in the third century BC, although the lack of written documents makes this date uncertain. Petra really started to develop as a city in the middle of the first century BC.

CHRONOLOGY OF NABATEAN KINGS
Aretas I (about 168 BC)
Aretas II (115-96 BC)
Obodas I (96-86 BC)
Rabbel I (about 85 BC)
Aretas III (86-62 BC)
Obodas II (62-59 BC)
Malchus I (59-30 BC)
Obodas III (30-8 BC)
Aretas IV (8 B.C.-40 AD)
Malchus II (40-70 AD)
Rabbel II (70-106 AD)

PETRA OF THE NABATEANS

The site of the ancient Nabatean capital is shaped like an amphitheater enclosed within high rock faces; it measures approximately one mile across from east to west and just over a mile from north to south. The bed of an often-dry river, Wadi Mousa, crosses this wide valley and, with its tributaries, circumscribes two low rocky plateaus on which used to lie the city proper, later swept away by earthquakes and disastrous floods. The Nabateans are known to have settled here because of the location's easily defended position. All the ancient writers from Diodorus Siculus to Strabo and Pliny the Elder agree on this point. Initially Petra must have looked like a vast camp of tents, the inhabitants of which, in the event of danger, took refuge on the impregnable peaks all around; in fact, the first ring of walls dates only from the first century BC. Favored by its geographical position, Petra became the hub of a profitable herb, spice and other luxury goods trade and soon became rich. Permanent dwellings built with stones and mortar appeared as early as the

16 top and bottom Although it is often hard to identify the actual function of hypogea known not to have been tombs, many were certainly dwellings. Most of these are grouped into districts on the mountain slopes overlooking the center of the city, but many are also found along Wadi Mataha and Wadi Siyagh.

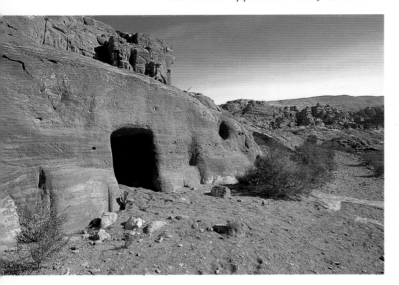

third century BC and with them came the first rock monuments. An age-old controversy surrounds the true function of the structures aligned along the rock walls around the urban center, but it has now been ascertained that many were dwellings, often consisting of a large central hall and a number of smaller rooms set around this. Judging by the few examples of wall decoration that have survived, the rooms were adorned with frescoes in geometrical frames, imitating architectural views or showing vegetable motifs.

What boosted Petra's rapid urban development was the presence of perennial water springs in the area, although these soon became inadequate for the growing population. The Nabateans therefore designed a highly complex system of cisterns and channels dug into the rock, aqueducts running through clay pipes, dams and artificial basins, in which the rainwater was collected. With their hydraulic engineering they managed to satisfy the needs of a metropolis that grew to at least 30,000 inhabitants and was situated in a desert area where the rainfall does not exceed six inches per year. In the first century BC, the Nabatean capital was an affluent city (it would later become opulent), at the crossroads of major trade routes. Filling the void left by the decline of Greece, Petra set out to dominate militarily and economically a vast area of the Middle East while, at the same time, absorbing extremely mixed cultural and artistic influences and acquiring uncommonly refined tastes. As well as trade, the inhabitants of Petra dedicated themselves to shepherding, breeding dromedaries and cultivating wheat, for which they created huge terraces on the heights around the city. No longer nomads, the Nabateans had organized a hereditary monarchy, which wielded military and perhaps also religious power, without being strongly conditioned by the latter like the nearby Jewish kingdom. Indeed there would appear to have been no great rivalry between the groups of priests, and the royal house was apparently very stable. The Nabatean state was democratic, something fairly unusual for the time. It is known that women could accede to the throne, because the names of some queens were passed down, the most famous being Shaquilat, mother of Rabbel II. The wives of the sovereigns bore the title of queen and must have enjoyed

considerable status, such to appear beside their consorts on numerous coins. Women were respected in Nabatean society and played an active role, as is confirmed by some funerary inscriptions inferring that they could own their own land, assets and employees. Merchants were at the top of the social pyramid, but sculptors, artists and craftsmen were also afforded some prestige and many artisans passed their trade on from father to son. Civil life was governed by laws and administered by legislators and magistrates.

As far as religion is concerned, the Nabateans venerated non-anthropomorphic gods and, hence, theirs was an aniconical culture; only in the first century AD, contact with the western world brought them to adopt figurative representations of their deities. The most important god was Dusares, who lived on the mountains and controlled natural phenomena; he governed the cycles of the seasons and fertility and was also the protector of the royal house. Later he was assimilated with Dionysus and Jupiter. Al Uzza was the mighty goddess, ruling on matters of life and love and, for this reason, later identified with Aphrodite-Venus. The Nabateans took the cult of the goddess Isis from the Egyptian pantheon.

ARCHITECTURAL MODELS

18 below An Assyrian façade – the style seen in more than half the tombs in Petra. The front is surmounted by one or two bands of crow-steps; in the latter case an undecorated attic level was added between them. Crow steps always include four steps on each side. Originally all the rock tombs in Petra must have had a walled entrance, covered with a layer of plaster inscribed with the name of the deceased. In some cases the plaster may have been replaced with a slab of carved stone.
No example of this type of closure has survived here, but it has been seen in the Nabatean necropolis of Hegra, in what is today Saudi Arabia.

The 19th of May, 363 AD marked the beginning of the end for Petra, when an earthquake razed part of the city, seriously damaging many buildings and bringing about the gradual de-population of the city. After the urban fabric shrunk, due to a number of factors, principally the loss of control of trade between the Mediterranean and the East, a second ring of walls was erected inside the older one and several areas were left in a state of ruin. More earthquakes struck Petra in the following centuries and it was no longer able to recover. When the Crusaders arrived in or around 1116, the superb Nabatean capital had already been reduced to a jumbled mass of ruins. This makes it very difficult to imagine what the Rose-red City looked like and, above all, to believe that the entire valley was once filled with a dense network of roads overlooked by a myriad of white-plastered houses, one or two stories high, each arranged around an inner courtyard full of greenery. As a whole, they must have resembled most of the old flat-roofed dwellings that form the nucleus of many villages in Jordan. At the height of its prosperity, not long after being annexed

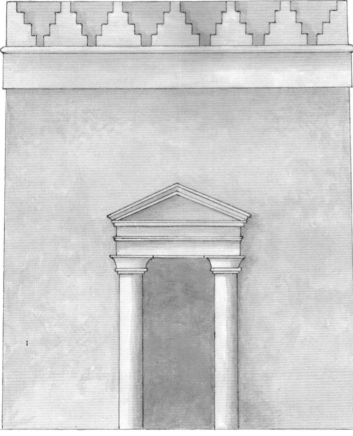

by the Roman Empire, Petra looked splendid. At that time, the paved main road, which started near a monumental fountain, ran alongside the bed of Wadi Mousa. On this elegant thoroughfare, flanked on both sides by a continuous colonnade, stood three large markets set on sloping terraces, lined with shops, two temples, palaces and sumptuous public buildings. On the other side of a majestic three-vaulted arch lay a vast sacred precinct, which culminated in an open-air altar and a relatively well-preserved temple, Kasr el Bint. At the mouth of the Siq gorge, the main route into the city, a large theater showed newcomers that the Nabatean kingdom also appreciated the tragedies of Aeschylus, Sophocles and Euripides, and the comedies of Aristophanes. Places of worship were located on the top of the surrounding peaks, as were

18 above A cavetto façade. The cornice that surmounts the lower attic is very similar to the crowning used on pillars in Egyptian temples. A band of multiple crow steps would, of course, have looked totally out of proportion and so two monumental crow steps were invented and also used in the more elaborate double cornice tombs.

19 This is a double-cornice tomb. Numerous variations were developed on this theme, some comprising various architectural elements such as pedimented doorways, taken from the Hellenized western world.

the outposts that formed part of an efficient defensive system. In many ways therefore, Petra resembled the great cities that were, in those years, the pride of Asia Minor and Palestine – Ephesus, Side, Caesarea – but it was also very different. Able merchants and great travellers, the Nabateans were like sponges that had absorbed new ideas from all the peoples they had come into contact with. Being of nomadic origin, and hence lacking building and decorative traditions of their own, they had adopted the figurative languages of others and come up with a highly distinctive art, which freely combined Syrian, Egyptian, Hellenistic and eventually Roman elements. Majestic religious buildings were erected in the center of Petra, similar to the classical temples, but clearly different in certain constructional respects from their models. Kasr al Bint, with its unusual square plan and three adjacent cella, reflects the essential independence that the local builders always managed to maintain with regard to the classical canons. Hundreds of still well-preserved rock faces prove this constructional heterodoxy and not just for their massive use of the so-called "Nabatean capital" (or "horn" capital), a local invention. You have only to observe the Palace Tomb to realize that the proportion of the "golden section" between the various parts – common to

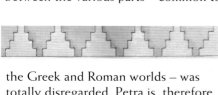

the Greek and Roman worlds – was totally disregarded. Petra is, therefore, unique and, unfortunately, has until now only been studied in part; it holds many surprises.

As almost nothing remains of the city of the living, the attention of visitors is focused on the "city of the dead," the splendid tombs that the Nabateans dug in the sandstone cliffs, sometimes 1,000 feet high or more. This attention is fully justified because it was indeed the rock architecture that made the Nabatean capital famous in ancient times. Scattered over an area of 350 square miles and linked by a dense network of paths and steps cut in the stone, Petra has more than 800 known tombs, temples and dwellings. Some of these structures are extraordinary works, even in comparison with the masterpieces created by the Greeks and

Romans in the same period. The building types are very different and many believe each one to be the expression of a different cultural influence, and of a different period in history. On the other hand, some scholars hold that the various types of façade do not correspond to a precise chronological sequence and that the simple forms continued to be used at the same time as the more elaborate ones. For the sake of convenience, however, the various Nabatean architectural styles are usually divided according to the following classifications.

The first graves used by the Nabateans – which can be dated to the fourth and third centuries BC – were the "ditch graves", usually rectangular, dug in the stone and seen virtually everywhere. The "pit tombs" are thought to be from a slightly later date and are subterranean funerary chambers reached along a sort of conduit; the bodies of the dead were laid inside graves closed with slabs. Very similar to these are the "dromos tombs" (or "rectilinear tombs"); in this case the pit is replaced by a horizontal passageway, the façade is smooth and the door framed with simple pilaster strips or the mere suggestion of an entablature. Far more complex funerary monuments made an appearance in the second century BC, and were known as "Assyrian tombs." The first of these

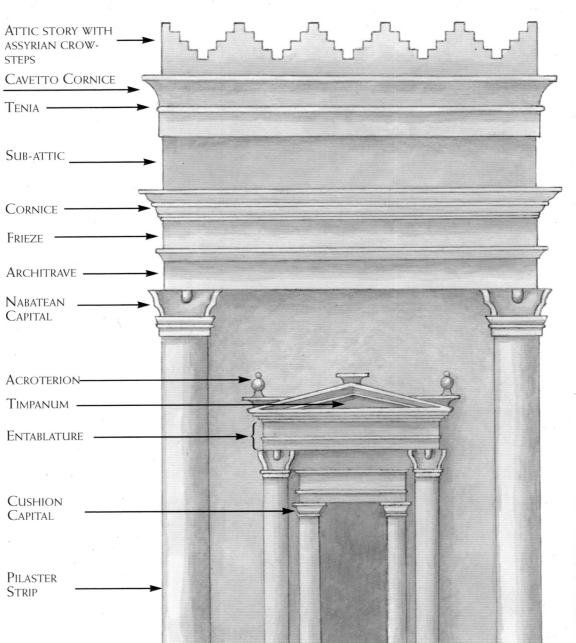

ATTIC STORY WITH
ASSYRIAN CROW-
STEPS

CAVETTO CORNICE

TENIA

SUB-ATTIC

CORNICE

FRIEZE

ARCHITRAVE

NABATEAN
CAPITAL

ACROTERION

TIMPANUM

ENTABLATURE

CUSHION
CAPITAL

PILASTER
STRIP

*20 left This drawing of
an imaginary double-
cornice façade shows the
names of all the various
architectural elements.
Actually there is only
one double-cornice tomb
in Petra topped with
Assyrian crow-steps. All
the others have the
standard monumental
ones.*

*20 below The Khasneh
is the most striking
example of the influence
exercised by the
Hellenistic culture on
Nabatean architecture. It
presents all the typical
features of the formal
language seen in the
Greek West: the broken
pediment, Corinthian
capitals, frieze decorated
with festoons and, above
all, a massive use of bas-
relief statues, totally
alien to the local
aniconical culture.*

*20 bottom left The
Deir, of which this is a
detail, is one of the most
remarkable monuments
in Petra. Although, like
the Khasneh, usually
classified as an example
of Nabatean Classical
style, it greatly differs
from it in the somber
expressive language
adopted, which seems
an attempt to break
away from Hellenistic
influence and formalize
an independent
Nabatean style which,
however, never
developed any further.*

probably had a very simple, smooth
façade crowned with a single band of
"crow-steps," below which opened a
door, sometimes framed with half-
columns; this type of tomb was a typically Nabatean adaptation of models
common in nearby Syria. Later, a
second band of crow-steps was added
above the first.

More sophisticated models developed over the next two centuries,
embracing Egyptian influences. In the
meantime a particular type had been
elaborated, called the "Nabatean
capital." The result of this evolution was
the "**cavetto tomb,**" with a façade surmounted by a large curved cornice
similar to "Egyptian molding," above
which are just two monumental crow-
steps (these are also called "stepped

tombs"). The front is often enclosed
between pilaster strips with Nabatean
capitals and the door crowned with
entablatures of varying complexity. An
elegant transformation of the previous
type is the "**double cornice tomb,**" in
which an additional classical cornice is
introduced below the cavetto cornice.
The attic between the two cornices may
be filled with short pilaster strips with
Nabatean capitals, and the façade is
usually marked with two or four pilaster
strips that frame an elaborate doorway,
often topped with a pediment with
tympanum and acroterions.

In the second half of the first
century BC Petra adopted architectural
motifs from the Hellenized west on a
wide scale (such as the Doric frieze and
the floral-Corinthian capital), probably

and exemplified by the Roman Soldier Tomb or the Wadi al Najr Tomb, are in **"Roman Classical style,"** subsequent to 106 AD.

The rock structures of Petra may seem to be the product of an incredible waste of energy but in many ways it is less demanding to dig a chamber in the sandstone than to erect a similar structure because the walls and ceilings stand up by themselves. Observation of the Unfinished Tomb has revealed that the digging proceeded from the top downwards. After constructing a wooden scaffolding, the workers first squared and smoothed the rock face with hammers, chisels and saws. Once the funerary chamber had been dug,

the external surface was divided into squares with plumb-lines and cords and the general outline of the various architectural divisions was marked. When all the parts in relief had been completed, the most important façades were probably given a thick layer of plaster as the fragile sandstone did not permit the execution of minute decorative detail. A projecting element in wood was inserted in special grooves to support the plaster (especially over the doors, where the molding was very thick).

The plaster was very possibly painted in bright colors, which must have given the façades a very different appearance from that of today.

introduced by artists from Alexandria. The splendid Khasneh belongs to this phase and was the first example of **"Nabatean Classical style."** From this point on, there was increasingly widespread use of structural elements for ornamental purposes, frequently placed one on top of the other, with chaotic results.

The provincial nature of Nabatean art, developed in a region fairly distant from the Mediterranean basin, in the middle of the desert, justified the continued use of native and obsolete elements of decoration, such as rosettes and contrarampant animals. After the middle of the first century AD, the extremely rich architectural figurative repertoire was joined by an unmistakable desire for scenic grandeur, and the rock façades reached colossal proportions, with orders of columns placed one above the other, imitating temple façades and theatrical backdrops. The Corinthian and Palace Tombs date from this period, while the Deir seems the fruit of an isolated attempt to assert the accomplished independence of Nabatean style from the Hellenistic formal language. Some pediment tombs, resembling the façade of a temple

Oblivion and Rediscovery

After 1189 – the year in which Saladin conquered Li Vaux Moise, the last crusader outpost to surrender to the Muslim armies – Petra was abandoned and memory of it was lost in the West.

Only a few scholars knew of the phantom city hewn into the rock, described by some Latin, Greek, Byzantine and Arab writers with a disheartening poverty of detail. The oblivion lasted longer than 600 years, until 1812, when the Rose-red City was rediscovered by a young Swiss explorer and Orientalist.

Born in Lausanne in 1784, Johann Ludwig Burckhardt is a fine example of that generation of heroic travellers who were half-scholar, half-adventurer. He helped to redesign geographical maps and knowledge in the early decades of the 19th century.

Having joined the Association for Promoting the Discovery of the Interior Parts of Africa, based in London and at least partially controlled by the British Foreign Office, he was officially asked to organize an expedition to Timbuktu in search of the source of the Niger; the British Foreign Office, however, was more interested in obtaining information on the political and economic situation and on transit routes across the Arabian Peninsula. So it was that Burckhardt was sent "undercover" to Cambridge to learn Arabic, as well as a little medicine and astronomy, the latter being essential if he was to trace a map of the region. The young Swiss man was so zealous in his preparation that – as well as sleeping on the ground and walking barefoot – he even had himself circumcised. Within a few years, spent travelling to Malta, Syria and Palestine, the metamorphosis was complete: Burckhardt had become Sheikh Ibrahim Ibn Abdallah, a pious scholar of the Koran and Islamic Law. Those who inquired about his strange accent were told he came from India, upon which he would break into the guttural Swiss-German that he passed off as his Hindustani mother tongue. No one ever doubted him. In the early months of 1812 he was in Amman and a few weeks later arrived at Shawbak, where the ruins of a crusader castle stand; here he was told of a "lost city,"

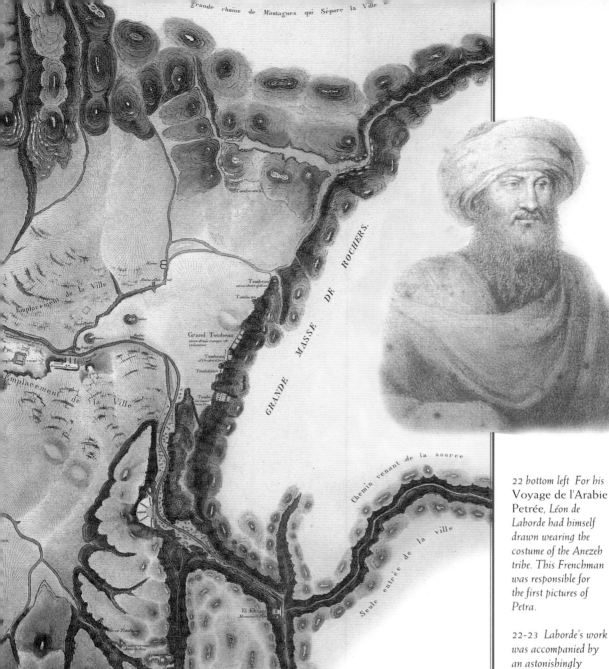

23 top So convincing
was Johann Ludwig
Burckhardt, the Swiss
explorer and
Orientalist who
discovered Petra in
1812, in his disguise
as an Arab scholar
that when he died in
Cairo in 1817 he was
buried according to the
Islamic rite with the
pseudonym of Ibrahim
ibn Abdallah. The
written account of his
adventure in the Rock
City was published
posthumously, in
1829, entitled Travels
in Arabia, although
news of his discovery
had spread long before
this.

22 bottom left For his
Voyage de l'Arabie
Petrée, Léon de
Laborde had himself
drawn wearing the
costume of the Anezeh
tribe. This Frenchman
was responsible for
the first pictures of
Petra.

22-23 Laborde's work
was accompanied by
an astonishingly
detailed and accurate
map of Petra.

23 bottom This view
of the ruins of the
three-vault arch
situated on Colonnade
Street is taken from
Léon de Laborde's
Voyage de l'Arabie
Petrée. The author
described the monument
as "decadent and
weighed down with
second-rate
decorations". The
temple known as Kasr
el Bint is visible in the
background.

inhabited by extremely belligerent
Bedouin tribes, not very far away.
Knowing that the tomb of Aaron was
on the top of Mount Hor, in the
immediate vicinity of the mysterious
city, Burckhardt expressed the desire
to sacrifice a goat on the tomb of the
venerated prophet and enlisted the
help of a guide. The ruse worked and,
although he had to pass in front of the
amazing rock monuments without
betraying the least emotion to avoid
arousing suspicion, he knew he had
found the fabulous Petra.

Burckhardt did not have time to
thoroughly inspect the ruins but the
Bedouins' secret had been exposed.
From that moment on, numerous
westerners set off for Petra in search

24-25 Laborde and Linant were the first westerners to see the Deir with their own eyes. Burckhardt had not even imagined its existence and Irby and Mangles had been able only to observe it from a distance through a telescope. Although Laborde was not overly enthusiastic about the proportions and style of the building, he was greatly impressed by its size, writing: "Carved in relief out of the rock, it is a compact mass, like a monolithic monument of huge proportions, a gigantic ornament set on the front of the mountain."

24 bottom This picture by Laborde is the first reliable survey made of the Khasneh. The result is truly remarkable as the artist lacked the proper measuring instruments needed to gauge the actual height of the construction. Laborde said that the reproduction of the decorations, friezes and group statues had not been too difficult as the monument was well preserved and very few details had been lost. The ornamentation must have been in better condition than it is today.

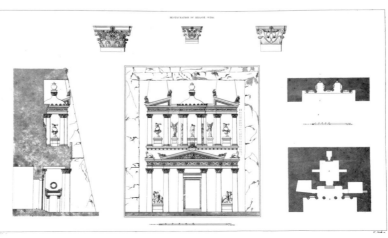

of adventure and improbably dressed in Turkish attire, in a pathetic attempt to pass unnoticed. What actually protected them were the "firmans" received in exchange for a generous reward from the various sheikhs who governed the region. Such xenophobia and hostile mistrust were justified by the long isolation in which the local tribes had lived, the fear of losing centuries-old privileges over passage through the dead city and, above all, by the conviction that the ruins concealed fabulous and as yet undiscovered treasures.

In 1818, just six years after Burckhardt's bold adventure, two British Royal Navy officers arrived in Petra; Charles Irby and James Mangles were accompanied by the painter William Bankes and travelled under the protection of a firman issued by the Sultan of Constantinople, whose jurisdiction included the region of Petra. Irby and Mangles left a vivid written account of their visit; in particular, they were bowled over by the sight of the Khasneh, stating that they did not know what to compare the monument with and that it should probably be considered a unique work.

The first reliable pictures of Petra were by the French Marquis Léon de Laborde and his travelling companion Louis Linant de Bellefonds.

The two reached the Nabatean city in 1828, after having met in Cairo and deciding to embark together on an adventurous expedition to the city discovered 16 years earlier.

Laborde, who was the son of a French diplomat and had considerable financial resources, was then just 19 years old. Bellefonds, son of a Breton naval officer, was 10 years older and already had an excellent reputation as an explorer, engraver, cartographer and expert on the Arab language and

customs. He had spent ten years travelling through Turkey, Syria, Palestine, Egypt, the Libyan Desert and Sudan, studying the local geography and drawing maps.

The two men's stay in Petra lasted a week and was marked by an unusual calm, for the simple fact that the local tribes had been decimated just a few weeks earlier by an outbreak of the plague. Despite the risks, the two decided to take advantage of the unusual situation and carefully drew all the main monuments around them; they also surveyed the interiors of several tombs. After their visit to the Rock City, Linant and Laborde headed for Aqaba where they took the caravan trail to Egypt.

On April 20th 1826 they

25 top Raised on the principles of neo-classical art, which idolized the Greek and Roman building codes, Laborde criticized several monuments in Petra and found the Roman Soldier Tomb out of proportion, although he did like the bas-reliefs on the façade.

25 bottom Laborde was far more enthusiastic about the "gracious form" of the Khasneh, which he defined as "the mark of the might and genius" of the ancient people of Petra.

26 top In line with current opinion, Laborde deemed the so-called Corinthian Tomb a "bad imitation of the Khasneh" although, despite being so bizarre, out of proportion and overloaded with broken lines, it could not be considered totally without grace. Almost as if to temper his judgement, the Frenchman then dwelled on the monument's crumbling appearance, eroded by water and almost suffocated by brambles, lamenting its condition and reflecting on the wretched fate of man's works.

26-27 Laborde admired the huge effort that was needed to dig the theater auditorium out of the cliff and the remarkable condition of the ancient seats. However, its unusual position, in the middle of a necropolis, touched his inner romanticism and he wrote: "What a strange attitude of the spirit is that of a people so accustomed to the idea of death as to become insensitive to it."

separated, as Linant had urgent business to do in Cairo and his companion wanted to stay longer in the Sinai desert.

Back home, Laborde – who would later become keeper of antiquities at the Louvre and then General Manager of the Archives of France – gave the press a report of the expedition, as well as dozens of lithographs based on drawings made by himself and by de

Bellefonds. Published in 1830, *Voyage de l'Arabie Petrée* marked the beginning of Levant's knowledge of science and, in particular, of Petra.

Although drawn with what would today be called vaguely naïve taste, the views represented an exhaustive record of Nabatean architecture and the copious notes that accompanied the pictures were filled with detailed observations. Indeed, Laborde was the

first to see the close link between many of Petra's façades and Egyptian and Assyrian monuments. By observing the obvious Hellenistic-Roman influence visible in other buildings, he underlined the derivation of local art.

Similarly, he was the first to describe the so-called "Unfinished Tomb," having guessed its importance from an understanding of the methods used by the ancient builders for these rock constructions, working from the top downwards. His book also contained an extremely detailed and accurate map of the site, used by numerous other travellers in subsequent years.

Laborde's notable work fascinated

Bellefonds, who gave him an exciting narrative of his experience and offered much generous advice.

In February 1836, after numerous adventures, Stephens at last reached "the Rose-red City, half as old as time," as it was later described by the poet John William Burgon. On his return to America, Stephens had his exciting travel journal printed. His *Incidents of Travel in Egypt, Arabia, Petraea, and the Holy Land* was a bestseller, and made the name of Petra known to the public at large, inspiring generations of readers on both sides of the Atlantic to dream of it.

Three years later, David Roberts also gained permission to camp at

27 right In his comment to this picture, Laborde expressed his regret at not having entered Petra through the Siq, but from the west, and having thus missed the thrill of the sudden and unexpected sight of what are today known as the Royal Tombs. Astonished by the scenographic effect of these colossal carved backdrops, he paused to consider the massive efforts required to construct the Urn Tomb, the first from the right, literally hewn into the cliffside.

a young American lawyer who was travelling across Europe: John Lloyd Stephens, later to become famous for having "discovered" the Maya civilization together with Frederick Catherwood.

In 1835 he was in Paris and happened to come across a copy of *Voyage*. The pictures of the fabulous Petra immediately captured his attention. After postponing his return home, the young American set off for Egypt, from where he intended to travel on to his destination through Sinai. In Cairo he was fortunate enough to meet Louis Linant de

Petra to study the monuments and he brought back exhaustive graphic documentation. Scottish and born in quite a modest social context, Roberts made up for his humble origins by becoming one of the most acclaimed artists of the time. After repeated trips to Europe, in 1838 he set off for Egypt and in the early months of the following year visited the Sinai peninsula, Palestine, Jerusalem, the coasts of Lebanon and Baalbeck.

The lithographs made from the drawings of that extraordinary journey, published in London between 1842 and 1849, brought him

fame that has lasted to the present day. Although a mere 14 in number, his views of Petra are some of the loveliest ever made by an artist; moreover, unlike Laborde's illustrations, the proportions are very accurate, with great attention to detail. It should be said that, unlike his predecessors, Roberts had the aid of a camera lucida, an instrument invented just a few years earlier by William Wollaston and already quite popular. This simple piece of apparatus used a glass prism to superimpose the outline of an object on a sheet of paper and this could then be traced; drawings thus obtained were true to reality.

Fortunately, this enterprising artist and traveller did not merely draw what he saw; he wrote his impressions down in a diary and carefully recorded a great deal of practical information

29 right This
picture by Roberts
depicts the
auditorium of the
great theatre, dug
entirely in the rock.
Enlarged after the
Roman conquest,
the building could
accommodate
approximately 6,000
spectators but its
raised stage collapsed
after an earthquake
and today only a few
well-restored parts
remain. Visible in
the background, to the
left, is the entrance to
the Siq; to the right
opens the valley and
path leading to the
High Place of
Sacrifice.

on the places he visited. Today, more
than 150 years later, there is still a
thrill in reading the description of his
adventures.

Roberts reached Petra on the 6th
of March 1839 and, thanks to the
good services of his local guides and
the payment of a conspicuous sum of
money, he was allowed to stay for five
days on what was the territory of a
still quite belligerent tribe. The sight
that greeted him was breathtaking and
the Scottish artist could not conceal

his excitement before such a wonder:
"I am increasingly astounded and
disconcerted by this extraordinary
city...; every ravine has been
inhabited, even the mountain tops.
The valley is dotted with temples,
public buildings, triumphal arches and
bridges, each of which has now
collapsed, with the exception of one
arch and a temple, although its
portico has been destroyed. The
architectural style is different from
anything else I have ever seen and

much of it reveals a curious
combination of Egyptian, Roman and
Greek styles. A stream still flows
through the city. Bushes and wild
flowers grow lush and prolific; every
crack in the rock is filled with them
and the air carries the most delicious
fragrance." As soon as the camp was
organized, Roberts decided to visit
the Khasneh, certainly the most
famous monument in Petra. He was
ecstatic: "... I do not know whether to
say I was more surprised by the
appearance of the construction or by
its remarkable position. It stands,
exactly as it was, in a huge recess in
the rock and the soft hue of the stone,
along with the perfect state of
conservation of even tiny details, give
the impression that it was only
recently completed."

The Siq also caught his attention:
"We explored the grand entrance to
Petra, which is approximately a mile
long and winds between high rocks.
These enclose the valley and are so
sheer that they seem almost to
meet…" This was the spectacular way
into the city, still used today by the
Bedouins.

Two days after admiring the
Khasneh, Roberts wanted to see the
other wonder of Petra with his own
eyes. Accompanied by a group of
armed men, he advanced into a deep

30 top Here Roberts drew the center of Petra, where the houses used to stand. Rising in the background is the rock now known as el Habis and at its foot lie the ruins of Kasr el Bint, the great temple that is the only remaining fairly well-preserved raised structure.

gorge along a very rough path which soon turned into a steep flight of steps; eventually he came to what is perhaps the Nabatean city's least visited but most impressive monuments: "After proceeding along a rugged gorge and climbing a crumbling flight of steps for roughly a mile, we reached a building called al Deir, or the Monastery, sculpted in the rock." The Scottish artist was enthralled by the stunning spectacle enjoyed from that balcony of rock extending over the valley below: "The panorama is superb here, the gaze sweeps over the valley, Mount

could do was retreat, and Roberts, after raising camp, continued on towards Jerusalem: a completely different picture from the hospitality that greets the large groups of tourists who come every day to visit what can be considered one of the great archaeological wonders of the world.

After Roberts, an increasing number of travellers came every year to the Rose-red City, but the first official study of its monuments was not conducted until 1898 by two German scholars, R. E. Brünnow and A. Von Domaszewski, who catalogued

30 bottom The remains of the great three-vault arch drawn by Roberts still stand at the eastern end of the great Colonnade Street, the city's main thoroughfare, on which stood the markets and some of the most important holy buildings.

Hor – crowned at the top with Aaron's tomb – and the entire mountain gorge, which winds among the highest rock peaks; the ancient city, in all its breadth stretches out along the valley."

Unfortunately, despite such enthusiasm, Roberts' stay in Petra was marred by minor incidents – including the theft of some crockery – culminating on the fifth day in an attack by marauders who, among other things, took guns and ammunition. At that point all they

more than 800 rock structures, giving each one a number that is still used today.

Until the end of the First World War, only German archaeologists studied the Nabatean City. The British followed them when the Trans-Jordan emirate was formed in 1921. In the meantime the first systematic reconnaissance of the zone was conducted and a reliable map of the urban area drawn up.

The first real excavation campaigns, this time directed by an

30-31 *Roberts was much impressed by the Royal Tombs, which he portrayed from several angles. That shown to the right,* *known as the Urn Tomb, is certainly one of the most interesting because of the way the façade is set back from the outline of the cliff in* *a clear attempt to create a scenographic effect. The result is made all the more effective by the perspective line of the two lateral colonnades.*

31 bottom *While in Petra, Roberts witnessed a dispute between Bedouins and decided to reproduce the scene. One of the men had been accused of theft* *and the authoritative opinion of three of the tribe's sheikhs was sought to settle the matter. The rock building seen behind the group is the Urn Tomb.*

32 top Roberts' picture shows the arch that used to span the Siq and marked its entrance. The lower part was cut into the rock and decorated with two deep niches, which presumably contained the statues of protective deities. The arch collapsed in 1896 following a minor earthquake.

32 bottom Visitors approaching the archaeological site of Petra today from the village of Wadi Mousa first encounter some of the most striking rock tombs in the area. These are large monolithic rocks, isolated from the slope of the mountain and now known as Djin or "Spirit" Blocks. A little farther ahead, on

the left, stand two singular rock tombs, one above the other: The upper one is known as the Obelisk Tomb, and the lower one is called the Bab el Siq Triclinium. This veduta is one of the few in which Roberts took some "poetic license," altering the actual arrangement of the monuments portrayed.

English team, date from 1929. Since then, numerous other archaeological missions – including those of Jordan, France and the United States – have succeeded one another in the dual and difficult task of preserving what remains and, above all, discovering what still lies beneath the sands of Petra. Indeed, an extraordinary and illuminating discovery was made in December 1993, in a room adjacent to the Byzantine church. Between 1992

and 1993 this religious building had already caused a great stir when splendid and well-preserved mosaic floors were uncovered. No one, however, imagined that a large number of charred scrolls, extremely fragile but still legible using the proper techniques, would emerge from the debris of the building. A preliminary study has revealed that they are mostly inventories, registers and land records written in Greek. The experts think

that at least 50 of them can be translated in the immediate future and will provide precious information on the economy of fifth- and sixth-century Petra.

Clearly, there is still a lot to be discovered in the city build in the rock.

32-33 On the morning of March 8th 1839, Roberts, escorted by a group of armed men, advanced into a deep gorge along a very rough path which soon turned into a steep flight of steps approximately a mile long. At the end of their climb, the group reached the stunning construction known as al Deir, or the Monastery, the most impressive monument in the Nabatean City and one of the best preserved.

33 bottom Like most modern-day visitors to Petra, Roberts fell under the spell of the Khasneh and decided to immortalize it in three vedutas. The subject of this one is its portico, at the time missing one of its four colossal columns. As well as by the size of the structure, the Scottish artist was struck by the splendid quality of execution of the friezes. It is not therefore surprising that he formulated the opinion that the true function of Petra's rock structures may have been merely to please the refined aesthetic taste of the Nabateans.

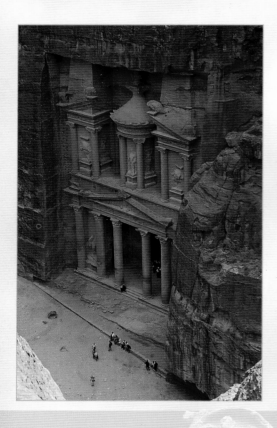

Petra

34 above The Khasneh seen from above; this splendid rock mausoleum has now become the symbol of Petra.

34 above right Detail of one of the semi-pediments of the Khasneh, with its festooned friezes and Corinthian capitals.

34 below right A detail of the tholos on the Khasneh, showing the bas-relief statue of the goddess Tyche - Al Uzza.

35 Some of the Assyrian tombs that line the walls of the Outer Siq.

LEGEND

1) *Wadi Mousa*
2) *Reservoir (al Birka)*
3) *Petra Forum Rest House*
4) *Entrance gate*
5) *Djin Blocks*
6) *Snake Monument*
7) *Obelisk Tomb and Bab el Siq Triclinium*
8) *Tunnel*
9) *Triumphal Arch*
10) *Little Siq*
11) *Khasneh*
12) *Tomb of Uneishu*
13) *Theatre*

WADI MATAHA

WADI MUTHLIM

JEBEL EL KHUBTHA

N

Before commencing a visit to the Rose-red City, a little time should be dedicated to the village of Wadi Mousa (or El Ji); this is visited every year by thousands of tourists but most are unaware that this agglomeration of white houses has a history of its own: one that goes back to the dawn of time, as it probably stands on the site of the ancient Gaia, first an Edomite settlement and then,

36 left In recent years, the government has built numerous houses in Wadi Mousa (seen here from Moghar al Nassara) to accommodate the Bedouins who until recently lived in the tombs of Petra. Some families, however, continue to live on the archaeological site.

in the sixth century BC, the home of the Nabatean kings before the court was moved to Petra. The inhabitants worshipped Dusares, the greatest god in the Nabatean pantheon, not surprisingly also known as the "god of Gaia."

In the upper part of the village is the famous Ain Mousa spring where, according to the Bible (Exodus 17:1-7), Moses struck the rock with his staff and brought forth water to quench the thirst of the people of Israel during their exhausting journey to the Promised Land.
As suggested by the many place-

names that contain the word Mousa (which means *Moses*), the entire region is permeated with the memory of the patriarch's passage. The spring supplies the river known as Wadi Mousa, after which the village is named, and is today protected by a white building that resembles a mosque. This spring made the birth of the Nabatean settlement possible, and it is easy to imagine how sacred it must have been in such an arid region.

Not far away from Wadi Mousa are the excavations of the Edomite settlement of Tawilan.

36-37 The name Wadi Mousa means literally "the Valley of Moses" and the village developed around the spring which the patriarch is supposed to have produced out of the rock to refresh the Jews during the exodus from Egypt. Once a major suburb of Petra, today it has numerous hotels, restaurants and other enterprises, all serving the flourishing tourist industry.

37 bottom right Until a few years ago, the area where the Petra Forum Rest House now stands was occupied by a government hotel that incorporated a fine Nabatean tomb. When the old structure was demolished, the tomb — now a luxurious bar — was restored and returned to the open air; its main attraction is the colonnaded courtyard before it.

37 top The first Nabatean rock tombs can be seen just a few dozen yards from the village of Wadi Mousa, along the normally arid course of the river; these were part of the necropolis of the ancient Gaia.

all its force against this and eventually opened a narrow passage – the Siq. Today there is no longer any risk because the flow of the water has been diverted a few meters before the mouth of the gorge, which is protected by a solid embankment. As will be explained later, this is exactly what the Nabateans had themselves already done.

THE TOMB OF PETRA FORUM REST HOUSE

A visit to ancient Petra can commence even before one passes through the entrance to the archaeological site. Indeed, attentive observers will notice some Nabatean tombs dug in the banks of white sandstone around the Visitor's Center. As they are greatly eroded, most of these look more like natural caves, but they are all that remains of the necropolis of Gaia. One monumental tomb is incorporated in the modern Petra Forum Rest House, to the immediate right of the entrance. Clearly visible from the parking lot in front, it has a double-cornice façade, which has lost its battlement; apart from this it is in

THE SIQ

The Siq, a narrow gorge eroded by water and wind over thousands of years, is the most spectacular, easiest and most popular way into the Nabatean capital. It seems incredible that a small trickle of water like Wadi Mousa – which also flows through the village of the same name and runs for a long stretch on the left side of the road between the entrance gate and the mouth of the gorge – could have produced such a phenomenon. Yet, during the rainy season and after the most violent summer storms this

pitiful little stream turns into a howling mass of water and has been responsible for numerous tragedies; in 1967 a flash flood took a group of tourists inside the Siq by surprise and most of them drowned. Observing the conformation of the valley around Wadi Mousa you will see exactly how such violent floods occur: Like a huge funnel, it gathers rainwater from the side valleys and gradually narrows until it reaches a colossal bank of sandstone; for centuries the kinetic energy of the river was discharged in

excellent condition partly because it had been used as a dwelling and stables for centuries. Known as *Al Khan*, it is particularly striking for the imposing colonnade that fronts each side, also carved into the rock. Also in the hotel area are the remains of a large Nabatean reservoir, known as Al Birka, into which some of the water from Ain Mousa must have been channelled. It seems certain that the precious liquid was carried from here, along a long pipe, to Petra, where it supplied the great nymphaeum at the beginning of Colonnade Street. The ruins of several kilns used to bake the characteristic Nabatean pottery have been discovered around the reservoir.

THE DJIN BLOCKS

38 It is easier to assess the amount of work that was needed to make the Djin Blocks from on high; these three structures were created from as many outcrops after a massive feat of excavation. At the top of the highest block, to the left, you will see a rectangular cavity which may have been a loculus. This would confirm the funerary function of these monuments. The sort of slanting plane, excavated in the wall behind and today much eroded, could have been used to hoist the sarcophagus, which was then put in place using a footbridge. Behind the three tower-

tombs is some of the audacious channelling that formed part of the complex hydraulic system designed by the Nabateans to supply Petra with drinking water. On the left, in the foreground, you will also see the mouths of unusual hypogea, devoid of external decoration, created by hollowing out some natural formations. The chambers thus obtained, probably used as burial places, are thought by some scholars to be among the oldest rock structures in Petra, dating from before the second century BC and therefore even older than the Djin Blocks.

Past the entrance gate, a two-lane dirt road descending to the southeast follows the bed of the river, in recent years controlled for safety reasons. This is Bab al Siq, the Gate to the Siq, the last stretch of the valley eroded by Wadi Mousa in a solid bank of white sandstone that creates a sharp contrast with the reddish hilltops. The scenery is already delightful, the rounded stones pockmarked with holes and cavities produced by the wind, and speckled with numerous shades of pink, salmon and saffron.

distant past, all that now remain are the holes and grooves they were fixed in. Although now they are thought probably to be tower-tombs (among the oldest in Petra), the word *Djin* in Arabic means "spirit" and these could indeed have been created as divine simulacra, containers of guardian spirits placed to protect the entrance

the Djin blocks, which vanishes in the distance at an almost constant gradient; this is what remains of the channel that conveyed the water from Moses' Spring to Petra.

It becomes a constant presence all along the Siq, and a little observation reveals that the mountain sides surrounding the Rose-red City are literally dotted with similar channels; as it has already been said, the Nabateans were exceptional hydraulic engineers.

The valley narrows gradually, enclosed by increasingly high cliffs and suddenly, three mysterious-looking structures appear to the right. These are the so-called Djin Blocks, huge monolithic cubes cut away from the slope behind in a colossal work of excavation. Dating perhaps from the first century BC and between 20 and 30 feet high, they stand solemn and majestic; one supports a pyramidal stepped structure at the top and the sides of another are adorned with four half-columns. The plinths, capitals, architraves and cornices must have been made in marble or bronze and then mounted in the rock. Wrenched away by some plunderer of the

to the Nabatean capital. Others believe that they represent the god Dusares, originally represented by the Nabateans in the form of a cube. However, the three monoliths are also known as *Sahrij*, which in Arabic means *water tank*. This idea may seem strange because these structures are totally unsuited to the function of cistern, but there are 23 similar cubes in Petra and the immediate vicinity, all situated near springs or rivers. The Djin may have been considered the homes or the containers of the spirits that guarded the Nabateans' most precious possession, water. It is interesting to observe a long horizontal cleft in the rock behind

39 *The true purpose of the Djin blocks is not yet certain but, as two of the three blocks in Bab al Siq have an internal cavity, they were probably tombs. In other cases, the burial chamber is thought to have been built on top of them.*

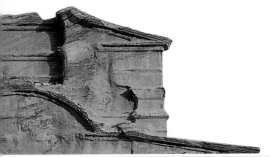

THE OBELISK TOMB

After the Djin blocks, the right side of Bab al Siq becomes a succession of rock tombs, most of which are Assyrian in type. Water channels and small cisterns dug in the rock can be seen. A few dozen yards farther down, on the left, stands the elaborate architectural elevation of Petra's first, great monumental tomb, which at first glance looks like a single monument. Actually these are two separate tombs, dug one on top of the other in different periods. There was probably a functional link between the two structures, but for the moment this possibility has not been investigated. The upper structure, unique in Petra and known as the Obelisk Tomb, owes its name to the four large pyramid-shaped obelisks that dominate it; approximately 20 feet high and sculpted in full relief out of the rock, these are probably of Egyptian influence. A niche in the wall behind the obelisks contains a standing male statue, dressed in Hellenistic fashion. A door flanked by pillars and surmounted by a Doric frieze leads into the funeral

chamber that contained five graves. The most important, in the back wall, is in the form of an arcosolium. A widely accepted theory holds that each pyramid, called *nefesh*, portrays one of the deceased; if this is so the tomb was probably initially constructed to house four people and a fifth laid here later had himself portrayed in the new fashion, the

arcosolium having been dug for him. If, on the other hand, the obelisks and statues were of the same period, this would demonstrate the continuing use of ancient funeral customs combined with the figurative language imported from the Greco-Roman West. This is only a theory, as other writers believe that the obelisks were actually intended as *mazeboth*, as described in the Bible, i.e. divine simulacra. Their presence at the very mouth of the Siq therefore served to exercise powerful protection over the city. Whatever the correct theory, it is common knowledge that the Obelisk Tomb dates from the first half of the first century AD, and the Triclinium from the second half.

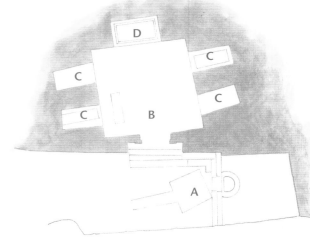

A PIT TOMB
B FUNERARY CHAMBER
C LOCULI
D ARCOSOLIUM
LOCULUS

40

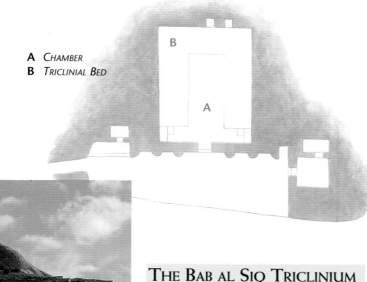

A CHAMBER
B TRICLINIAL BED

THE BAB AL SIQ TRICLINIUM

The monument dug immediately below what has just been described is in far poorer condition, although it is a few decades more recent. It is attributed to the reign of Rabbel II (71-106 AD), the last Nabatean king, or his immediate predecessor, Malchus II. As the name says, this is not a proper tomb, but a room used for the wakes and feasts held to honor the deceased; Petra has numerous other similar places, of clear western influence. The Roman *triclinium* consisted of three adjacent beds or benches arranged around the three sides of a table, and two or three persons lay on each bed; by extension, the term later came to mean the dining room itself. The deceased for whom the monument was built may have been buried in the two graves on the sides of the façade, or even in the Obelisk Tomb above. In stark contrast with the elaborately marked front (very similar to the lower part of the Corinthian Tomb), the interior is extremely bare, save for the great stone *triclinium* that runs around three sides of the simple rectangular chamber. An inscription in two languages, Nabatean and Greek (in reduced form), is visible on one of the rocks that face the two structures. It reads as follows: "This is the funeral site chosen by Abdmank, son of Akayus, son of Shullay, son of Utaih for the construction of a tomb for himself, his heirs and the heirs of his heirs, for eternity and beyond. He did this during his life, in the ... year of the reign of Malchus." Given the position of the epigraph, many scholars no longer believe it is related to the Obelisk Tomb and think that it pertains to some pit graves situated nearby. Doubts remain and it is also impossible to ascertain which Malchus the inscription refers to; the uncertainty surrounding the date is quite considerable as Malchus I reigned from 59 to 30 BC and Malchus II was king from 40 to 70 AD. The use of Greek, moreover, shows that, between the first century BC and the first century AD, Petra had become a cosmopolitan city.

An unusual burial place lies a short distance before the two tombs, again on the left of Bab al Siq; this is known as the Snake Tomb because of a very worn bas-relief, the interpretation of which is still dubious.

A path that is extremely rugged and at times rather difficult to see starts from the Triclinium Tomb and leads through what looks almost like a moonscape to El Madras, once one of Petra's suburbs. From this area, dotted with rock structures, you can choose to continue to the northwest and return to the Siq later along an extraordinary number of flights of steps cut in the rock, directly to the left of the Khasneh. This is a tiring route suited to expert hikers and is tackled by the adventurous few.

40 bottom left The four massive obelisks marking its front make this tomb unique in Petra.

40-41 Although the Obelisk Tomb and the triclinium below seem to be one structure, they are actually two separate monuments dating from different periods, as demonstrated by the fact that the two façades are not vertically aligned.

41 top left Although the elements have caused considerable damage to the façade of the Bab al Siq Triclinium, it is still readable and constitutes a fine example of what is known as "Nabatean classical style." It has much in common with the other broken pediment Nabatean tombs and, above all, with the Corinthian Tomb.

Continuing down along the dirt track, after no more than 300 yards it suddenly turns left into the proper Siq or Interior Siq. Before entering this spectacular gorge, you should stop a moment to observe a few details. First of all, you will see that a huge dam, reconstructed in 1963 and again in 1991 bars the mouth of the Siq, and that the course of Wadi Mousa has been diverted to the right, towards a tunnel. The modern road crosses the riverbed on a bridge, also recently constructed, and starts to descend in

the narrow fissure. This is a fairly true reconstruction of what the Nabateans did to control Wadi Mousa between the first century BC and the beginning of the first century AD. This is when the bottom of the Siq was paved with stone and, to prevent the disastrous winter floods, Wadi Mousa was conveyed into a deep channel dug into the rock; a tunnel (280 feet long and known as *al Muthlim*) was built to carry the waters to a side valley. In this way Wadi Mousa – first along Wadi Muthlim, then along Wadi Mataha – is forced to circumnavigate the mountain of El Khubtha before returning to its ancient bed in the

Petra valley, at the beginning of Colonnade Street. This is a brilliant and extremely complicated work of hydraulic engineering. Moreover, in order for the canal from Bab al Siq to enter the Siq and continue on towards the city, it had to cross the river. It probably did so in conduits in the bridge that was used by caravans on their way to Petra. Near the tunnel, to the right, a Djin block confirms the link between this type of monument and places of flowing water. Once past the tunnel there are interesting monuments to visit, described under the Little Siq. The entrance to the Siq is marked by the remains of a monumental arch, of which only the two abutments cut into the rock face and decorated with two niches (which must have housed votive statues) and some hewn stones of the arch itself have survived. This daring construction – a sort of triumphal arch, or perhaps a form of defense with heavy wooden doors – collapsed in 1896 following an earthquake, but its appearance is known thanks to some lithographs by David Roberts and other contemporary artists. The monument reveals Greco-Roman influence and dates from the latter half of the first century AD. The two fissures visible in the walls that enclose the passage are the channels that carried water from Moses' Spring to the city; the water flowed at first in the open air before being forced through cylindrical clay pipes, lodged in the rock channel with plenty of mortar. Some sections of this piping, very similar to its modern equivalent, are on display in the New Museum. Large sections of the aqueduct were exposed and restored during excavation work conducted along the Siq between 1997 and 1998. At the same time tons of gravel and sand that had accumulated after the floods provoked by the collapse of the Nabatean dam were removed and large sections of the original flooring were discovered. This paving, most of which was considered lost, probably dates from the first century AD, but may even go back to the Roman conquest; this suggestion is supported by the fact that the *Via Nova Traiana* –

a straight road to Aqaba – had already been completed and the Siq had become the main way into Petra.

The Interior Siq is a spectacular natural fault – produced perhaps by tectonic forces and then worn smooth by the waters of Wadi Mousa – approximately one mile long. Of a mysterious and disquieting charm, it is a very narrow (in some points no more than 10 feet wide) winding passage, perpetually steeped in shadow and enclosed between 300-to 600-foot high walls that at certain points seem to touch and block out the sky. At intervals they suddenly separate to form natural projecting roofs. These areas were used as caravanserai by caravans arriving in Petra. Along both walls of the fissure are a number of votive niches and stelae, which suggest that the Siq was sacred not only for the Nabatean people, as numerous

42 top left and top right All that remains of the great monumental arch that marked the entrance to the Siq are the abutments carved in the rock and adorned with pilaster strips and niches.

42 center right Two aqueducts are dug into the rock on both sides of the Siq.

42 bottom right More than 50 votive niches containing baetyli (up to 10, as in this picture) have been found along the Siq. Sometimes accompanied by inscriptions, they are probably manifestations of religious beliefs left by Nabatean merchants on their way to and from Petra.

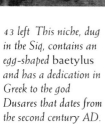

43 left This niche, dug in the Siq, contains an egg-shaped baetylus and has a dedication in Greek to the god Dusares that dates from the second century AD.

43 right This quite elaborate religious niche in the Siq is one of many carved in the form of an aedicula with pilaster strips and a pediment.

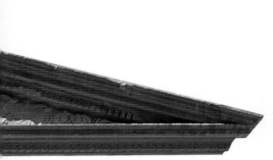

44 bottom left The Siq is a spectacular fissure created by tectonic motion and then worn smooth by the waters of Wadi Mousa. So close are the walls that in many parts they block out the view of the sky.

44 center top Halfway along the Siq is an outcrop of sandstone, with a large votive aedicula on one side, containing two baetyli, one adorned with a stylized face.

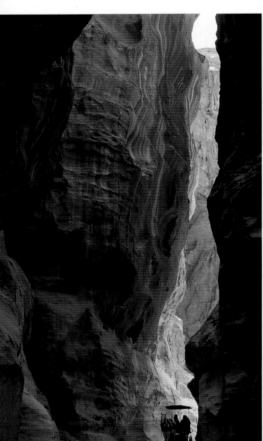

44 center bottom Along the Siq there are also some underground chambers, the function of which has not yet been clarified. The possibility that they were tombs has been excluded but it also seems difficult to believe that they were dwellings. More probably they housed the guards that defended the main entrance to Petra.

feet and the legs of the two men. The figures are almost twice lifesize, and it is easy to imagine the thrill this unexpected vision must have stirred in those arriving in Petra for the first time.

The Khasneh appears farther on, at a point where the Siq veers to the right. This rock monument is unequalled anywhere else in the world and however well-prepared you may think you are for the spectacle, its sudden appearance – a remarkable contrast between the delicately pink façade and the dark gloomy Siq – will take your breath away. With its totally symmetric front and exquisite proportions, the Khasneh is certainly one of the wonders of antiquity.

inscriptions date from the second and third centuries AD. Many niches contain just one *baetylus*, but some have several, up to a maximum of 10. Halfway along, where the passage widens considerably, stands a solitary sandstone block shaded by a single wild fig tree. The side facing those leaving Petra has a large niche framed by two pillars with Nabatean capitals, surmounted by an elegant architrave with a Doric frieze. Inside, side by side, are two *baetyli*; the smaller right-hand one is smooth, whereas that on the left features a highly stylized face with square eyes and a straight nose. This niche, the largest known in the Siq, dates from the reign of Malchus II (40-70 AD). Not far ahead, on the left-hand wall, is a remarkable group of statues uncovered in 1998 when digging was conducted to lower the road by more than six feet. Although the whole upper part is greatly eroded, it is still possible to recognize the figures of two merchants each leading two dromedaries. The animals' feet are still perfectly distinguishable, as are the *caligae*-clad

44-45 and 44 bottom right A group of statues portraying a caravan was found in the spring of 1998 in the Siq. Unfortunately, as no one could have known it was there, the hooves of the animals were broken during excavation work by the bucket of a digger. The pieces will shortly be returned to their original place.

45 The sudden sight of the Khasneh as you enter Petra from the deep fissure of the Siq is a unique experience. So much perfection seems truly of another world.

THE KHASNEH

Without doubt Petra's most famous monument, the Khasneh is also the best preserved thanks to a protected position that has saved it from the elements. This amazing structure is carved deep into a sheer rock face at the point where the Siq makes an unexpected and sharp right turn. The best time to admire the Khasneh is between 8:45 and 10:15 am, when the rock takes on the most fantastic colors. The proportions are formidable. The façade, 130 feet high and 92 feet wide, is divided into two stories, the lower one consisting of a portico with a pediment and six

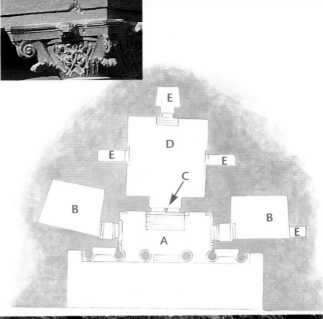

46 top The delicate ornaments carved in fragile sandstone to embellish the façade of the Khasneh are an eloquent demonstration of the skill acquired by the Nabatean artists.

A VESTIBULE
B SIDE ROOMS
C PURIFYING BASIN
D GREAT HALL
E NICHES (OR LOCULI)

46-47 The Khasneh is fronted by an open space scattered with alluvium. Recent surveys have shown that the ancient paving of this area lies at a depth of more than 13 feet. The monument was therefore probably originally reached from a high flight of steps.

46 bottom The intercolumns of the upper floor contain carved bas-reliefs of female figures. Six of them, although extremely worn, can be identified as amazons thanks to their short tunics and axes brandished above their heads. In the past, however, they were thought to be Maenads.

47 top left The external intercolumns of the vestibule contain relief figures of the Dioscuri.

47 top right The roof of the tholos is sumptuously adorned with a crown of frontal palmette tiles.

Corinthian columns 40 feet high. Despite appearances, only the two central columns are free-standing, the other four being connected to the mass behind. Two huge equestrian groups carved in high relief between the external pairs very probably represent the Dioscuri. These sculptures are very worn as are the other nine relief figures that adorn the façade, but the damage is only partially ascribable to natural erosion, the main culprits being Christian and Muslim iconoclasts; careful observation reveals holes left on and around the figures by rifle shots. The design of the frieze running above the

columns consists of foliage and volutes alternating with vases framed by facing griffins; a scroll decoration completes the *tympanum*, which had at the center a Gorgon's head (interpreted by some writers as an eagle with outspread wings). In the corners of the architrave two lions (or sphinxes) have the function of acroteria. The upper part of the attic that separates the two stories presents an unbroken row of rosettes. The second story, of aerial elegance, is divided into three parts. At the center is a *tholos*, or round templet, with a conical roof topped by an urn. This is what gave the building its Arab name,

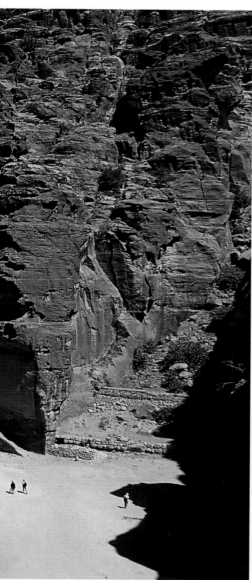

47 center The tympanum of the pediment is decorated with a much-ruined figure, interpreted as the bust of a Gorgon emerging from a background of foliage.

47 bottom The monument's full Arab name, Khasneh al Faraoun (the Pharaoh's Treasury), is based on a legend totally devoid of historical foundation.

the Treasury; the Bedouins believed that it contained immense riches and, in an attempt to gain possession of these, repeatedly fired their rifles at it, with the intention of smashing it. The *tholos* is flanked by two semi-pediments, each one supported by corner columns; the two niches to the rear, set against the back wall, stand between two pairs of paired semicolumns. The four figures adorning the semi-pediments and the two at the sides of the *tholos* are identifiable as amazons brandishing axes in their right hands. The two sculptures in the two rear niches represent winged Nikes. Far more problematic was the interpretation of the female figure in the central intercolumn of the *tholos*.

The figure is holding a cornucopia in her left hand and a patera in her right, typical of the goddess Tyche (Destiny, but here meaning Fortune); moreover, slightly below, the acroterion around the apex of the pediment is in a solar disk set between ears of wheat and framed by another two cornucopias. Such symbology is closely related to the goddess Isis. On this basis there is a tendency today to see her as the goddess Isis assimilated with Tyche and at the same time the Nabatean goddess Al Uzza, in accordance with a form of syncretism widely recorded in Hellenistic times. This identification is supported by a comparison of the way the goddess is posed with similar portrayals of Tyche-Isis on vases of Alexandrian production, in particular a Ptolemaic jug worked in relief and housed in Stuttgart. An unbroken entablature with a frieze depicting garlands of leaves and nuts runs above the capitals of the second story and four huge eagles served as acroteria. The interior of the building – quite disappointing compared with its grand façade – consists of a large vestibule or pronaos, 46 feet wide and 19 deep, with eight steps leading to the central chamber; this is a large cube, 40 feet

square, flanked on three sides by smaller rooms. The only decorations are the pedimented surrounds to the three doors. Another two smaller rooms, also reached via steps, flank the vestibule. The exceptional architectural type seen in the Khasneh, as well as the complex and refined decorations, would suggest the work of craftsmen from afar, probably from Alexandrian cultural circles or at least influenced by Greek artistic style, who worked side by side with the local stone cutters. Equally, it could be a design by a Nabatean artisan trained in Hellenistic spheres. This dilemma is closely related to the age-old debate as to the date of the monument. Today there is a tendency to reject the idea that the Khasneh was erected at the time of the emperor Hadrian's visit to Petra (in 129 or 130), with a more likely date being a period between the middle of the first century BC and the middle of the first century AD. There is also an open debate as to the purpose of the Khasneh: tomb or temple? The arrangement of the

internal rooms and the presence of niches that could quite easily have contained sarcophagi would suggest it was used for burials rather than as a sanctuary. Such a fine monument could only have been the tomb of a king and, considering the date proposed, this monarch may have been Aretas III Philhellen, Obodas II or Aretas IV, responsible for Petra's urban renewal. The matter is so far unresolved.

48 bottom left One of the pillars of the pronaos, the third from the left, collapsed at an unknown time and was restored in 1960.

48 center top The vestibule, 46 feet wide and 20 deep, leads to a large chamber and two small rooms that open on each side of it.

48 center bottom The interior of the Khasneh consists of a large room, 40 feet square with huge doorways leading to three smaller rooms.

48 top right The capitals that adorn the Khasneh are a local interpretation of the classical Corinthian modules, imported from the Greek world.

48 bottom right There is a magnificent view of the narrow mouth of the Interior Siq from inside the large chamber.

49 left You will see a hemispherical hollow on the threshold of the large chamber linked to a second basin via a small channel dug in the rock; this is a purifying bowl which collected the blood of sacrificed goats.

49 right Superb, spectacular and well preserved, the Khasneh has become the symbol of Petra.

50 left Tomb 70, situated on the left side of the Outer Siq, is easily recognized thanks to its singular appearance. Considerably out from the back wall, it is surrounded by a crown of battlements and has three identical sides.

50 top right On the side opposite the façade of the Khasneh, on the right wall of the Siq, is a large opening without a façade. This was presumably a triclinium and is one of the largest in Petra.

51 top left High up along the walls of the Outer Siq runs the channel which contained the earthenware pipes of the aqueduct; the water flowed through these at high pressure.

51 bottom left Tomb 67 is one of the group of four adjacent tombs dug in the left-hand wall of the Outer Siq, not far from the Khasneh. Of the "double-cornice" type, it is known for the remarkable funerary chamber on the attic level, between the two crow-stepped battlements. The square-plan chamber is totally bare.

The gorge veers to the right from the clearing on which stands the Khasneh and starts to descend sharply towards the ancient city.

There are tombs on both sides, dug at a certain height from the ground and now in quite bad condition. On the left not far beyond

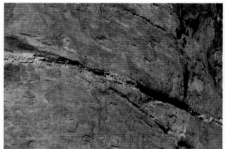

a large square chamber (which could have been a *triclinium*) opened in the opposite wall, the most attentive observers will see the remains of a façade (number 66 in Brünnow's classification) with a still-preserved circular and diamond-shaped base, surmounted by a right-hand pilaster strip. Part of the structure collapsed in 1847 destroying its Greek epigraph; this, however, had been copied and is known to be the tomb of Arriano, who died at the age of 27 of "an illness that overwhelms all" and was mourned by his elderly mother. Initially still confined between high walls (the course of the aqueduct is easily distinguished on the right, high

above the ground, with several terracotta pipes still in place), the gorge then widens suddenly. For this reason it here takes the name of Outer Siq. The most striking structures include, to the left, a large double-cornice tomb, its portal framed by four high pilaster strips, and the subsequent Tomb 70, the main body, which is crowned with a crow-step battlement and juts out significantly from the rock face. The road now runs beside the normally dry bed of a seasonal river, created by the streams that descend during the winter rains from the side valleys. The inconsistent stream now carries tons of pebbles and sand downstream, but at the height of Petra's splendor – starting from the reign of Aretas IV – the Siq looked very different. First, the road level was six to nine feet lower than now and the road was paved.

The river was robustly channelled and perhaps later even covered; the waters surfaced hundreds of yards downstream and joined those of Wadi Mousa and Wadi Mataha near a *nymphaeum*, described later. To the right and left, dozens of tombs created a backdrop of great scenographic effect. You can imagine the thrill that this sight must have stirred in the merchants arriving in Petra with their caravans from distant lands after crossing boundless deserts. Approximately 200 yards before the theater, the Siq forms a natural arena; on the sides of this – to the left in

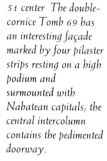

51 center The double-cornice Tomb 69 has an interesting façade marked by four pilaster strips resting on a high podium and surmounted with Nabatean capitals; the central intercolumn contains the pedimented doorway.

51 top right Numerous arch-headed tombs stand along the "Streets of Façades" in the Outer Siq; these are hard to date but may be from the first century BC.

51 center right and bottom The "Streets of Façades" are true compendiums of Petra's most common architectural styles. There are cavetto and double-cornice façades, with battlements on top, some with double battlements and arch-headed ones. Such variety indicates that the Nabateans were open to influence from various cultures.

52-53 *This view of the hollow that opens along the Outer Siq, shortly before the Theater, clearly highlights the characteristic rows of tombs cut into the rock. To the rear rise the mountains that surround the urban area.*

52 bottom *Standing out amidst the myriad of façades crammed along the mountain walls are some highly elaborate and large tombs, which were the burial places of Petra's richest families.*

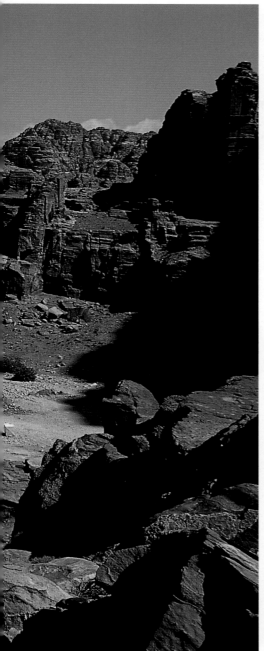

particular – are aligned dozens of tombs in several rows. Most are crowned with single and double battlements but several are arched; others are of the cavetto or double-cornice type. These tombs are linked to one another by narrow passages and flights of steps, giving the impression of streets lined with buildings; not surprisingly they are known as the "Streets of Façades." The fact that many of the tombs on the lowest levels seem half-buried by alluvial detritus (such that you can no longer see the entrance to some of them), demonstrates how violently Wadi Mousa returned to the Siq after the collapse of the Nabatean dam built at its mouth.

53 top The ceaseless erosive action of the elements has devastated many of the façades that once adorned the sides of the Siq, though they have now become splendid works of abstract art.

53 center In some parts (such as the valley that opens to the left of the Outer Siq, top), as well as the customary rock tombs, there are quarry faces from which the Nabateans obtained their building materials.

53 bottom This spectacular aerial view of the Outer Siq demonstrates that the rock tombs flank the main valley on terraces at various levels, achieving

spectacular effects. These were originally joined by flights of steps, which earned this particular stretch of the Siq the nickname of "Streets of Façades."

54 top *Inside, the tomb of Uneishu is a vast roughly square-shaped chamber, as usual completely bare, with three loculi in the back wall and another four in each of the two side walls. Spacious and dry because of its raised position above the bottom of the Siq, the tomb was long inhabited by the Bedouins. Indeed, until the middle of the 20th century, a similar form of reuse was common among most of the Nabatean necropolises.*

THE TOMB OF UNEISHU

54-55 To the extreme right in the picture is the Tomb of Uneishu, not to be confused with a similar tomb that stands not far from it (visible at the center).

55 top The Tomb of Uneishu has a double-cornice façade and the doorway, between pilaster strips with Nabatean capitals, is crowned with an elegant pediment. The monument was preceded by a colonnaded courtyard, onto which opened a triclinium.

55 bottom The rock wall of the Outer Siq near the Tomb of Uneishu contains a large number of rock structures, most with very severe façades, crowned with the typically Assyrian crow-stepped battlements. At the corners there are sometimes pilaster strips with characteristic Nabatean "horn" capitals, and simple pediments of classical inspiration may surmount the entrance doorways. The various burial places were linked by flights of steps and paths, some of which are still usable.

By rights this tomb should be included on the next itinerary, because it is one of the so-called "Royal Tombs;" however, its location suggests inclusion here for the visitor's convenience. It is entered from the road that runs along the bottom of the Siq, by climbing up a path to the right, before the theater. Its majestic double-cornice façade, set slightly back from the edge of the mountain, is very easy to identify. Known as Tomb 813 in Brünnow's classification, it was given its present name by a loculus cover slab, found in the vicinity in the 19th century; the inscription sculpted on the stone bears the epitaph of Uneishu, minister of the queen Shaquilat. She was the wife of Aretas IV and mother of Rabbel II, during whose childhood she reigned for six years. This and other fragments of inscriptions found inside have allowed the monument to be dated to a period between 70 and 76 AD. The large number of loculi present in the funerary chamber would suggest that the tomb was used for at least three decades by Uneishu's direct relatives, in keeping with a widely ascertained custom. This rather elaborate tomb is preceded by a courtyard and has a *triclinium*, visible to the left.

THE THEATER

Not far from the Tomb of Uneishu, on the left of the Outer Siq, the visitor's attention is drawn to the huge auditorium of the theater, one of the most spectacular rock structures in the Rose-red City. Despite the monument's standard Roman plan (with a perfectly semi-circular orchestra), its date of origin is not certain. It is thought to have been built during the reign of Aretas IV (8 BC-40 AD), when Petra was still independent, but already strongly influenced by the art and

tangible evidence of this gigantic excavation work; the orientation of the surviving façades, visible to the right and left, indicate where the above-mentioned street ran.

It is conceivable that these vast apertures were in fact walled up and that the filling collapsed during the earthquakes that struck the city repeatedly, although there is no visible evidence to support this hypothesis.

As it appears today, the auditorium, most of which is carved into the rock, has 45 rows of seats, divided into three horizontal sections and six vertical ones by steps that allowed the spectators to reach their seats.

An ingenious drainage system – achieved with complex channelling – carried the rainwater away. The theater is thought to have seated between 6,000 and 8,500 people, but some writers raise this limit to 10,000, a third of the city's entire population. The orchestra, 82 feet in

culture of Rome. In this initial phase the theater must have reached the height of the second annular passage visible today. This large building reflects Petra's wealth. Later, after Trajan had annexed the Nabatean kingdom to the empire in 106, the structure was extended greatly at the expense of those tombs along the road behind it. They were ruthlessly carved away to accommodate a new auditorium sector.

The huge holes left halfway up the back wall – what remains of the original burial chambers – are

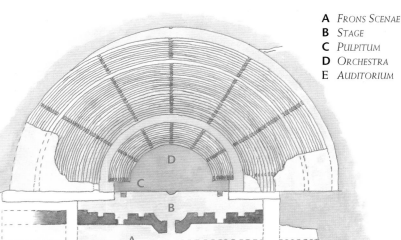

A   FRONS SCENAE
B   STAGE
C   PULPITUM
D   ORCHESTRA
E   AUDITORIUM

56 bottom left The position of a theater inside a necropolis is quite unusual, but it must be remembered that the Nabateans had a different relationship

with death. Suffice to observe how the entire city center was surrounded by the façades of hundreds of tombs, giving the city perspective views that

its particular position would otherwise have made impossible. Moreover, the structure must have been an integral part of the monumentalization

desired by Aretas IV of the paved road that ran through the Siq and which, then as now, constituted the favorite approach road to Petra.

56 top right The auditorium of the theater, dug in a particularly beautiful bank of polychrome sandstone, has exceptional acoustics.

diameter, was also carved from the emerging rock. The stage platform was raised according to Roman custom but only a few traces have survived earthquakes and floods.

The well-restored stage, fronted by the traditional *pulpitum* (a low wall with niches), was 124 feet wide. Behind it the *frons scenae* (the back stage), with three entrances, must have had two colonnaded levels and been sumptuously enriched with frescoes, statues and marble friezes.

Two barrel-vaulted passages,

once plastered and painted, are visible at the sides of the stage and led via covered passages and steps to the orchestra and the auditorium. From the exterior, the theater must have looked very somber and solid, a blind wall no less than 82 feet high and approximately 195-210 feet long, that completely blocked the view of the auditorium.

The great earthquake of 363 probably destroyed the theatre, but many scholars believe that performances had already ceased to be staged here some time earlier.

56 bottom right and 57 top The images present two views of the vault-covered passages that led to the auditorium and orchestra.

56-57 Some believe that, as well as staging tragedies, the theatre was also used for funeral services.

58 top Detail of the
Tomb of Sextius
Florentinus; it has an
arched pediment adorned
with a gorgon's head.

58 bottom Detail of the
entrance to the Urn
Tomb, showing the
Doric frieze interpreted
in the local style.

58 center An unusual
view of the Jebel el
Kubtha rock face, in
which are carved the
façades of the Royal
Tombs.

59 The Urn Tomb,
fronted by a short
colonnade and high
two-story substructures.

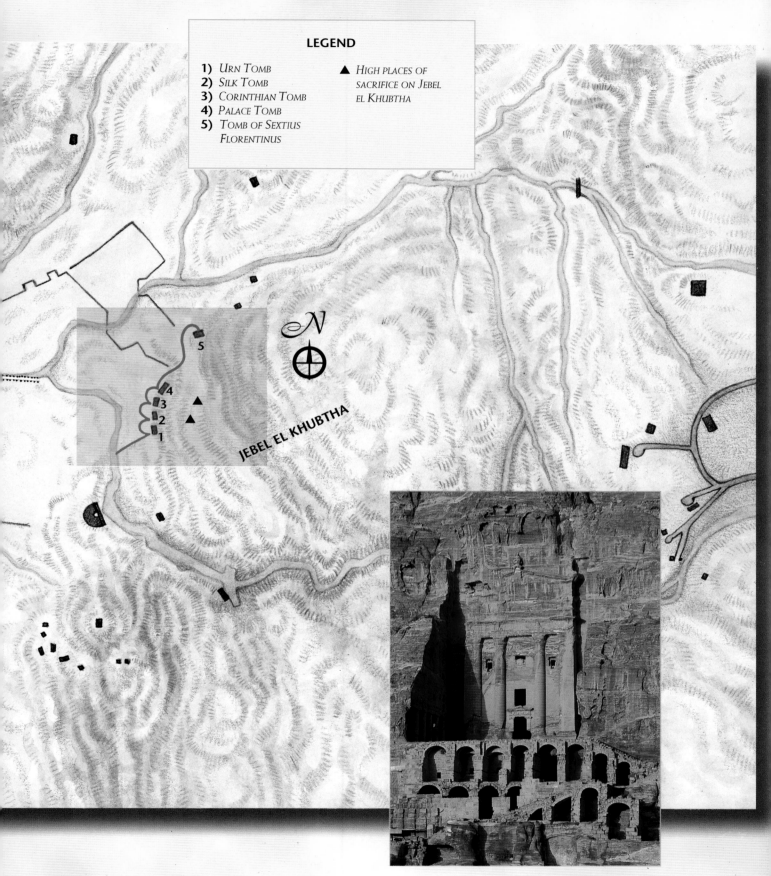

LEGEND

1) URN TOMB
2) SILK TOMB
3) CORINTHIAN TOMB
4) PALACE TOMB
5) TOMB OF SEXTIUS FLORENTINUS

▲ HIGH PLACES OF SACRIFICE ON JEBEL EL KHUBTHA

N

JEBEL EL KHUBTHA

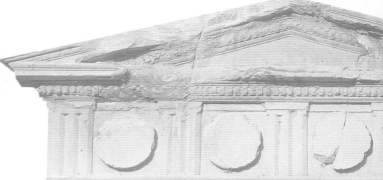

THE URN TOMB

Not far from the theater and just past the refreshment kiosk, on the right-hand side of the road that leads from the Siq to the center of Petra, an easily spotted path climbs up the rock face of Jebel el Khubtha to the so-called "Royal Tombs." Although there is no written evidence or archaeological find to confirm that these are indeed the burial places of the Nabatean sovereigns, their size – and

platform, the arches visible today being all that remains. The soaring façade is structured like the front of a temple and framed by two corner pillars against which are set quarter-columns; the two central half-columns on the podium flank the entrance, surmounted by a Doric frieze (the metopes of which are replaced with circles) and a small pediment. The upper part of the intercolumns contains three loculi but

consequently, the high estimated cost of their construction – would suggest that this assumption is correct.

The most striking if by no means the largest of these structures is the Urn Tomb, easily recognized by the great substructures that front it and the extraordinary way the façade is set back from the natural profile of the mountain. Similar in plan to the Petra Forum Rest House tomb, it is preceded by a large courtyard, 70 feet wide and enclosed on two sides by low colonnades dug into the rocks. The front of this open space was widened with the construction of a raised

only the middle one has preserved its closing stone, adorned with a much-deteriorated male head and torso, identified by some as the effigy of King Malchus II (40-70 AD).

The large tripartitioned attic story (the lower architrave immediately above the capitals also reveals the presence of four bas-relief busts, presumably deities) sustains a pediment with tympanum devoid of decoration. On the very top of this pediment is the acroterion, in the form of an urn, after which the tomb was named.

Although, as always, very austere and devoid of ornamentation, the

61 top *The Urn Tomb is a splendid example of a' pedimented building, its façade imitating a distyle in antis temple. On the basis of stylistic and architectural analysis this is thought to be the tomb of King Malchus II (40-70 AD) and his family. Recently however, it has been suggested that it may be the tomb of Aretas IV (8 BC-40 AD). Unfortunately, the three loculi are empty and there are no specific elements to support one or the other of the theories.*

61 bottom *In 447 the Urn Tomb was turned into a church, as shown by an inscription in Greek painted on the wall beside the niche in the left wall of the underground chamber. This records the consecration of the building by the bishop Jason. The holes seen in the floor in front of the central apse housed the small pillars that supported the balustrade all around the altar, typical of the tradition of the Byzantine period. The pulpit stood to the right of the altar.*

interior deserves a visit; it is a massive chamber, approximately 62 feet wide and 56 deep and the unplastered walls look as though they have been covered with watered silk. It was probably used as a *triclinium* and altered when the monument was converted to a church, in 447. At this time the triclinial beds were destroyed, the floor levelled, a large window opened above the door, two side doors hewn out and the back wall – which originally had four niches – was given a sort of *arcosolium* apse by joining the two central recesses.

A *SUBSTRUCTURES*
B *COURTYARD*
C *PORTICOES WITH DORIC COLUMNS*
D *LARGE CHAMBER OR TRICLINIUM*
E *ARCOSOLIA*
F *NICHES*

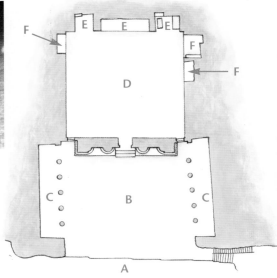

62 left The striking appearance of the Silk Tomb, also known as the Rainbow Tomb for the multitude of colors in its fine sandstone façade, has stirred the imagination of many writers and poets.

62 center The beautiful color combinations seen in the bank of fine sandstone lying beside the Silk Tomb are highlighted by the low rays of sunset or after a storm, when the rock is still wet.

62 left This picture permits a comparison between the façade of the Silk Tomb and an adjacent crow-stepped tomb; not only is the former seen to be brightly colored, it also has a more complex architectural design, particularly evident on the attic level.

62-63 Unfortunately, the position of the Corinthian Tomb has done little to help its preservation. Despite being seriously damaged, it remains extremely interesting for its remarkable blend of different architectural styles.

THE SILK TOMB

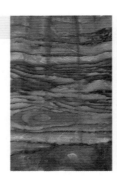

A few yards past the Urn Tomb (keeping the rock face to your right), you come to a monument that is considered one of the most photogenic subjects in Petra. This is the Silk Tomb, thus named for the spectacular polychrome veining of the stone it was dug into. The finely streaked sandstone contains bands of color that range from powder pink, salmon and white, to pale

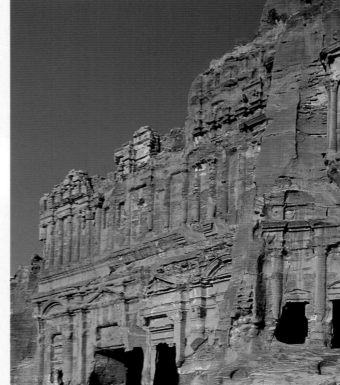

blue, ochre and saffron yellow, creating an enchantingly beautiful spectrum. As well as for its brilliant coloring, the tomb deserves careful observation for the elaborate crow-step façade which is still visible although fairly eroded. The lower part is marked by four prominent pilaster strips, topped with the characteristic Nabatean capitals; the lateral intercolumns frame two niches which, quite unusually, contain numerous relief figures, now too worn to be identified with certainty. The attic level, that sustains the Assyrian-style battlements, is divided by four short pilaster strips with capitals in line with those below; this lend a highly animated appearance to the whole.

THE CORINTHIAN TOMB

Standing adjacent to the Silk Tomb, the Corinthian Tomb is a monument of considerable architectural interest but unfortunately has suffered more than others from the ravages of time and the elements. Exposed to strong winds and falling rocks, the structure is greatly damaged but nonetheless remains impressive: 80 feet wide by approximately 92 high. It was given its name by two of the first visitors to Petra – the Englishmen Irby and Mangles – because of the style of the capitals, similar to those of the Khasneh. For its similarity to this building, the Corinthian Tomb is often hastily dismissed as a sort of bad copy. Actually, devoid of

projections and avant-corps and hence purely decorative, more careful inspection of the architecture of the Corinthian Tomb reveals that it differs greatly from the Khasneh, and the similarity lies mainly in the division of the upper story. As a whole it is far more precise to say that it represents an attempted compromise between traditional Nabatean and imported Hellenistic styles. The entire lower order was clearly designed in accordance with traditional local canons: the very squat half-columns, the semi-circular crowning of the main portal, the broken pediment and the repetition in the large attic story of horizontal (cornices) and vertical

(pilaster strips) lines closely resemble the Bab al Siq Triclinium. The upper story, with its two semi-pediments and central tholos, floral capitals and the soaring verticality of the whole is instead a tribute to Hellenistic taste and the Alexandrian imprint already applied to the Khasneh. This eclectic combination may appear hardly organic and even discordant to our eyes, but the ancient inhabitants of Petra may not have shared this opinion. Standing in a privileged position in line with the great Colonnade Street, at the height of its splendor this building must have been a backdrop of considerable scenographic effect.

Once again, the interior is disappointing and, as it is also difficult to reach, you are advised against visiting it. Strangely, the doors lead to many different-sized chambers, separate from one another. Given the presence in the main room of numerous niches for deposition, it is thought to have been a collective tomb, destined to accommodate the remains of a high-ranking figure and his family. In the absence of inscriptions or other historical evidence and on the basis of mere supposition related to its architectural style, some believe that this person was king Aretas III whereas other historians think it was Malchus II, making the dating of the monument open to debate.

A *FUNERARY CHAMBERS*
B *LOCULI*

63 top right and center As illustrated clearly in these photographs, the two smaller doors in the left-hand intercolumns, not balanced by similar ones on the right, constitute an incongruous disturbance to the symmetry of the Corinthian Tomb's façade.
Another extremely anomalous presence is that of the two large windows (only the right one is still intact) set at the sides of the main doorway. They seem unrelated to the presumed funerary use of the monument and it is thought that they may have been opened in the Byzantine period, when the building was adapted for a different use.

63 bottom right The upper order of the tomb, with the tholos between two semi-pediments, betrays obvious links with the late Hellenistic architectural tradition already experimented with in the Khasneh. Unlike the latter, however, the Corinthian Tomb is totally devoid of group statues or bas-relief figures.

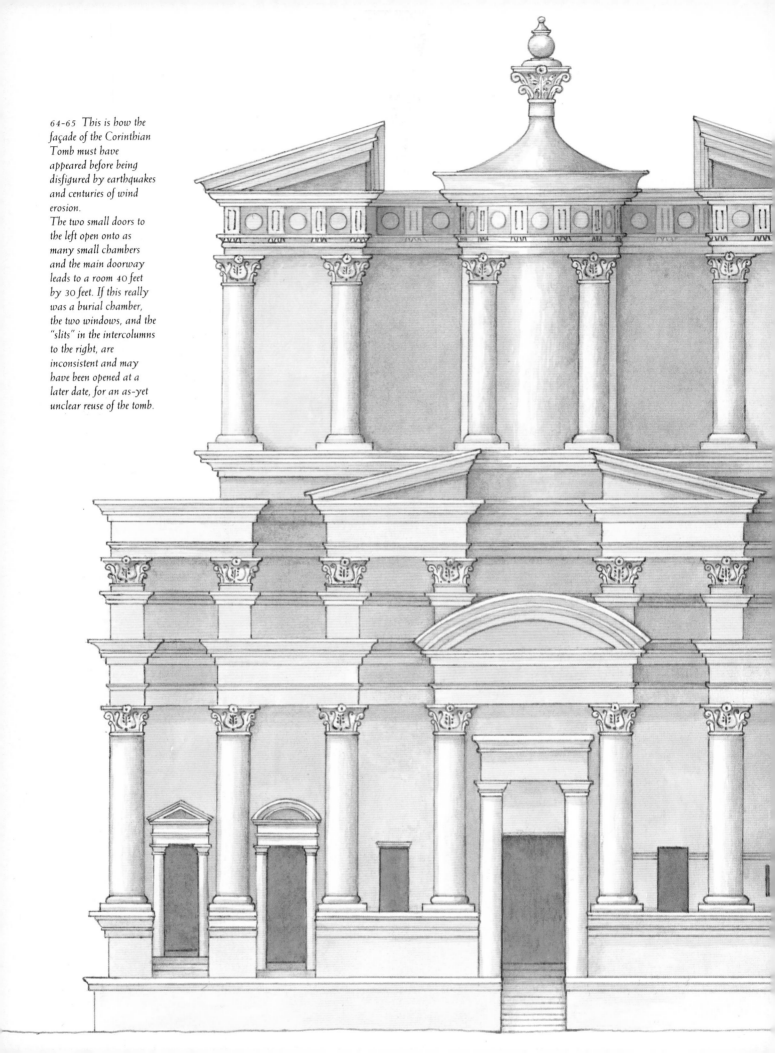

64-65 *This is how the façade of the Corinthian Tomb must have appeared before being disfigured by earthquakes and centuries of wind erosion.*
The two small doors to the left open onto as many small chambers and the main doorway leads to a room 40 feet by 30 feet. If this really was a burial chamber, the two windows, and the "slits" in the intercolumns to the right, are inconsistent and may have been opened at a later date, for an as-yet unclear reuse of the tomb.

65 right The photograph highlights the serious damage caused to the Corinthian Tomb by the ravages of time.
The section of façade surrounding the main doorway seems particularly eroded, such that the opening looks like a natural cave. Inside the door, there is a great gaping hole in the floor of the main room, making access almost impossible. There would seem to be an underground chamber below and this may have been uncovered when part of the walls collapsed as a result of centuries of unfavorable weather conditions. Nonetheless, the cavity, blocked by rubble and never properly investigated, may merely have been produced by erosion. Again, because the monument has been so eroded, it is very hard to say whether the room to the left of the large doorway was a separate one, or part of the main chamber — a sort of very large niche. The plan drawn by Laborde, who saw the tomb in 1828, showed just three unconnected rooms.

THE PALACE TOMB

66-67 As it has been pointed out by several writers – including Browning – the façade of the Palace Tomb resembles the frons scenae of a theater, more so than any other in Petra.

66 bottom The picture shows how the attic storey (or "third story") presents the unusual juxtaposition of decorative elements repeated again and again.

The last of the Royal Tombs true and proper is the colossal Palace Tomb, situated right beside the Corinthian Tomb. Although the façade has lost most of its upper part, it is still the most imposing in Petra, 160 feet wide and approximately 150 feet high.

This name is used because by tradition the architecture of this tomb is thought to imitate that of the large Hellenistic palaces. Although some believe it was inspired by the Golden House in Rome, Nero's sumptuous palace, there is no specific evidence to bear out this supposition. It is clearly very different from the other known pediment tombs of the Nabatean City; indeed it can be considered unique, for the stereometric plan, its decoration and the striking difference

between the ground floor and the upper levels. Fronted by a large balcony of sorts, and originally entered up steps cut into the sandstone, the four huge doors are framed by half-pillars with Nabatean capitals below double molding with a smooth frieze. Each aperture stands between two pillars flanked by a quarter column and "horn" capitals, which support a double-dentilled cornice that soars vertically; the side ones support a pediment with triangular tympanum and the inner ones a semi-circular pediment. The whole appears majestic and well balanced. The second story, separated by a highly unusual and completely smooth unbroken entablature, seems to be the result of a change in the original project.

66

The architectural decoration consists of the juxtaposition of repeated identical elements, intended to create a disconcerting overall effect. The 18 half-columns, also with Nabatean capitals, are not at all aligned with the vertical elements of the story below. Divided in pairs, they support a double, alternating recessed and advanced entablature without frieze. Above this was a third story – or attic – divided into several registers by short pilaster strips which were the continuation of the half-columns of the lower story. Except for the right-hand section, this story was constructed in masonry, as the front of

the cliff was too low for the whole building. Unfortunately, much of this, built with large stones, collapsed during earthquakes. High up to the right, there appears to be a fourth story, slightly set back from the vertical line of the façade and marked by pilaster strips partially hewn into the rock. In the spring of 1998, this writer noticed what looks like the bases of as many columns in line with each of the above pilaster strips, speculating that the façade may have ended with a continuous gallery sustaining a crowning entablature. This is merely a hypothesis and awaits investigation by the experts.

Yet again, the interior of the Palace Tomb is quite bare, the four doors leading to as many unadorned rooms, which were undoubtedly originally plastered and frescoed. Only the middle two chambers are open to one another. There is no documentary evidence, but this is thought possibly to have been the tomb of Rabbel II, the last Nabatean king.

68-69 The drawing shows how the massive Palace Tomb may originally have looked. Up to the upper cornice of the attic story (or third story), its reconstruction presents no great difficulties because the upper-right-hand corner of the monument is relatively well preserved. This gives a good idea of what the structure must have looked like before the constructed masonry collapsed. The top story is more difficult to picture. The way the rock was cut (to the right) at the top and the presence of the pilaster strips carved in the recessed story would suggest that the building originally rose a good bit higher.

Halfway up the second story, a large natural fissure, on the left side of the monument, was filled, with a wall resting on a relieving arch, still visible. Such a large substructure must have had to sustain considerable weight while what remains of the façade betrays a programmed repetition of identical structural elements. The way the top story, partially dug in the stone, is set back would seem to avail the hypothesis of a gallery, a replica (three-dimensional this time) of the mock colonnade on the second story. This gallery would date the Palace Tomb to the time of Trajan, or at least to a period after the Roman conquest.

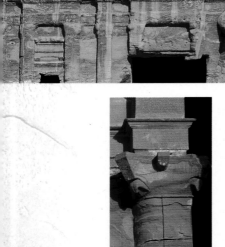

68 top The façade clearly denotes the presence of six niches in the intercolumns on the second story. Their function is unknown but some writers believe they contained marble slabs bearing memorial inscriptions; these, however, would have been practically impossible to read and their presence would have broken the rhythm of solids and voids suggested by the mock colonnade. The mystery therefore remains.

68 bottom The use of Nabatean capitals bears witness to the syncretism between local traditions and imported architectural tastes.

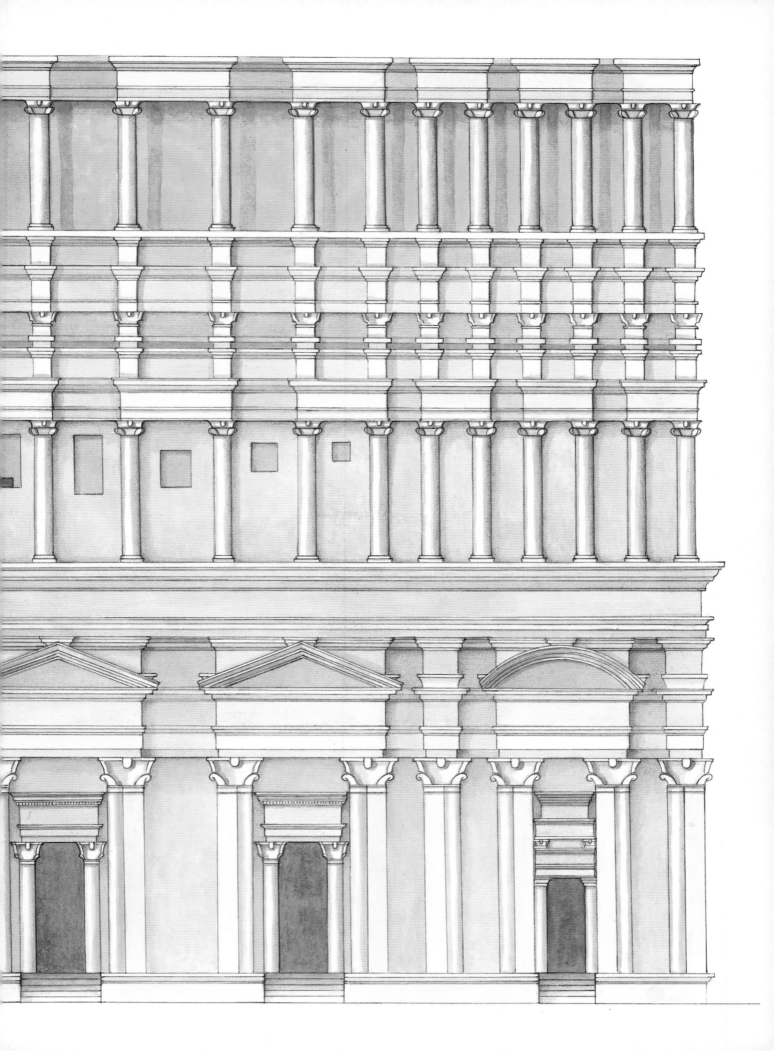

THE TOMB OF SEXTIUS FLORENTINUS

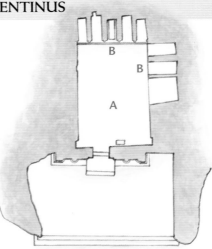

A few minutes from the Palace Tomb is a monument of considerable interest, although very small compared with the giants described previously. Technically speaking, this is not one of the Royal Tombs, but its importance and beauty prompt its inclusion on this itinerary. Follow the track that descends into Wadi Mataha, on the side of Jebel el Khubtha, which drops to become a sort of promontory. To the left you will see the ruins (here hardly visible) of the Roman-Byzantine ring of walls, while to the right a spectacular

A *FUNERARY CHAMBER*
B *LOCULI*

70 right The tomb of Sextius Florentinus shows the continuing application of Hellenistic architectural language in Petra even after the Roman conquest.

71 The gorgon's head that adorns the semi-circular tympanum seems to be based on a similar decoration on the pediment of the Khasneh. This would confirm that the latter does not date from the time of Hadrian's visit (129-130), as the tomb of Sextius Florentinus dates just from 129 or 130.

70 top left Half-pillars with quarter columns leaning against them are very common in Petra. The composite style of the Tomb of Sextius Florentinus denotes local, Hellenistic and very marginal Roman influence.

70 bottom left Although he was Roman, the Governor Sextius Florentinus must have loved the city in which he spent the last years of his life; this is confirmed by the appearance of his tomb, totally consistent with the repertoire of Nabatean architecture.

flight of steps cut into the stone rises towards the "High Place of Sacrifice" on Jebel el Khubtha.

A few yards farther on, at the end of the northernmost tip of the rocky massif, appears the splendid façade of the Tomb of Sextius Florentinus. Hardly ever in the sunlight and much ruined by the passage of time, it conveys a mournful elegance and, in its most eroded parts, displays a stunning range of colors. It is highly elaborate and divided into two orders: the lower one has a doorway framed by four pilaster strips and topped with a pediment and triangular tympanum; the upper one, above the continuous entablature, on which is a large arch, has an attic story divided into several registers by four cornices and short pilaster strips and crowned with a triangular pediment. The bas-relief that adorns the semi-circular

tympanum, surmounted by an eagle, depicts a gorgon's head set against a background of foliage. A porticoed courtyard probably extended in front of the building, as indicated by some fragments of column half-buried in the sand. The interior consists of a funerary chamber, the back wall of which is divided by pilaster strips framing five loculi; another three loculi open in the right-hand wall.

This is the only tomb in Petra that can be dated with relative accuracy, thanks to a very worn funerary inscription in Latin carved on the lower entablature. The text states that his son dedicated the burial place to Sextius Florentinus, legate of Hadrian and Proprietor of the Province of Arabia between 126 and 129 or 130 AD.

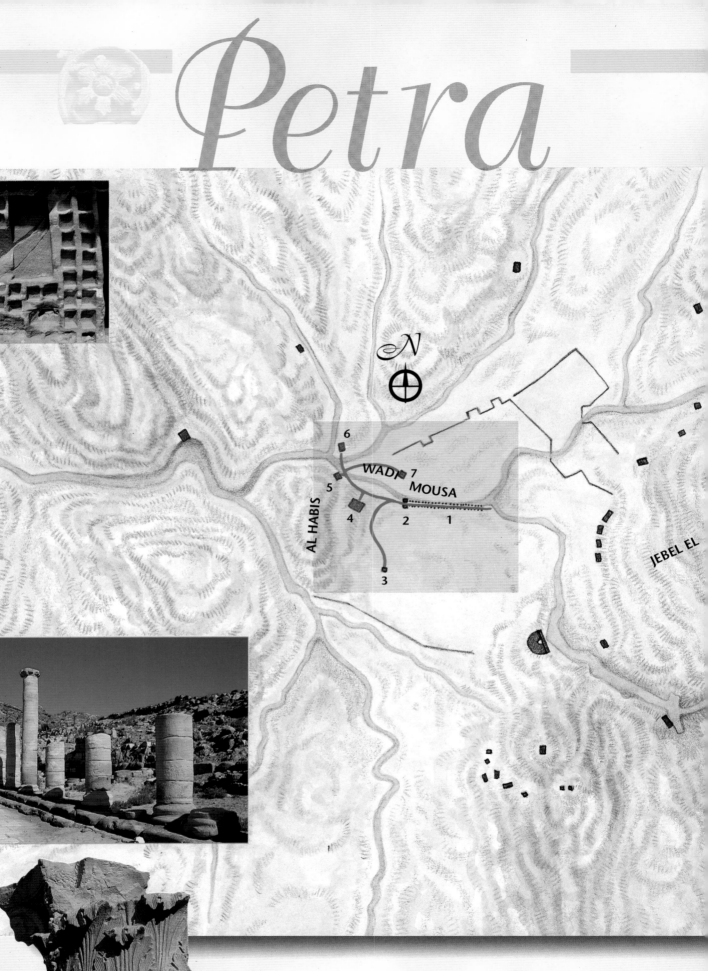

Petra

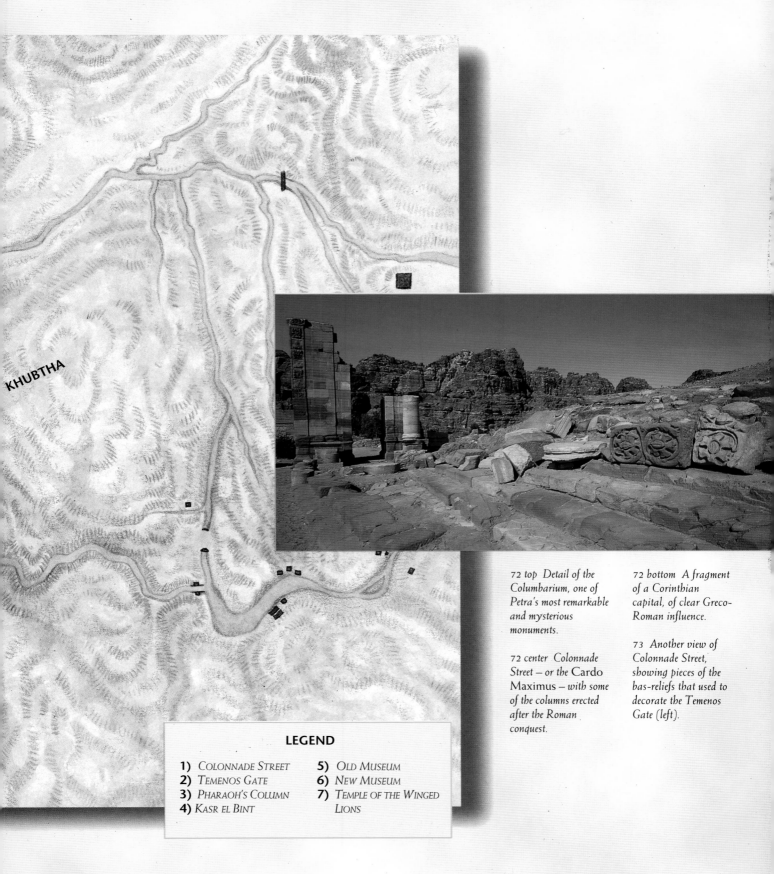

KHUBTHA

72 top Detail of the Columbarium, one of Petra's most remarkable and mysterious monuments.

72 center Colonnade Street – or the Cardo Maximus – with some of the columns erected after the Roman conquest.

72 bottom A fragment of a Corinthian capital, of clear Greco-Roman influence.

73 Another view of Colonnade Street, showing pieces of the bas-reliefs that used to decorate the Temenos Gate (left).

LEGEND

1) COLONNADE STREET
2) TEMENOS GATE
3) PHARAOH'S COLUMN
4) KASR EL BINT

5) OLD MUSEUM
6) NEW MUSEUM
7) TEMPLE OF THE WINGED LIONS

THE COLONNADE STREET

At the present stage of archaeological excavation, what remains of the city proper extends along the course of Wadi Mousa, between Jebel el Khubtha and the al Habis rock. The ruins start just past the lower mouth of the Outer Siq, to the left, approximately 400 yards from the Theater.

The urban layout consisted mainly of an expanse of small flat-roofed houses and occupied much of the valley,

A	COLONNADE STREET	**L**	BATHS
B	NYMPHAEUM	**M**	TEMENOS GATE
C	SHRINE	**N**	SMALL TEMPLE
D	UPPER MARKET	**O**	TEMENOS
E	MIDDLE MARKET	**P**	KASR EL BINT
F	LOWER MARKET	**Q**	GREAT ALTAR
G	PROPYLAEUM	**R**	TEMPLE OF THE
H	GREAT TEMPLE		WINGED LIONS
I	ROMAN HOUSE	**S**	ROYAL PALACE
J	PHARAOH'S RUINS	**T**	BYZANTINE TOWER
K	PHARAOH'S COLUMN	**U**	BYZANTINE CHURCH

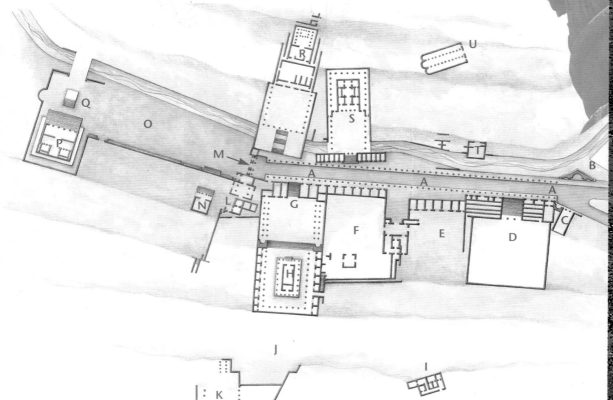

now reduced to a stretch of sand, bushes and well-squared stone ashlars. Two strong rings of walls with incorporated towers, very probably built towards the end of the first century BC, defended the city to the north and south. Several archaeologists believe that a considerable number of ancient structures still lie quite well preserved under a foot or so of rubble and sand. If this is so, future generations will be kept busy. At the moment, however, it is Colonnade Street that attracts visitors' attention.

The street commences at the point where Wadi Mataha joins the seasonal river coming from the Outer Siq, but it probably used to start slightly farther east. From this point on, the waterway is, by common accord, once more known as Wadi Mousa and passes through the entire urban area from east to west. Colonnade Street runs parallel to it for approximately 300 yards, and sections of the strong embankments built by the Nabateans to contain the *wadi* can still be seen. This had probably become the city's main

thoroughfare well before the reign of Aretas IV, but this monarch gave it its first monumental design. It seems certain, however, that the stone paving and the two colonnaded porticoes of which some sections have survived can be attributed to the emperor Trajan (98-117 AD), who had conquered the Nabatean capital and wanted to embellish it according to western tastes. Having, in keeping with Roman tradition, adopted the name of *Cardo Maximus*, the street became the bustling center of the metropolis. All the major

74 top Colonnade Street was paved and flanked on both sides by colonnaded porticoes, beneath which were shops and bars. The picture shows, to the left, one of the flights of steps that led to the markets.

74-75 This sweeping view covers the entire length of Colonnade Street with the Temenos Gate near the foreground and the Great Temple compound to the right; the Temple of the Winged Lions is seen to the left.

75 top The fact that the paving of Colonnade Street – or Cardo Maximus – dates from Roman times was confirmed in 1958 when a dedicatory inscription to Trajan dated 114 AD was found.

public buildings stood along it and business was conducted, money exchanged and people ate and drank here chatting idly in the refreshing shade of its porticoes. Colonnade Street starts at the point where a lone tree grows on the ruins of a *nymphaeum*, a large public fountain, supplied by the aqueduct from Moses' Spring. On the left-hand side, preceded by a wide flight of steps, were three large markets, but these are now reduced to heaps of rubble and are very difficult to decipher.

75 bottom This picture clearly shows that, seen from Colonnade Street, the façades of the Royal Tombs acted as a sort of spectacular backdrop. The columns seen to the left, along the street were returned to their original position by the Department of Antiquities in 1960.

THE GREAT TEMPLE

76 top A wide flight of
steps in the western sector of
Colonnade Street leads
through the remains of the
Propylaeum to the vast
sacred precinct in which the
Great Temple stood.

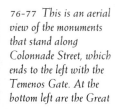

76-77 This is an aerial
view of the monuments
that stand along
Colonnade Street, which
ends to the left with the
Temenos Gate. At the
bottom left are the Great
Temple and, to the right,
the Roman House.
Visible at the top left are
the Temple of the
Winged Lions and, to
the right, the Byzantine
Church.

the Greek goddess assimilated by the Nabateans into Al Uzza) mentioned in a document from 124 AD is sheer conjecture. Behind the Great Temple, at the top of the hill, are the ruins of what must have been a palace, temple or a monumental structure of some importance. The ruins are known as the "Pharaoh's Ruins" and, as usual, this name is based on a Bedouin legend. Here the eye is drawn to a solitary column of rather surreal appearance not far away, standing beside another long fallen to the ground. The "Pharaoh's Column" and its companion must have formed some part of the nearby complex, although their purpose is not at all clear. In 1988, excavation work started to the east of the Pharaoh's Ruins on a large house from the Roman period, built on the foundations of an older dwelling; the Roman building, on two storys, was probably knocked to the ground by the earthquake of 363 AD.

At the end of Colonnade Street, on the left, an impressive flight of steps climbs to a vast quadrangular terrace, once passing through a monumental propylaeum, the foundations of which can still be seen. This courtyard, surrounded on its east and west sides by colonnaded porticoes ending with two exedra, was the *temenos* of a great peripteral tetrastyle temple, which was entered up a flight of steps that filled the entire south side of the courtyard. The sacred building stood at the center of a second colonnaded courtyard, in a spectacular raised position. Although the monument – conventionally known as the "Great Temple" – is still being excavated, it almost certainly dates from the middle of the first century AD. The Nabatean-style capitals with floral motifs and architectural fragments found *in situ* relate to a building phase prior to Roman domain. As can easily be deduced from the position on the ground of the sections of columns, the Temple collapsed after an earthquake. Some finds seem to demonstrate that the sanctuary remained in use until the sixth century and the earthquake was therefore probably that which struck Petra around the middle of the same century. That the temple was consecrated to the goddess Al Uzza and was the *Aphrodiseion* (a temple dedicated to Aphrodite,

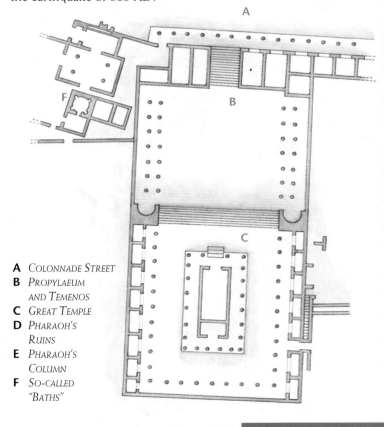

A COLONNADE STREET
B PROPYLAEUM AND TEMENOS
C GREAT TEMPLE
D PHARAOH'S RUINS
E PHARAOH'S COLUMN
F SO-CALLED "BATHS"

78 left *On the motab was perhaps venerated the simulacrum of the goddess Al Uzza, to whom it is presumed that the temple of the Winged Lions was consecrated.*

78-79 *The Temple of the Winged Lions was probably erected in the first half of the first century BC and then repeatedly altered. The picture shows how the* excavations have uncovered, in the area around the building, the foundations of various rooms, including some craft workshops.

78 top *The inside of the Temple of the Winged Lions is marked by a real forest of columns; according to Nabatean building customs, these are very close to each other and are made of very small drums.*

THE TEMPLE OF THE WINGED LIONS

On the westernmost part of Colonnade Street, on a rise opposite the Great Temple, stands the ruins of the "Temple of the Winged Lions." The monument, of which the massive foundations are still visible, was originally approached on a bridge built across Wadi Mousa. It was preceded by two vast terraces on different levels, the lower of which was apparently surrounded by a colonnaded portico. Typically Nabatean in design, the temple itself consisted of a large portico *in antis* erected on strong vaulted substructures (uncovered during the

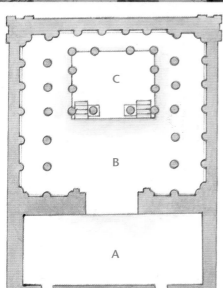

A PRONAOS   **B** CELLA   **C** MOTAB

excavations commenced in 1974), which led to the cella through a wide portal. The walls of the square-plan interior were marked by half-columns framing deep niches. Five free-standing columns, in line with the pilaster strips, were aligned some way from the side walls, to form two aisles. At the center was a high square platform, surrounded by 12 columns in the manner of a peristyle, reached via two flights of steps on the front, between the external intercolumns. The platform, which served as an altar, was called a *motab*: The interior, entered from the rear, contained a small chamber, perhaps used as storage for sacred ornaments and vestments. The floor of the temple was covered with marble slabs, as was the *motab* and the base of the walls; the upper half, the shafts of the

columns and perhaps also the ceiling were covered with painted stuccowork. The monument was named after the unusual decoration on some capitals found during excavations; the usual Corinthian volutes were replaced with the figures of winged lions. Pieces of masonry are visible to the east of the temple, scattered over an area full of architectural fragments and regular-shaped stone ashlars. A large monumental structure stood here, fronted by a terrace approached from Colonnade Street across a bridge and similar to that of the Temple of the Winged Lions. Although the area has never been systematically explored, the building has been given the charming name of Royal Palace. This definition is, however, not very convincing.

THE TEMENOS GATE

Colonnade Street ends to the west, towards the al Habis rock, with the remains of a three-vaulted monumental arch. Razed by an earthquake, this monument has been partially and painstakingly reconstructed and may be further restored using original material found nearby. Until a short time ago the ruins were thought to belong to a triumphal arch erected at the end of the *Cardo Maximus* in honor of the emperor Trajan (98-117 AD), but recent studies have contradicted this theory. It has now been established that, despite resembling a triumphal arch in form, this structure was actually a gate, with heavy wooden doors, as demonstrated by a stone curb placed across the central opening and the sockets in which the metal hinges rotated.

This gate separated Colonnade Street, and hence the bustle of

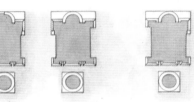

everyday life, from the silent *temenos*, overlooked by Kasr el Bint, one of Petra's most important temples. *Temenos* is a Greek term used in antiquity to define a consecrated, enclosed open-air space where ceremonies in honor of the deities were held. The fact that the three-vault gate served this vast square is confirmed by its position, slightly oblique to the line of Colonnade Street, but perfectly aligned with the short sides of the *temenos*. Archaeological excavations have shown that this gate, built in Roman times (which explains its unusual shape) after the completion of Colonnade Street, stands on an older structure that served the same purpose. The monument's spectacular effect was heightened by its richly carved decorations and the four free-standing columns on the front, facing the *Cardo Maximus*.

The Temenos and the Kasr el Bint

The great Temenos gate, flanked on its short sides by two towers still being studied, provided access to a vast rectangular square set on an east-west axis. The left-hand "tower" acted as a vestibule for a colonnaded chamber which opened onto three rooms, in part subterranean and with domed ceilings; these are not yet entirely open to visitors because they are still being excavated. At the time of their discovery they were thought to be part of a bath complex, but it now seems clear that this was not the case. They were probably part of a larger religious building, perhaps connected with the Great Temple. On the subject of unresolved dilemmas, fragments of carvings and some panels carved with the effigies of gods of the Greco-Roman pantheon (two of these are reproduced on pages 12 and 13) have also been found at various stages around the Temenos gate. Accurate

80-81 *Of all the buildings constructed that were the urban fabric of Petra, the Kasr el Bint is the best preserved, alone in having resisted the earthquakes that razed the rest of the Nabatean capital.*

80 bottom *In recent years, the Kasr el Bint has been subjected to proper restoration work, which has addressed mainly the rear southeast corner and the steps built into the back wall.*

versions of western models made by local artists, it is not yet clear whether these were part of the decoration of the gate or of an adjacent building. On the south side (on the left arriving from Colonnade Street) the *temenos* was closed by a long retaining wall; two unbroken rows of seats stood against this, where worshippers used to sit during the sacred celebrations. The north side must have presented a similar arrangement but, once the embankment erected by the Nabateans had worn away, the disastrous floods of

A Pronaos
B Cella
C Adyton
D Side Cellas
E Steps

Nabatean inscription to king Aretas IV (8 BC-40 AD); as this must have been the base of a statue, it is thought to be one of a row of statues on this side. The discovery of this inscription has made it possible to date the present design of the *temenos* to the first years of the first century AD.

Standing at the back of the great square, to the left of the north-south axis, is the most conspicuous constructed monument still visible in Petra – the Kasr el Bint, a great tetrastyle temple *in antis*. Its full name, Kasr el Bint Faraoun or "Palace of the Pharaoh's daughter," is yet again the fruit of a Bedouin legend totally devoid of historical foundation.

Attributed until a few years ago to the Roman period, the monument actually dates from the second half of the first century BC, probably from the reign of Obodas III (30-8 BC). Because of its superior position and majestic structure, it is common opinion that the temple was consecrated to the two most important local deities, Dusares and Al Uzza, although there is no evidence to support this theory.

The wall ran all the way around the *temenos* in the manner of a peribolos and then continued to the east, where it

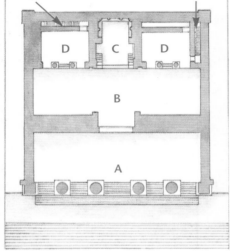

Wadi Mousa eliminated all traces of such structures. Also on the south side of the square are the remains of an altar, a small prostyle temple (raised above the level of the *temenos*), a small water basin and a monumental gate, leading to a flight of steps, the function of which is unknown. Set in the back wall is a block of sandstone bearing a

formed an exedra before meeting up with the north side of the square.

The remains of a huge sacrificial altar, preceded by steps and now just under 10 feet high, stand between the façade of Kasr el Bint and the bed of Wadi Mousa. Given its position, this was obviously closely connected with the temple.

81 left On the left door on the façade, part of the stucco decoration is still visible; the niche to the right of the door perhaps housed a slab with an inscription or a holy image.

81 top right The great doorway of the temple is still surmounted by an arch, which neither the earthquake of 363, nor the subsequent tremors managed to destroy. This is a relieving arch which served the purpose of easing the pressure exercised by the masonry on the lintel of the door below. As this was a monolith, it could not resist the tremors and shattered.

81 bottom right In the adyton, that is the holiest part of the temple, the image of the deity was housed.

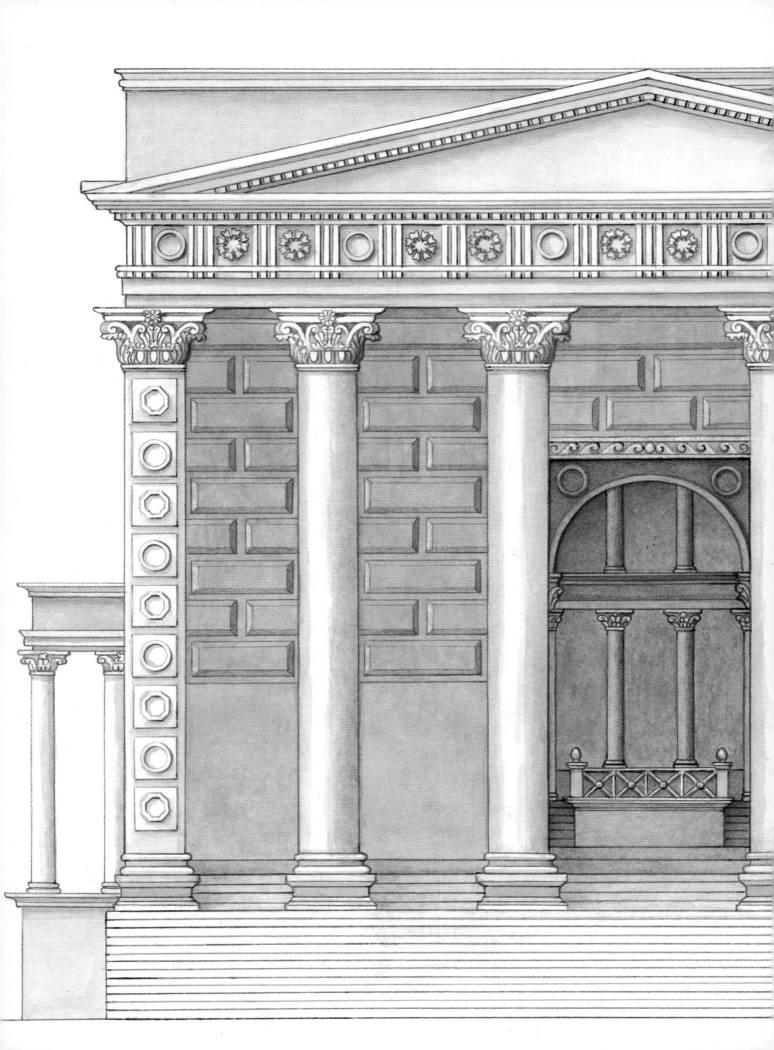

82-83 This is how the temple known today as Kasr el Bint must have looked. With a square plan, built in ashlars of sandstone bound with mortar, it measured 105 feet per side and rose on a high podium fronted visible on the rear wall of the temple. From the great pronaos, three steps led to the cella: This vast rectangular hall was illuminated by two large windows, opened high on the short sides. Three adjacent

by a flight of steps covered with slabs of marble. The overall height was approximately 95 feet. The façade was of the in antis type with four ungrooved columns crowned with capitals, perhaps similar to those of the Khasneh; in the frieze on the entablature, the metopes consisting of busts of deities alternated with pairs of rosettes. Unfortunately, as it can be seen in the detail at the bottom left, the medallions containing the bas-reliefs were obliterated by the iconoclasts; only the metope depicting Helios (today in the Archaeo-logical Museum in Amman) has survived intact. The external face was covered with a thick layer of modelled and painted stucco: part of this decoration (picture top right) is still rooms opened onto the cella: the central one was the adyton, which housed the effigy of the deity. Approximately a foot and a half higher than the cella, it was reached via two side staircases; the front was bordered by two pillars surmounted by an arch, whereas the walls were adorned with half-columns. The side rooms – in which were held the symposia in honor of the gods – were articulated on two stories. In each of these, two columns between pillars supported the mezzanine floor, reached by a staircase built into the back wall. One or both staircases led to the flat roof where the holy ceremonies were officiated. At a later stage, on the east and west sides of the temple were constructed two colonnaded porticoes.

THE UNFINISHED TOMB

The impressive rock of al Habis, defined as the "citadel" of Petra by some and the "acropolis" by others, rises behind Kasr el Bint. Much of the city of Petra lay at its base and extended up the rocky slopes. Many of the caves dug in its sides were actually rock dwellings and some minor traces of their plaster and wall decorations have been preserved. One of the most interesting monuments in this sector is, however, the so-called "Unfinished Tomb," already mentioned in the chapter on architectural models, which provides a fundamental explanation of the techniques adopted by the Nabatean workers. This monument shows that, after the rock face had been duly squared, the excavation work proceeded from the top

downwards. The only completed parts of this hypogeum are the architrave and the four capitals below it: two to crown the lateral half-pillars and two for the central columns. Once they arrived at this stage, the stone cutters started to hollow out the internal chamber, leaving a diaphragm which would later be used for the shafts of the columns. Had it been finished, the façade would have had the appearance of a huge portico *in antis*, the largest of its type in the Rose-red City. Why work was interrupted remains a mystery. The door cut at ground level is manifestly the fruit of later intervention, as the opening is set perpendicular to the spot where a column should have been.

84 center This detail shows how, after having outlined architrave and capitals of the great façade in antis, the Nabatean stone cutters had already started to dig the internal chamber of the Unfinished Tomb.

THE COLUMBARIUM

84 bottom Without doubt, the Columbarium has a strange appearance. The largest recesses carved in the façade may have contained divine effigies

and in the niches all around, the worshippers would therefore have placed their ex votos, but this is merely a supposition.

Not far past the façade of the Unfinished Tomb, towards the southernmost tip of al Habis, is what is perhaps the most mysterious monument in the whole Nabatean capital. The hypogeum known as the Columbarium has, in fact, been interpreted in various manners but no plausible explanation has so far been found. Quite simply, no one knows the purpose of this extravagant rock structure. The walls of the façade, set back from the rock

profile, and the internal chamber are literally covered with square niches, arranged tidily in rows one above the other. The effect is truly disconcerting. *Columbarium* is a Latin word used to indicate a particular type of burial chamber with semi-circular or square niches on the walls containing cinerary urns, and thus resembling a dove-cote or pigeon house. The definition would seem to apply, but the niches here are too shallow to house any type

84-85 As can be seen in this picture, the niches are not cubical in shape, and the back surface slants forwar. This would have made them totally unsuited to hold urns, however small.

85 top Many have wondered whether the Columbarium was not just that, a dove-cote. But the niches are too small even for this purpose and, moreover, there are no traces of guano.

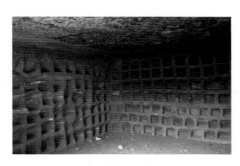

of urn. Some believe these small recesses have a religious function and that the worshippers placed votive tablets, tiny baetyli or, perhaps, simulacra of deities in some form inside them. This is similar to modern sanctuaries, where the believers amass huge quantities of ex votos. It is a lovely idea but there is no proof to support it. The mystery, therefore, remains.

85 bottom
The Columbarium remains an inexplicable mystery; it is as if the Nabateans wanted to play a trick on future generations. However, the structure must have had a specific function; its existence shows that archaeology must still resolve countless questions. This is part of what makes it so fascinating.

THE MUSEUMS

To the right of Kasr el Bint, close to the refreshment area set in the shade of some trees, an easily identified flight of large stone and concrete steps leads to the Old Museum, housed in a hypogeum dug in the side of al Habis. The terrace in front of the entrance – on which are arranged bas-reliefs, friezes and fragments of carvings – affords a splendid view of the valley below and the Royal Tombs. The original purpose of the three adjacent chambers (illuminated by large windows), which house the archaeological collections is the subject of conjecture. The rock complex was probably not a tomb but a temple. Beside the door there is a lovely headless statue of Hercules, found during the excavation of the theater; above the entrance is a magnificent bearded head, very possibly a Roman copy of a Greek original depicting Zeus. Inside (the extraordinary polychrome walls alone are worth a visit) are several carvings, pieces of friezes and festoons as well as bas-reliefs; most of this material is of Hellenistic inspiration although some

pieces are Roman copies or imported works. The high quality of execution demonstrates that the inhabitants of Petra – unique for the Nabatean kingdom – had absorbed cultural influence from the Greco-Roman west and loved to surround themselves with beautiful objects. The museum also houses pottery of typically Nabatean production, coins and other artifacts. Not far from the Old Museum, in a flat area near the point where Wadi

Turkamaniya joins Wadi Mousa and 250 yards from Kasr el Bint, a structure built in the nineties houses the New Museum and restaurant. The spacious and well-lit rooms display the most recent finds (including pottery, coins, gold jewelery, and semi-precious stones), some of the carved fragments and objects previously housed in the Old Museum, as well as a considerable number of finds discovered in the Petra area and, until a few years ago, kept in the Archaeological Museum in Amman.

87 top left This bas-relief, depicting a sphinx, is also housed in the Old Museum.

87 center This male bust should perhaps be identified as the god Serapis, and is situated above the door of the Old Museum.

87 top right Housed in a modern purpose-built building, the New Museum contains works of art and everyday objects — dating from various periods — found during the numerous archaeological digs conducted in Petra.

86 top The old Museum is set up in a hypogeum, consisting of three adjacent rooms, presumed to have been a temple. This hypothesis is supported by the fact that a sacred street starts from this area, cut in the side of the al Habis rock and leading to a "holy place" in the Wadi Siyagh valley.

86 center This winged head in sandstone is part of the collection of the Old Museum: Alien to Greco-Roman figurative languages, on the contrary it displays markedly Oriental facial characteristics. This is probably a local interpretation of the god Ermes.

86 bottom Along the comfortable flight of steps up to the Old Museum, this bas-relief bust has been placed in a circular cornice, and is thought to be the effigy of Zeus (Jupiter), the chief deity of the Greco-Roman pantheon. The Nabateans probably assimilated this god with Dusares.

86-87 On the terrace overlooking the Old Museum you can admire this sandstone panel, on which is carved in bas-relief a cupid between two facing winged lions. The fragment must have been part of a balustrade situated inside a temple.

88 top *The Byzantine church of Petra was a building with three aisles, supported by rows of columns and concluded to the east by as many apses. In one of these, the marble balustrade adorned with bas-relief crosses that stood before the altar has been reconstructed.*

88 - 89 and 88 bottom The mosaics of Petra bear witness to the permanence, in the Christian-Byzantine cultural spheres, of iconographic elements taken from the classical world. It is no accident that the subjects of the pictures depict the Seasons, personified according to the stylistic features of Greco-Roman art.

89 Of excellent workmanship, the floors of the two aisles date from the golden era of mosaic art in Jordan, which ideally began in 530 AD and ended in the first decades of the seventh century. Until the time of the discovery made in the Byzantine church of Petra, it was common opinion that

the great tradition of mosaic had developed in Jordan mainly in the northernmost part of the country, in particular at Madaba and Gerasa. Although they have yet to be carefully analyzed, the mosaics of Petra are quite clearly the work of highly specialized artists, masters of a figurative lexicon extremely well evolved. Some subjects, such as the personification of Ocean recognizable at the bottom right, had not been identified before in any other mosaic of the same period in Jordan. Also of great interest is the rich repertoire of animal species in both aisles.

North of the Colonnade Street and east of the temple of the Winged Lions stands a large tensile structure, visible for miles: This shelters the remains – still being studied and restored – of a large Christian church dating from the sixth century AD, the Byzantine period. At the time, Petra was the seat of the metropolitan bishop of the province of *Palaestina Tertia* and it is thus highly likely, also considering the size of the building and its rich decoration, that this was a cathedral. The monument was discovered in 1973 by the American archaeologist Kenneth Russell, but digging did not commence until May 1992 and has continued in subsequent years. From the very beginning it was clear that the church – with a basilica plan, three apses facing east and an atrium on the opposite side – was destroyed by fire and an earthquake shortly after its construction. The tremor was probably the disastrous one of 551, which shook much of Petra to the ground. Despite the collapse of most of the structures, archaeologists have been able to ascertain that the apses

and walls must have been richly decorated with mosaics in polychrome tesserae of vitreous paste, regrettably nearly all lost. The floor of the nave, in slabs of marble with local sandstone inserts, is also greatly damaged but the mosaic floors of the two aisles were more fortunate and are only slightly damaged. These portray numerous figures, animals and symbols bound to Christian rites and subjects taken from classical tradition, enclosed in geometrical frames of various forms. Paradoxically, the ruin of the church has saved these splendid floors, as the layer of debris saved them from further damage by the elements and the fury of the iconoclasts, who disfigured many other mosaics in Jordan. Fragments of the altars and the marble transennas that stood before them have been found in the apse; one of these has been recomposed there. In December 1993 numerous ecclesiastical manuscript scrolls were found in a chamber adjacent to the church; although damaged by the fire that devastated the church, they are still legible.

90 top A group of
Nabatean rock
dwellings along the
sides of Wadi Siyagh.

91 top Subterranean
houses in Wadi Siyagh,
once a residential
suburb of Petra.

90 bottom Rock
dwellings dug in the
western slopes of al
Habis.

91 bottom Another
view of Wadi Siyagh
at the point where it
meets Wadi Thughra.

Petra

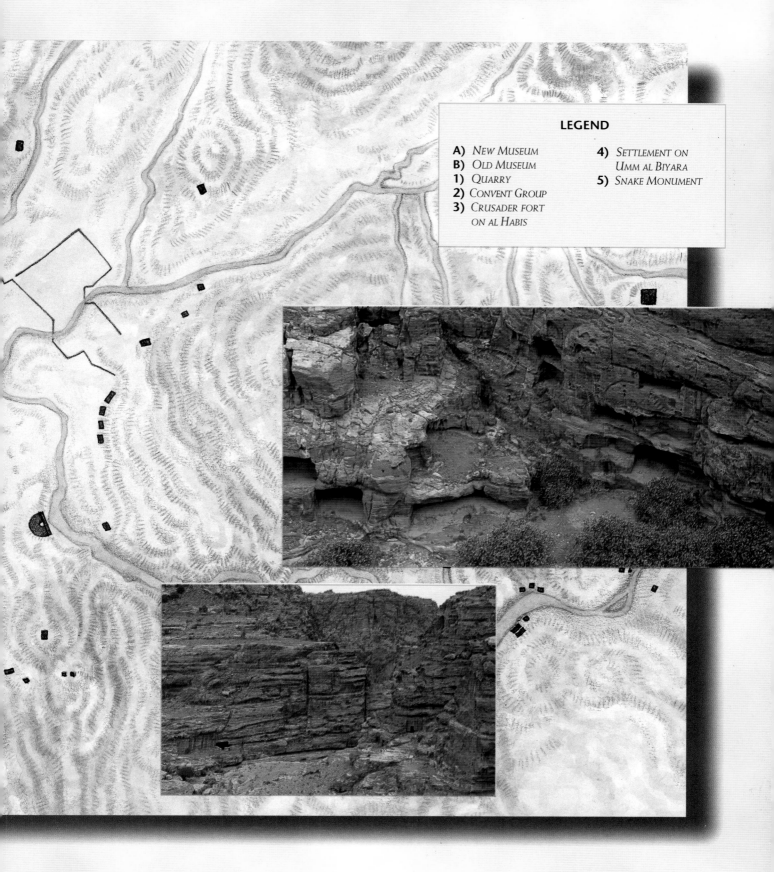

LEGEND

A) *New Museum*
B) *Old Museum*
1) *Quarry*
2) *Convent Group*
3) *Crusader Fort on al Habis*
4) *Settlement on Umm al Biyara*
5) *Snake Monument*

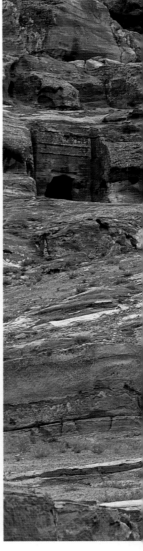

WADI SIYAGH AND WADI THUGHRA

Interesting excursions can be made from the Old and New Museums into the Wadi Siyagh valley, where one of Petra's major suburbs used to lie, and along Wadi Thughra, to the so-called "Southern Graves." Those with more time can plan a visit in the same area to the top of al Habis or Umm el Biyara, but these are by no means easy excursions. Because no monuments of fundamental importance are situated there, these trips are recommended to

south, along the Wadi Thughra valley. Here the eye is immediately drawn to a Nabatean tomb preceded by a flower garden and a vegetable patch. This is the home of a very courteous Bedouin family and your presence should be discreet. Behind their unusual "house" is the fine pediment façade of a *triclinium*. Not far ahead, several feet below the level of the road, which here allows the passage of vehicles, is the so-called "Convent Group."

92 top This holy place is also dug in the rocky outcrop that juts out over Wadi Siyagh.

92 bottom The "Convent Group" would seem to have had a specific function, but the tombs may have simply been dug in a disused quarry.

those who are able to spend several days in Petra. A processional way dug into the side of al Habis departs from the terrace of the Old Museum and leads west; the route is quite frightening for several yards but is safe. This favorable spot affords splendid views of Wadi Siyagh down below and the point where Wadi Thughra flows into it from the southeast. For a few hundred feet all around the path, the rocks abound with channels, cisterns and holy sites. At a certain point the processional way turns sharply to the left and heads

This remarkable complex comprises a large square courtyard, dug at a depth of approximately 18 feet in a sandstone shelf. The walls are lined with tombs devoid of decoration, save for one with a simple cavetto façade. The overall appearance resembles that of a convent and hence the name. Access is down a flight of steps, from the south side; a second flight, on the north side and now badly eroded, used to descend to a larger courtyard, with a niche and a baetylus. On the rocky plateau that forms the west side of the

Convent Group is a holy area – or "place of sacrifice" – with the base of the altar on one side. Some believe that the processional way led here and that the Convent housed the priests responsible for the sacred duties. Visible from this spot, along the course of Wadi Siyagh, is the Nabatean quarry described below. If you return to the dirt road you will see it continues southward, along the sides of al Habis, skirting numerous tombs. By following this for a few hundred yards then bearing left again, you can go all the

92-93 and 93 bottom right A cavetto tomb situated along the processional way from the Old Museum to the Convent Group is still inhabited by a Bedouin family.

93 top The beautiful pediment façade of a triclinium is carved on the northwestern spur of el Habis. Visible just above it is a deep channel, along which flowed one of the many Nabatean aqueducts.

93 bottom right Only one of the chambers in the Convent Group has a cavetto façade; the others are totally devoid of decoration but were probably tombs nonetheless.

94 top left The sides
of the Wadi Siyagh
gorge open into dozens
of subterranean
dwellings where
oleanders and aloe
bushes abound.

94 bottom left In the
shade for much of the
day Wadi Siyagh
enjoys a pleasant
climate. For this
reason it was a suburb
for the wealthy.

way around the mountain. Shortly before reaching the Columbarium you will see a flight of recently opened steps, the easiest way to climb to the top of al Habis. Here are the sparse remains of a crusader's fort, some Nabatean ruins and a place of sacrifice cut in the stone. Actually the true reward for climbing this far up is the splendid view over the Petra valley. Continuing along the road and then

breathtaking. The dirt road along Wadi Thughra continues south toward the so-called "Southern Graves" (where the Snake Monument and two Djin Blocks also stand), the Nabatean suburb of el Sabrah (not yet extensively explored) and Jebel Haroun, on the top of which is the white tomb of Aaron. The latter two are some distance away and it is essential to go in the company of a guide.

crossing the bed of the river, you will come to a group of tombs carved into the walls of Umm el Biyara. A gorge opens to the left of the great double cornice façade, marked by four pilaster strips, and a spectacular but difficult road cut in the rock leads to its top. To climb this you need good footwear, a water supply and, if possible, a local guide. Initially the path crosses a number of screes, before turning into a smooth ramp, once marked by an arch, which forms a bend. Farther on, the way becomes precipitous and rather dangerous. On the flat top of the mountain are some enormous cisterns and the partially excavated remains of several Edomite and Nabatean installations. Once more, the view is

The Wadi Siyagh valley can also be visited from the New Museum, following the banks of the river. The gorge is dotted with rock dwellings, some of which still preserve part of the external walls and entrance steps. One of the subterranean houses is closed with a locked door (permission to enter must be obtained from the Department of Antiquities). The internal walls can be seen through the cracks in the door frame and are frescoed in brightly colored panels containing architectural perspectives. Nearby, at the end of a right-hand bend in the river, the side of the mountain seems to have been cut in a bizarre fashion. This is one of the quarries from which the Nabateans procured material for the construction

of their homes and public buildings.

Approximately 500 yards ahead there is a perpetual spring, where the Wadi starts to become an ever-narrower gorge. All around, the rocks are dotted with the customary Nabatean channelling, religious niches and baetyli. One of these has stylized eyes and nose and an inscription identifying it as an effigy of Atargatis, the Syrian goddess of water and fertility. A few hundred yards on is the unexpected spectacle of a waterfall, but the way is by no means easy and indeed can be dangerous.

94 top right To the rear of the picture is the great Nabatean quarry along Wadi Siyagh.

94 center right The looming walls of Umm al Biyara, in the Wadi Thughra valley, are dotted with tombs.

94 bottom right The sides of a Djin Block in the Southern Grave area are carved with Assyrian crow steps.

95 The so-called "Southern Graves" are dug in a light-colored sandstone platform between the courses of Wadi Thughra and Wadi Nmeir. One of the most striking structures in the necropolis is this Djin Block, called a "tower tomb" by some, a temple by others; it is the only known two-story monument of this type in Petra. Carved on a rocky spur not far away is the Snake Monument, a monolithic block — much worn and not particularly photogenic — which can be identified as a coiled reptile. It may be an apotropaic symbol or the symbolic effigy of the god Dusares... or something else completely.

Petra

96 top The Lion Triclinium, one of the most elegant examples of a pediment façade.

96 bottom A detail of the façade of the Deir, the most important monument in Petra.

97 top A sweeping view of the Deir, preceded by a deep courtyard.

97 bottom The processional way that leads to the Deir passes through landscapes of untamed beauty.

JEBEL AL DEIR

WADI KHARAREEB

WADI MA'AISERAT

WADI SIYAGH

N

THE ASCENT TO THE DEIR

LEGEND

A) *NEW MUSEUM*
1) *LION TRICLINIUM*
2) *EL DEIR*
3) *MONUMENT 468*

+ *CHRISTIAN HERMITAGE*
■ *QATTAR AL DEIR*

98 and 99 top A bridge
originally stood before the
Lion Triclinium, providing
access to its chamber up a
flight of steps. The wind
has eroded the rock
between the doorway and
the oculus above it,
creating an unusual
"keyhole" aperture.

THE ASCENT TO THE DEIR

Winding through the ruins of Petra, a visit to the Deir is one of the loveliest here. This excursion is a must, not just because it visits one of antiquity's most spectacular monuments, but also for the untamed beauty of the surrounding scenery. The route may be rather long and involves a considerable climb, but the path is easy to follow. We do recommend against commencing the hike in late morning, to avoid exposure to the burning sun on the steepest section. The path starts in front of the New Museum and is marked.
The path runs northwest from the New Museum along the bed of a stream called Wadi Kharareeb.

THE LION TRICLINIUM

Surrounded on both sides by rock structures, the valley gradually narrows and the track comes to a fork, half-concealed in the bushes. The path to the left leads, in a very short time, to the Lion Triclinium. Often erroneously identified as a tomb, this is of considerable interest because it is one of the few underground triclinia to have survived intact. Dug into the head of the small wadi, beside a crack that turns into a waterfall in the rainy

season, the façade is much eroded, but still comprehensible. Pedimented in type, it stands between two half-pillars with engaged quarter columns and capitals with vegetable motifs. The badly damaged portal is flanked by the two figures of lions in bas-relief that gave the monument its name. The entablature is decorated with a Doric frieze, in which triglyphs alternate with *paterae*. Carved at the ends are two Medusa heads. The pediment, its *tympanum* decorated with foliage, supports an *acroterion* in the form of an urn.

99 bottom left The left wall of the Lion Triclinium has a niche containing a baetylus dedicated to Dusares and two tombs (one of which is seen in the photograph). The presence of these burial places explains the existence of the triclinium, needed for the funeral rites held in honor of the dead.

99 right Because of the refined decorations developed over the façade of the triclinium (this function being confirmed by the presence inside of a triclinial bed) the monument has been ascribed to the rule of Aretas IV (8 BC-40 AD). Others, however, believe it dates from the Roman period. Lions were sacred to the goddess Al Uzza.

THE PROCESSIONAL WAY AND THE CHRISTIAN HERMITAGE

To proceed towards the Deir from the Lion Triclinium, first return to the main path, which from the fork, becomes gradually steeper. After veering to the west along the gorge excavated by the Wadi al Deir, the sandy trail very soon turns into what used to be a processional way, hewn into the rock at numerous points. To reach your destination you must be prepared to climb more than 800 steps and follow sections cut into the side of the cliffs, but the natural scenery, the incredible colors of the sandstone and the scenic spots that follow one after the other justify the effort. Besides the natural beauty, along the way you can also admire some interesting monuments. Where the path enters Wadi al Deir – on the wall to the

100-101 Petra is not only rock tombs and temples, as nature quite rightly also plays a leading role – for the monuments carved by man would lose much of their charm without these amazing settings.

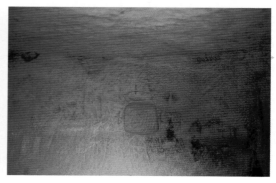

100 top The climb along the ancient processional way from Petra to the Deir takes approximately an hour and passes through scenery of unequalled beauty. All around you, fine sandstone walls streaked with multicolored veining are a delirium of surreal forms that have been shaped by erosion.

101 left An amazing staircase carved in a zigzag is visible right opposite the Christian hermitage, on a knoll of light-colored sandstone. Impossible to climb now because the first flight is so badly worn, this once led to cisterns supplied by a complex system of channels.

101 right Steps, steps and more steps. Those wishing to admire the grandest monument in Petra have to accept some hardship, although the processional way also affords no lack of delights: banks of rock in the most incredible colors, stunning views and even a passage below a huge boulder.

right, as you climb – you will see a tympanum façade, the highly eroded door of which is framed between two characteristic Nabatean half-pillars. The two benches inside suggest this was not a tomb but a *biclinium* and the loculus dug in the floor dates from a far later era. Three-quarters of the way towards your destination, a turn to the right will lead the more curious up a side valley to Qattar al Deir, a rock balcony near a huge cistern that is supplied by underground springs and remains full all year round. This is yet another eloquent example of the remarkable water reserves accumulated by the Nabateans.

Continuing along the processional way, after a fairly steep section full of bends and flights of steps, you reach a white sandstone promontory which affords a splendid view of the Royal Tombs and the surrounding valleys. To the left opens a deep gorge, wedged between sheer walls, which meets up with Wadi Siyagh. To the right towers a pinnacle of rock with some artificial cavities. One of these doorways leads to a semi-hypogean chamber extending out into the void, the external masonry wall of which has partially collapsed; the other entrance leads to a room with crosses and other Christological symbols carved into the back wall. This is thought to have been a Christian hermitage in the Byzantine period. At its foot, the way continues along the edge of the chasm before starting to climb again.

100 bottom The so-called "Christian hermitage" is situated in a spectacular position not far from the Deir. Christian symbols have been found carved inside the main chamber, very probably a Nabatean hypogeum adapted for a different use in the Byzantine period.

THE DEIR

The Deir is visible from some distance away, when the gigantic urn that decorates the top of the *tholos* appears suddenly from behind a curtain of rocks. The contrast between this perfectly geometric form and the incoherent mass of eroded sandstone that surrounds it, is truly surreal. A last flight of steps, enclosed between high pinnacles, dotted with oleanders and junipers, and the processional way comes to an end, in a saddle at the foot of Jebel al Deir, the mountain that dominates the Petra valley to the west. The monument's façade is set a good few feet back from the side of the mountain, so that it is not seen until the last minute. The emotional impact produced by the appearance of this superb construction is unforgettable. The Deir stands out against the rocky ridge behind it as if recently freed from the embrace of the natural matter. Virtually intact, spared from the fury of

102-103 *The Deir is perhaps the Nabatean architects' most astounding and grandiose creation. The façade of this huge construction seems to come forth from the rock, as if proudly asserting the victory of human genius over natural matter.*

102 bottom *Certainly the most impressive monument in Petra, the Deir stands in an isolated position on the top of a mountain spur. The photograph shows the enormous and mysterious round clearing that lies just a short distance from the rock construction.*

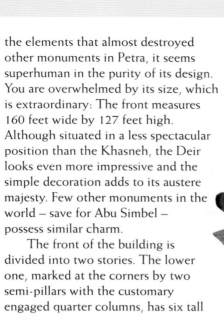

the elements that almost destroyed other monuments in Petra, it seems superhuman in the purity of its design. You are overwhelmed by its size, which is extraordinary: The front measures 160 feet wide by 127 feet high. Although situated in a less spectacular position than the Khasneh, the Deir looks even more impressive and the simple decoration adds to its austere majesty. Few other monuments in the world – save for Abu Simbel – possess similar charm.

The front of the building is divided into two stories. The lower one, marked at the corners by two semi-pillars with the customary engaged quarter columns, has six tall half-columns crowned with Nabatean capitals. The central intercolumn contains the pedimented

doorway, once preceded by a flight of constructed steps, whereas the external intercolumns have two deep rectangular niches, each crowned with a semi-circular tympanum. A high broken entablature, devoid of ornament, supports the second story, carved in very high relief out of the mountainside. The large central *tholos*, with a conical roof and crowned with an urn, is enclosed at the sides by two semi-pediments. The *tholos* and semi-pediments are supported on half-columns with Nabatean "horn" capitals and, in the intercolumns, present deep rectangular niches. Like those on the lower story, these must have housed statues. The whole is closed, at the ends, by two avant-corps, each marked by a half-pillar with a quarter column leaning on the inner side. The half-pillars and half-columns on the upper floor are aligned with those below. A long, very elegant, Doric frieze in which the metopes are replaced by very low-relieved disks links the various architectural elements of the second floor with each other. Not surprisingly, compared with the magnificence of the façade, the interior appears strikingly bare. It consists of a huge almost cubic

chamber, 36 feet square, without ornament. Only in the back wall is there a large arcosolium niche, flanked by half-pillars, the stucco frame of which suggests that the whole chamber was originally plastered and painted. At the center, raised above the floor and reached via two flights of steps on the sides, is a sort of altar, or platform. The foundations of two benches have recently been found along the walls of the room, half-buried in the debris. Their presence would suggest that the

104 top *The huge doorway of the Deir leads to a large chamber approximately 36 feet square, devoid of ornament save for the arcosolium niche dug in the back wall. Several Christian crosses carved inside (now difficult to see) bear witness to the fact that the mausoleum was used in the Byzantine period as a church or perhaps a monks' refuge. Indeed, the Arab name for the building, al Deir, means "the Monastery."*

104-105 *The façade of the Deir is set deeply in the mountain and was preceded by a large courtyard made by excavating the rock for a distance of approximately 200 feet in front of it. For an idea of the true size of the monument, suffice to think that the temple of Abu Simbel, in Nubia, is 125 feet wide and 101 high. As it is a monolith, the Deir — and all the other rock structures in Petra — should be thought of more as a huge piece of sculpture than as a building.*

Deir was used as a *biclinium* or a *heroon*, a mausoleum constructed to commemorate the figure of a deified monarch. The great room would thus have served for ceremonies and symposia. It is common theory that the mausoleum was consecrated to king Obodas I (96-86 BC), who died at Advat, a Nabatean city in the Negev Desert. This assumption is supported by the presence, on a rocky wall not far from the Deir, of an inscription naming Obodas and mentioning a confraternity set up in his honor. On the basis of these considerations, the monument should date from the first century BC, and thus be the same age as the Khasneh. The appearance of the building would, however, seem to contradict this theory. Often people have stressed the similarity between the Deir and the Khasneh, but it is a matter of impression rather than of substance. Firstly, in the Deir the height and width ratio is inverted compared with that of the "Treasury"; secondly, the pronaos of the Khasneh rests on free-standing columns, which lead to a deep vestibule, whereas here there is only the slightest suggestion of a portico. Lastly, the decoration of the Deir is totally untouched by the Greek influence so obvious in the Khasneh; the capitals are

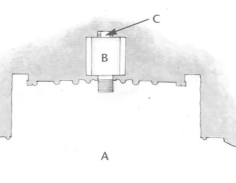

A COURTYARD
B CHAMBER
C ARCOSOLIUM
 NICHE

typically Nabatean and even the Doric frieze looks like a local interpretation. It could be said that the builders of the Deir set out to intentionally assert their independence from the languages of Alexandria and the Greek world in general. The play of voids and solids, the rhythmic alternation of straight and curved lines, the chiaroscuro effect produced by the broken line of the entablature between the two stories, the convex line of the *tholos* contrasted with the concave one of the exedra of the lower story, which contains the portal,

his people to their ancient splendor, rejecting all links with foreign influences.

In the absence of concrete evidence, the matter remains open to debate. Another element still to be investigated is the presence of the huge courtyard in front of the building, usually hastily defined as an area used for mass holy ceremonies. Interestingly, however, both the rocky slopes bordering the courtyard were clearly levelled at the edges and two pilaster strips (see the plan here and the drawing on the next pages) on the two walls thus obtained were spared. Moreover, the debris half-buried in the sand, 30 yards from the façade reveals several column drums, some still covered with a thick layer of fluted stuccowork. It is therefore possible that a raised block stood before the building, a colonnaded portico surrounding a sort of *temenos*. This too is, at present, mere supposition.

all give the monument a great sense of modernity. It almost appears that, overcoming the conventions of Hellenistic art, the Nabatean builders managed to anticipate Baroque style. It is therefore more likely that the Deir was indeed conceived as a heroon in Obodas I's honor, but long after his death and, more precisely, during the reign of the last Nabatean king, Rabbel II (70-106 AD), who set out to return

105 The bell-shaped roof of the tholos is reached up a flight of steps carved in the sandstone, to the right of the façade of the Deir. In the back of the

picture, to the right, is the huge cavity known as Room or Monument 468, which contains the finest and best-preserved religious aedicula in Petra.

106-107 This hypothetical reconstruction shows a colonnaded portico in front of the Deir that marks a vast holy area or a temenos, in which the followers of the confraternity honoring Obodas celebrated their rites. Some writers (including Bachmann) have already presumed the existence of enclosed spaces in front of some of Petra's rock structures; the Tomb of Uneishu and the Roman Soldier Tomb are the most obvious examples. If this is so, the substructures in front of the Urn Tomb may originally have supported a colonnaded block that was the continuation of the two porticoes dug in the rock in the front of the building. These enclosures seem most commonly associated with triclinia or at least with tombs having such chambers. It is above all true that both triclinia and enclosures were essential to carry out funeral and convivial rites. This would confirm the function of the Deir as a cenotaph of the deified king Obodas, because its sole chamber was indeed a biclinium.

MONUMENT 468

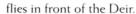

The area around the Deir has been little explored and, consequently, little studied. Yet, it is full of very interesting remains. The rock wall to the left of the great rock sanctuary is lined with water channels, cisterns, hypogeums and religious niches. A bas-relief group portraying two figures leading a dromedary, situated at the entrance to a side gorge, resembles the similar group recently discovered in the Interior Siq. Almost in front of the Deir, in a slightly raised position, is a huge circular clearing, partly obtained by excavating the rock and partly marked by a low wall, now half destroyed.

The function of this area, whether as *temenos*, open-air sanctuary or place of sacrifice, is completely unknown. At the northeastern end of the hill where the Deir stands, a heap of almost incomprehensible ruins is perhaps all that remains of a temple or a *tholos*. Nonetheless, the most interesting monument – number 468 in Brünnow's classification – is carved in the striking rocky hummock that stands just over 500 yards as the crow

108 bottom left
The aedicula inside Monument 468 is splendidly preserved and consists of a niche – which must have contained the statue of a deity – crowned with an entablature and Doric frieze, framed between two pilaster strips supporting a second entablature with two busts at the ends. Obviously of Hellenistic influence, the whole is topped with a pediment and three acroteria.

flies in front of the Deir.

Today it is a vast square cavity, totally devoid of a façade, its sole interest lying in the splendid tympanum niche dug in the back wall. This chamber must have been the cell of an enormous religious building – perhaps the most impressive in Petra – razed by one of the numerous earthquakes that have struck the region in the past. As you approach the rock you will notice that the terrace in front of the room is artificial, once reached up one or two monumental flights of steps; this substructure very probably supported a gigantic pronaos comprising 10 or 12 columns in front, the bases of which are still visible.

The whole appearance of the mountain was very different in the past. If you climb to the top – extremely carefully — you will see a sweeping section of Wadi Arabah and the Deir, but you will also see large sections of wall, the basement of a small *tholos* (or a circular chamber at

108 top right In front of the Deir in the map drawn by Laborde is the plan of Monument 468, with a large pronaos in front of it. David Roberts (see the drawing on pages 32-33) also noticed the remains of the building and drew the bases of the columns.

108 bottom right This photograph, taken in spring 1998 on the top of the rock in which Monument 468 is dug, shows the bases of some half-columns that were part of a circular chamber.

109 top left The left wall of the Deir is filled with aedicula and votive niches, an indication that the hill at the foot of Jebel al Deir was considered a particularly sacred place.

109 top right Erosion has produced a bizarre shape in a tomb near the Deir.

least) and even the remains of a mosaic floor in black and white tesserae. Clearly, Monument 468 and the structures above it must have been part of a monumental complex of considerable importance, especially given its raised position overlooking the saddle of Jebel al Deir and its monuments. It is known that the Nabateans liked to erect their holiest sanctuaries on the tops of mountains. When and to whom the complex was consecrated are mysteries still to be investigated.

109 center It is very hard to imagine what Monument 468 and the structures above it must have looked like, although it was certainly an architectural complex of considerable size.

109 bottom In the vicinity of the Deir are some platforms cut into the rock, usually adjacent to small basins. These places must have been used to hold offertorial ceremonies.

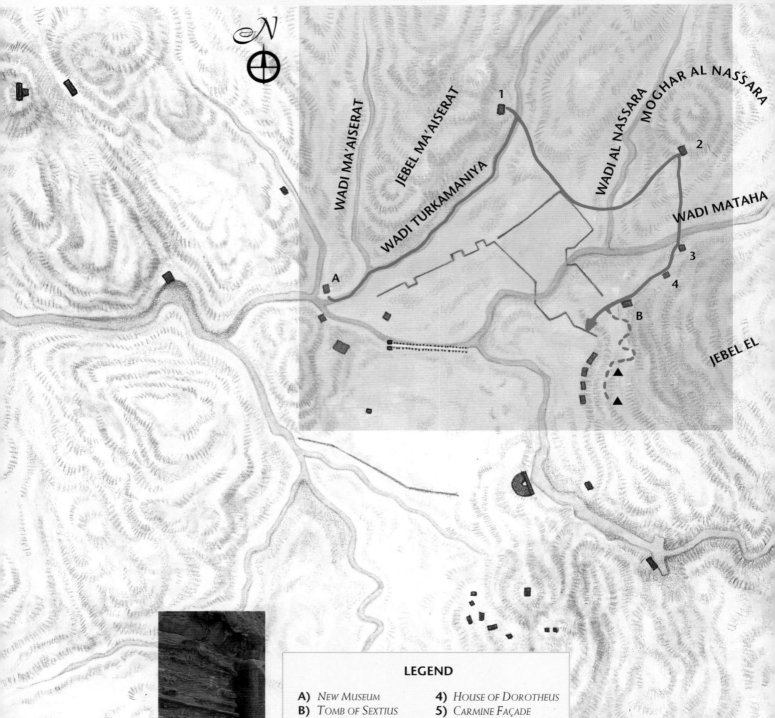

Petra

N

WADI MA'AISERAT

JEBEL MA'AISERAT

WADI TURKAMANIYA

WADI AL NASSARA

MOGHAR AL NASSARA

WADI MATAHA

JEBEL EL

A

B

1

2

3

4

LEGEND

A) *New Museum*
B) *Tomb of Sextius Florentinus*
1) *Turkamaniya Tomb*
2) *Conway Tower*
3) *Armor Tomb*

4) *House of Dorotheus*
5) *Carmine Façade*
▲ *High place of sacrifice on Jebel el Khubtha*

Wadi Turkamaniya, Moghar al Nassara and Jebel el Khubtha

KHUBTHA

110 bottom The Carmine Façade is carved on the northern slopes of Jebel el Khubtha; its function is unknown.

110-111 The rocks of Jebel el Khubtha feature particularly bright colors; the shades are produced by the different chemical compositions of the various layers of sandstone.

111 top Numerous niches and other rock structures with distinctive bright coloring are scattered within a hundred feet or so around the Carmine Façade.

111 bottom The spectacular rock-carved flight of steps that leads to the holy place on Jebel el Khubtha provides picturesque views.

THE TURKAMANIYA TOMB

The itinerary proposed here is quite long but can be divided into small sections, according to the time available and specific personal interests; it does cover three areas that differ greatly from one another. The monuments visited, although not of primary importance, are very interesting. For logistical reasons you are advised to start the excursion from the New Museum, climbing to the northeast along the dirt track that skirts the bed of Wadi Turkamaniya. This pleasantly green valley has a plentiful water supply and was already farmed in Nabatean times. On both sides the rock slopes are studded with tombs and places of sacrifice. After twenty minutes or so, you will come to a tomb that is easily recognized, as it has lost the whole bottom half of its façade, swept away over the centuries by violent river floods. This is the Turkamaniya Tomb, also known as the Tomb with the Nabatean Inscription.

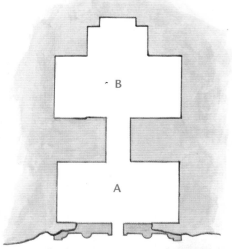

A VESTIBULE
B FUNERARY CHAMBER

The darker area shows the parts of the façade lost forever.

112 top The lovely façade of the Turkamaniya Tomb was seriously damaged by the violent flooding of the nearby wadi (Who the Turkman who gave his name to the tomb and the valley was remains one of Petra's many mysteries). Soon, a major restoration operation will consolidate the structure and make the important Nabatean inscription safe from any further damage.

Deemed one of the most elegant examples of the double-cornice façade, the front is divided by two half-columns and two lateral half-pillars with engaged quarter columns. The sub-attic is divided by four short pilaster strips, in line with the half-columns and, like these, crowned with Nabatean capitals. The main reason for its interest, however, is the long inscription carved in the central intercolumn above the door at a height of more than 20 feet. Although it does not bear the name of the owner of the tomb, nor mention any king, the style of writing dates the

monument to the reign of Malchus II (40-70 AD). It contains a formula that was used to place the tomb and all its ancillaries under the eternal protection of Dusares. The inscription is of fundamental importance because the first part lists all the structures that evidently formed an integral part of the tomb of a wealthy person: a porticoed courtyard, a triclinium, gardens, wells and other ancillary chambers. Clearly the vast majority of Petra's tombs that have survived to the present day are missing their constructed parts, razed by earthquakes and floods.

112 center left and bottom right The Nabatean language is classified in the Aramaic group. Unfortunately no literary works have survived, only rock inscriptions. That adorning the façade of the Turkamaniya Tomb is the only one of some length found in Petra. It states that the tomb and all its ancillaries are under the protection of the god Dusares and that "no one else except him who has in writing

a contract" may be buried here. This privilege was usually extended to the owner's children and closest relatives.

MOGHAR AL NASSARA AND THE ARMOR TOMB

112-113 The photograph shows the central part of Moghar al Nassara. The Armor Tomb is clearly visible to the left.

113 top right A vast necropolis lies among the rocks of Jebel Ma'aiserat, to the east of Wadi Turkamaniya. Numerous interesting structures surround this double-cornice tomb.

After the Turkamaniya Tomb, those with a few hours to spare can explore the tombs that stud the slopes of Jebel Ma'aiserat above, on the left side of Wadi Turkamaniya. There is a complete range of Nabatean architectural models: well-conserved tombs, holy ways and courtyards dug in the rock, sanctuaries and "places of sacrifice" where lambs were offered to the gods. The area is lovely but extremely vast and it is advisable to carry a good supply of water with you. If, on the other hand, you wish to reach the Moghar al Nassara necropolis, leave the Turkamaniya

purpose. Walk northeast from the Conway Tower and cross the bed of Wadi Nassara to eventually reach the Moghar al Nassara heights. This major suburb of Petra, which for some inexplicable reason was never included within the ring of walls, was named for the numerous crosses carved in the hypogea, probably during the Byzantine period. "Nassara" means "Nazarene," the term used by the Arabs for the Christians. There are all kinds of tombs in this area, but the most famous is the Armor Tomb. Facing south, this has a lovely double cornice with a sub-attic divided by four short pilaster strips and crowned with Nabatean capitals. In the spaces between these are carved two Medusa heads and trophies; one depicts the armor which gave the monument its name. This highly unusual frieze is unique in Nabatean architecture.

113 bottom right The Armor Tomb – actually it might have been a triclinium, probably preceded by the customary porticoed courtyard – is famous for the unusual frieze that adorns the sub-attic. This monument may date from the second half of the first century AD.

113 center right The Moghar al Nassara ridge is full of rock structures – from the oldest pit tombs to some examples of the so-called "Nabatean Classical style." On the west side of the rock is a section of the old road that climbed to the suburb of el Barid; a "place of sacrifice" is situated in the northernmost area.

Tomb and cross the bed of the *wadi*, then head southeast. After hiking approximately 20 minutes, you will notice the clearly visible remains of the Nabatean ring of walls, built to defend Petra's northern districts. The area overlooking the walls is occupied by the partially explored Turkamaniya Necropolis. In the northwest corner of the wall stand the massive foundations of a round tower, known as the Conway Tower, named after the archaeologist who commenced the excavations in 1929. Approximately six feet thick, the wall was built around a projecting rock, and evidence suggests that it was built for a defensive

THE WADI MATAHA AND THE HOUSE OF DOROTHEUS

The large Moghar al Nassara ridge is bordered to the southeast by the course of Wadi Mataha; the waters of Wadi Mousa, diverted at the mouth of the Siq, flow into this wadi. It is quite easy to descend to the bed of the river from the Armor Tomb, but you must beware of the pit graves dug in the banks of sandstone. The panorama is particularly agreeable; growing amidst rocks in surreal colors and shapes are thick oleander bushes; in the hottest hours of the day the air is filled with their fragrance. This slope is also studded with façades, most of the "cavetto" or "double cornice" type. Opposite rises the great rock wall of Jebel el Khubtha, at the bottom perforated with a myriad of shady apertures; above this runs the straight

114 right The House of Dorotheus, as well as the other rock dwellings dug in the slopes of Jebel el Khubtha, is reached via daring flights of steps and rather vertiginous passages and must be approached with great care.

114-115 The House of Dorotheus consists of about 20 connecting rooms. This was probably the home of a wealthy man and his family. The Nabatean aqueduct is also visible in the photograph.

114 top left Some of the chambers that make up the so-called "House of Dorotheus" are illuminated by large windows on two stories — their similarity with modern buildings is disconcerting.

114 bottom left The entrances of some rooms are flanked by one or more windows and preceded by a terrace; the stone is so worn that it is difficult to know whether the façades had any architectural decorations.

line of an aqueduct, like a thin wound cut in the side of the mountain. As can be gathered from their appearance, most of the hypogea were used as dwellings as this must have been a heavily populated suburb of Petra. The rock face is in the shade for much of the day and the area is rich in water, so living conditions were particularly good.

A complex of connecting chambers, reached via a steep flight of steps, is known as the House of Dorotheus, after two Greek inscriptions mentioning this name found on the inside walls. Here, as everywhere else in the area, erosion and earthquakes have seriously damaged the rock houses but you can still picture what this unusual district looked like: well-plastered façades, terraces and flights of steps flanked by wooden parapets, roof and vegetable gardens kept lush by the water collected in the large cisterns, the course of the *wadi* closed between strong embankments and a good road descending to the center of the metropolis. The river was crossed by masonry bridges and fields and meadows lined the shores. Although conditions have changed since then, some still appreciate the Nabatean residences, and Bedouin families continue to occupy hypogea in the western part of the valley. Several families belonging to the Bdoul and Liyatheneh tribes reside on Petra's archaeological site. They are the modern-day inhabitants of the Rose-red City. The government has built them modern homes near Wadi Mousa, but they seem to prefer their traditional lifestyle, living off shepherding and small-scale trading. They are proud, reserved, courteous and the elderly are slightly xenophobic. Please respect their privacy.

116 The rock face around the Carmine Façade, as well as the entire western side of Jebel el Khubtha, is literally studded with tombs, votive niches, rock dwellings, cisterns and channels. This area is a true paradise for trekking enthusiasts; there are miles upon miles of paths and steps carved into the rock which often lead to outstandingly scenic spots. It must, however, be remembered that many routes are eroded and in poor condition, others end abruptly in thin air (literally, on frightening overhangs), and others disappear into great expanses of rock where orientation becomes rather difficult. Those who are not accustomed to the mountains or to long difficult hikes, should keep to the main paths, because a wrong turn could have serious consequences.

THE CARMINE FAÇADE AND THE ASCENT OF JEBEL EL KHUBTHA

Along the course of Wadi Mataha on the way towards the old inhabited center, not far past the House of Dorotheus, stands the structure known as the Carmine Façade. It is not easy to find at first, as it is dug in a recess in the rock wall and blocked by a thicket of oleander bushes. As in the case of the Silk Tomb, this mysterious monument is of interest for the bright coloring of the rock it is carved in. Of the pediment type and adorned with a Doric frieze, the façade has lost its door; hence the function of the structure is unknown. Approximately 200 yards farther ahead is the Tomb of Sextius Florentinus. From here it is easy to reach Colonnade Street and

the New Museum, or return to Wadi Mousa along the Siq. A fascinating alternative for the hardier hikers is the spectacular processional way, which starts right behind the tomb enclosed between the walls of a narrow *wadi* where some Nabatean metalworkers must have once had their workshops. Entirely dug in the rock, the path passes beneath an arch (thought to have originally had two heavy wooden doors) before becoming a treacherous flight of steps. It ends on the flat top of Jebel el Khubtha where an important "place of sacrifice", a reservoir, partially covered with a vault, and the remains of other installations stand.

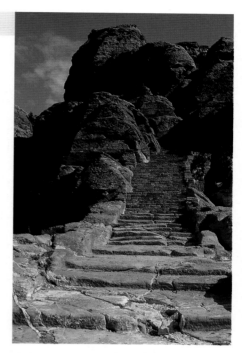

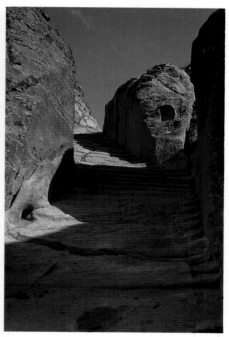

117 left Its colored veining makes the Carmine Façade an ideal subject for photographers, but it remains a mystery to archaeologists. It is unlikely to be an unfinished tomb or triclinium, because the chambers were dug before the architectural decoration was completed. Given its size it could hardly have been a votive niche either.

117 right Although the place of sacrifice and the other remains on Jebel el Khubtha are of some interest, the holy way that leads to them is far more spectacular. Once at the top of the mountain, walk south to a point that commands a breathtaking view of the façade of the Khasneh below. This area is home to an unusual bright blue lizard, the Agama sinaita.

Petra

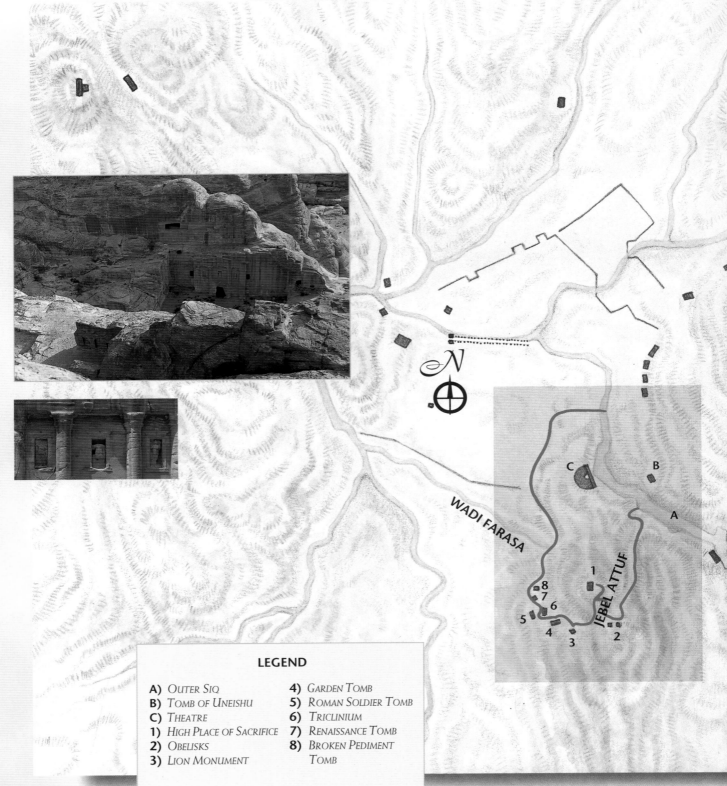

WADI FARASA

JEBEL ATTUF

A

B

C

1

2

3

4

5

6

7

8

N

LEGEND

A) Outer Siq
B) Tomb of Uneishu
C) Theatre
1) High Place of Sacrifice
2) Obelisks
3) Lion Monument
4) Garden Tomb
5) Roman Soldier Tomb
6) Triclinium
7) Renaissance Tomb
8) Broken Pediment Tomb

JEBEL ATTUF AND WADI FARASA

119 top The Broken Pediment Tomb, an austere example of "Nabatean Classical Style."

119 bottom The portal of the Renaissance Tomb, crowned with an unusual segmented open pediment.

118 top A sweeping view of the Roman Soldier Tomb; in the foreground, to the left, is a large triclinial chamber.

118 bottom Detail of the façade of the Roman Soldier Tomb showing the three bas-reliefs which adorn the niches between the intercolumns.

The Ascent of Jebel Attuf

The ascent to the top of Jebel Attuf is perhaps the most demanding and tiring of those proposed in this book, but it is of fundamental interest for several reasons: first, because as well as visiting the Holy Place it also passes some of the most fascinating rock constructions in the area; secondly, because the route offers spectacular sweeping views of the Petra valley and surrounding mountains. This excursion should not be missed. As it takes at least three hours it is preferable to set off in the morning, to avoid walking in the hottest part of the day, although the view from the top of Jebel Attuf at sunset is breathtaking to say the least. Expert hikers can start the climb in the late afternoon and descend before the archaeological site closes. The best route is that on the Outer Siq side; the sanctuary on Jebel Attuf can also be reached from the Wadi Farasa valley,

120 left When they carved the colossal obelisks in the Jebel Attuf rock, the Nabateans had to shift no fewer than 113,000 cubic feet of material. The blocks are aligned on an east-west axis.

120 top right Overlooking the entrance to the "High place of sacrifice" are the ruins of a fort built by the crusaders. Not all agree on this, however, and some believe it was actually a Nabatean or Byzantine construction.

but in this case you may have difficulty finding the right path. The holy way that commences just past Tomb 70, on the left side of the Siq, is well marked. The starting point for the ascent is unmistakable, immediately appearing as a never-ending flight of steps; in parts these become ramps, also carved in the rock. Looking to the left, you will see how the mountain was literally carved to pieces by the Nabateans. A double row of square niches (similar to those seen at the sides of the Khasneh) carved on the quarry face led the way to the higher terrace: a truly amazing, absolutely vertical flight of steps. You then follow a narrow valley, closed between sheer rock walls.

The processional way emerges

The Obelisks

abruptly in a saddle, a crack between two spurs dominated by two unusual obelisks that are visible from some distance. The top of Jebel Attuf, the highest point of which is 3,414 feet, is actually divided in two: the northern part is known as the "High place of sacrifice" (or Jebel Madhbah), the southern one as the "Obelisk ridge." Slightly less than 23 feet tall and 30 yards from each other, the two monuments stand isolated on a level area created by excavating the top of the mountain. These monoliths are commonly thought to represent Dusares and Al Uzza, but there is no conclusive evidence for this theory.

From the obelisk area it is possible,

The High Place

on the northern side of Jebel Madhbah, to observe the remains of strong walls and towers constructed on the edge of high, artificially squared rock faces. These walls are thought to be what remains of a crusader fort, probably erected on older foundations or possibly on the site of a Nabatean quarry. The path to the "High Place of Sacrifice" passes straight through the ruins before veering left, onto the bare rock. The objective is a hundred yards or so ahead, on the highest point of the mountain. The open-air sanctuary – preceded by a large cistern cut in the rock plateau – occupies a fairly small area, but is the best preserved of all those situated on the peaks around

120-121 *Their appearance and the Arab name they are known by (Zibb Attuf, or "Merciful Phallus") suggest that the two obelisks may have been symbols of fertility or divinity linked to the concept of mercy.*

A COURTYARD
B MENSA SACRA
C ALTAR
D LUSTRAL BASIN
E CISTERN

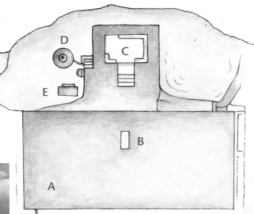

121 top The subject of this photograph is the large round basin situated to the left of the altar; the priests perhaps used it to collect the blood of the sacrificed lambs, which was then sprinkled all over the holy area.

121 Top This large water tank, just over three feet deep, is nine yards south of the courtyard and cut into the stone. It probably held the water required for the holy ceremonies.

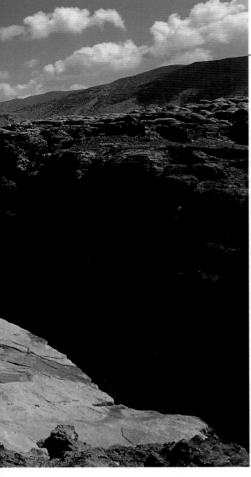

preceded by three steps, is situated right in front of the offerings table in a recess dug in the sandstone on the west side of the courtyard. On the top is a square hole, into which the baetylus symbolizing the divinity was almost certainly inserted. To the left of the altar is a large circular basin, approached up four steps, with a drain that discharged onto the steps. This may have been a basin where the blood of the victims sacrificed to the gods was collected, or where the priests washed after the ceremonies. The adjacent rectangular water tank perhaps contained pure water for the cleansing of the vessels used during the ceremonies. In ancient times the offering of blood to the gods bore great symbolic significance because blood was the symbol of life. Rites involving blood strengthened the bond between the gods and humans.

121 bottom The "High place of sacrifice" could not accommodate great masses of worshippers, a characteristic common to all the open-air holy places around Petra.

Unfortunately very little reliable evidence has survived as to the Nabatean religious practices, which in many ways resembled those of the Jews.

Petra. Given its position, so exposed to the elements, it seems incredible that it has not been totally eroded and that in many parts the rock seems only recently cut. The "High place of sacrifice" is a rectangular courtyard approximately 48 feet by 21 feet, surrounded by a low step that perhaps served as seating for those participating in the holy rites. In the middle of this perfectly levelled area is a platform, also rectangular, just six inches high. This is the "Mensa Sacra," where non-blood offerings to the gods – food, drink, stalks of wheat and perhaps also precious objects – were placed. The single block altar, approximately three feet high and

122 top right Along the path that descends from Jebel Attuf into Wadi Farasa are numerous dedicatory inscriptions in the Nabatean language; this one, fronted by a level area, is just a few minutes from the top.

THE LION MONUMENT

The view over the Petra valley from the "High place of sacrifice" and indeed from the entire Jebel Madhbah plateau is stunning. To the west is the towering mass of Umm el Biyara and, to the south, you can see Aaron's Tomb, gleaming white on the top of Jebel Haroun. It seems impossible to descend to the west into the Wadi Farasa valley from here, but simply

return to the obelisks, walk south for a hundred yards or so and then turn right, where an unexpected path – or rather, a holy way – starts to wind across the rock wall. Along the path you will see numerous inscriptions left by Nabatean pilgrims, a few baetyli, and some of the most spectacular color combinations in the entire region. On the sides of a rocky outcrop, to the right, is a rectangular baetylus, crowned with a medallion and bust. A few hundred yards past this stands the Lion Monument. Actually, this must have been a fountain, judging from the remains of channelling found. The now-headless animal is 15 feet long and eight feet tall.

122 top left Minus its head (which was perhaps in bronze) and so eroded it looks like an elephant, the Lion Monument was a fountain with water gushing from the animal's mouth. The lion was an animal sacred to the goddess Al Uzza.

122 bottom left It is very hard to interpret with certainty the bust that tops this baetylus cut in a rocky spur overlooking the holy way that runs along the western side of Wadi Farasa. Some believe it depicts the god Dusares, others the goddess Al Uzza. In either case, it would be one of the few known figurative representations of a Nabatean divinity.

122-123 The Garden Tomb is a mysterious monument; it could not have been a burial place, therebeing no trace of loculi or graves, but the suggestion that it was a triclinium does not seem very convincing either, particularly because there are no triclinial beds inside. It may have been a temple, built to "protect" the nearby cistern.

THE GARDEN TOMB

Although at times quite treacherous the path never becomes dangerous and offers magnificent views over the Wadi Farasa valley and, in the distance, over Wadi Nmeir and Wadi Thughra. It also provides an opportunity to see the monuments below from an unusual angle: the façade of the Roman Soldier Tomb, a cistern and adjacent chamber (now without its roof), with niches in the walls. The latter two structures can be reached directly along a very steep path, but it is far safer to follow the main route which, in a few minutes and after some last bends, will bring you to one of Petra's loveliest monuments. Known as the "Garden Tomb" it is not large, nor architecturally elaborate, but it is dug in an extraordinary position on a promontory that juts out over the valley. The backdrop to this splendid setting is the Petra valley in the distance and a blue sky that contrasts splendidly with the warm colors of the sandstone. The Tomb consists of an elegant, simple portico with two columns *in antis* leading to a sort of vestibule, which then opens onto a simple, totally unadorned square chamber.

The structure owes its charming name to the fact that when the 19th-century visitors saw it, the courtyard in front was partially covered with soil fallen from above and full of oleander bushes and other plants. Actually, this was not the intention of its builders, who did not conceive the hypogeum as a tomb. It was probably a temple, similar to that dug in the el Barid Siq, described later, although some interpret it as a triclinial chamber. The age of the monument is also disputed; some

123 bottom left and top right The pictures show details of the lovely façade in antis of the Garden Tomb and clearly show the use of the characteristic Nabatean capital.

123 bottom right The chamber opposite the great cistern – perhaps a triclinial chamber – was covered with a barrel vault, quite a rare architectural feature in Petra.

A COURTYARD
B VESTIBULE OR PRONAOS
C CHAMBER OR NAOS

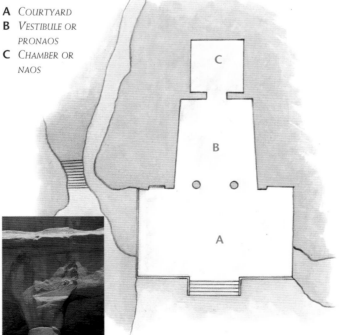

suggest that it dates from the reign of Aretas IV (8 BC-40 AD) or the second half of the first century AD, but according to others it may have been part of the nearby Roman Soldier complex. A great wall stands to the right of the courtyard in front of the portico; to discover its purpose you must climb a steep flight of steps that leads to the edge of a huge cistern (now dry), more than 60 feet long and half as wide. The wall is its south side. At the opposite end is the chamber, mentioned above, with walls containing niches. This was once covered with a barrel vault and must have served as a *triclinium*.

A MAIN FUNERARY
　CHAMBER
B SECONDARY FUNERARY
　CHAMBER
C LOCULI
D COURTYARD
D TRICLINIUM

THE ROMAN SOLDIER TOMB

A flight of steps descends to the left of the Garden Temple towards the bottom of the gradually widening Wadi Farasa valley. After a hundred yards or so, the processional way opens in a vast courtyard, partially dug into the sides of the two opposite mountains. The great façade of the Roman Soldier Tomb is carved in the rock wall to the left, facing west. Of dignified elegance, this is the most famous example of the

124-125 Seen from above, it is easier to gauge the amount of excavation required to create the courtyard in front of the Roman Soldier Tomb. The hypogeum situated above the façade is also clearly visible here.

124 left Although the façade of the Roman Soldier Tomb is obviously of classical inspiration, typically Nabatean elements such as the capitals and the half-pillars with quarter columns continued to be adopted.

"Roman Classical style" introduced to Petra after it was conquered by the emperor Trajan. The front resembles that of a tetrastyle temple. It is flanked by the customary half-pillars with leaning quarter columns and the portal is framed between two half-columns. The capitals appear to be in the usual Nabatean style, but are greatly eroded by the rain and wind. The entablature, devoid of a frieze, supports a low tympanum placed against a rectangular parapet on which perhaps were three acroterions; the stone is so worn, however, that this hypothesis is very uncertain. Above the portal is a tympanum with a Doric frieze extremely similar to that of the Urn Tomb. The truly striking features of

125 The Roman Soldier Tomb was most certainly destined for an important figure and his family. On the basis of the type of armor worn by the bas-relief statue that adorns the niche in the central intercolumn (center picture), he is presumed to be a high-ranking officer of the Roman army or even an imperial legate. According to this interpretation the two men represented in the side niches (pictures top and bottom) would have been his sons. The design of the façade, which contains motifs typical of Greco-Roman funerary architecture, suggests a date around the first decades of the second century AD.

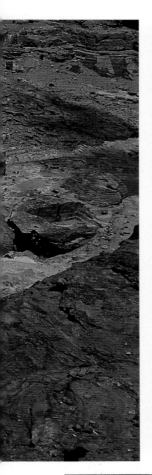

this tomb are the three unusual niches high up, in each of the intercolumns. Framed by a simple cornice with a smooth entablature, they were adorned with numerous bas-relief statues. The central one, unfortunately headless and without its legs, depicts a man in a heroic pose and wearing elaborate armor, similar in design to that used by Roman soldiers. It most certainly portrays a high-ranking figure and the statues in the side niches, apparently wearing short military-style tunics, are presumed to portray the sons of the deceased. Traces of plaster are still visible in the folds of the cloaks which would suggest that the statues were originally richly colored.

Above the façade, to the left, is a deep rectangular hollow, probably that of a grave demolished during the construction of the new tomb. Lower

down, to the right, is a row of four recesses, of unknown purpose (perhaps niches housing numerous baetyli), and two obelisks are traced in very low relief on the right-hand wall of the façade. Inside, the tomb consists of two simple funerary chambers; some arcosolium loculi are dug along the walls of the first, in which the bodies were laid, wrapped in shrouds or enclosed in wooden sarcophagi (this too is still open to debate). The courtyard that lies in front of the tomb was created by partially excavating the sides of the mountain and levelling the bottom of the valley. To do this the builders had to construct a strong

126 top Niches and conduits for water are found all around the Roman Soldier Tomb.

126 center The groove above the three doors that lead to the triclinium supported the pitch of the colonnaded portico roof, thus making room for the three windows that illuminated the inside chamber.

retention wall and, very probably, force the course of the *wadi* through a vaulted tunnel. However small the seasonal stream may have been, its flow increases dramatically during the violent winter and spring rains. This mass of water, no longer properly controlled, has over the centuries caused serious damage to the monumental complex. The front of the hypogeum immediately opposite the tomb, which is totally devoid of architectural elements, shows its effect. The doorways have been misshapen by

erosion and the interior is also severely ruined. Nevertheless, the vast square chamber is one of the most fascinating in all Petra; the walls, with their magnificent colored veining, are remarkable in themselves and are decorated with a harmonious alternation of fluted pilaster strips and niches dug in the intercolumns. The elegant half-columns – surmounted by capitals that seem to represent a new syncretism of Tuscan, Ionic and Nabatean orders – sustain an entablature devoid of a frieze, but which

must originally have been covered with multicolored stuccowork. Plaster moldings also framed each niche, as is revealed by grooves that housed the wooden corbels used as reinforcement. The low unbroken dais running around three sides of the room proves that this was a triclinium. This chamber, with such refined decoration, is the only surviving example of its kind in Petra and is a true exception. During inspections conducted in the early twentieth century, the German archaeologist W. von Bachmann

126 bottom This imaginary reconstruction, inspired by those of W. von Bachmann and I. Browning, gives an idea of what the monumental complex of tomb, triclinium and large courtyard surrounded on three sides by porticoes must originally have looked like.

126-127 and 127 bottom The triclinium is a large square-plan chamber, measuring approximately 35 feet on all sides. Refined banquets were held here in honor of the deceased and his forefathers. With its fluted pilaster strips, entablature and niches, this is the only known internal chamber so magnificently decorated in Petra. While observing what has survived, you must picture the walls as they once were, plastered and frescoed.

(on the basis of the remains of walls still visible *in situ* and the description given on the front of the Turkamaniya Tomb) formulated the hypothesis that the courtyard between the tomb and the *triclinium* was surrounded on three sides by a colonnaded portico. His guess has been proven right by the latest studies of Nabatean funerary architecture, which confirm the close link between tombs, porticoed courtyards and *triclinia*.

THE RENAISSANCE TOMB

128 Situated where the rock walls of Wadi Farasa become more distant, the Renaissance Tomb is unique among all the examples of rock architecture in Petra for its unusual open pediment, an arch devoid of the usual sub cornice. A vast courtyard dug in the rock mass precedes the façade. The remains of masonry on the terrain would suggest that a porticoed courtyard and, perhaps, a raised triclinial chamber also preceded this tomb.

As it moves away from the Roman Soldier Tomb, the processional path continues for a short stretch as a flight of steps before turning into a sandy track, only in parts cut in the rock. On the left side of the gorge, to the south, is a wadi dug deep in the spurs of Jebel al Najr. Those with 20 minutes to spare and plenty of breath should make a detour to a rather interesting but little-visited tomb. Known simply as the al Najr Tomb, it has a very well-preserved classical façade that closely resembles the Roman Soldier Tomb. Dating from the same period, it differs in that there are no niches in the intercolumns; as a result, it appears more compact, less vertical and very similar to the front of a tetrastyle temple.

At the point where the Wadi Farasa valley opens unexpectedly, the eye is drawn to a particularly elegant,

westward-facing façade on the right. This well-proportioned structure is known as the Renaissance Tomb and, on observation, it is easy to understand why. The front is framed with the customary half-pillars with quarter columns and supports an entablature with a smooth frieze and a low tympanum, adorned with three urn-shaped acroterions. The doorway is the most striking feature of the composition and resembles the pure architectural designs of the Italian renaissance. The inner cornice of the door is of the standard type but the outer one presents the usual half-pillars with Nabatean capitals supporting not a normal entablature but an open pediment, consisting of a segmental arch with three urn-shaped acroterions resting on the extrados. The whole is very similar to the Tomb of Sextius Florentinus and, for this reason, it is thought to be from the first half of the second century AD.

THE BROKEN PEDIMENT TOMB

A short distance beyond the Renaissance Tomb the Wadi Farasa valley widens further and is full of rounded sandstone outcrops and large oleander bushes. The surrounding mountain slopes contain numerous façades, most of the step type, and the ever-present channelling which

129 top The dignified and austere Broken Pediment Tomb stands on a terrace approached up a flight of steps; the adjacent room, altered over the centuries and used as stables, must have been a triclinium.

129 center left The entrance to the Broken Pediment Tomb is preceded by a flight of steps dug in the rock; unfortunately, the architrave of the door is seriously damaged, but it must have been of the standard kind, with a simple entablature. The two slits in the outer intercolumns seem unrelated to the original project and probably date from a time when the tomb was turned into a dwelling or stables. In the past, this was the fate of many of Petra's rock structures.

carried rainwater to cisterns cleverly hidden in the subsoil. On the same side as the Renaissance Tomb and just a few dozen yards from it, is one of the stylistically most successful pieces of architecture in Petra. Carved in a rocky ledge, facing north, the Broken Pediment Tomb shows that the Nabatean builders managed to totally resolve the sharp contrast between formal schemes imported from the Hellenized west and the local passion for abundant decorative elements. The façade is divided by four half-pillars with leaning quarter columns, surmounted by a simple entablature sustaining a broken pediment. This same scheme was observed in the Bab el Siq Triclinium and in the Corinthian Tomb, but total equilibrium is achieved here, far from the muddle of lintels, cornices and short half-pillars that needlessly weigh some compositions down.

The Broken Pediment Tomb

must have belonged to a highly influential family and stands at the top of a flight of steps, above the path. The front is preceded by a large terrace, in which are dug two tanks, one octagonal and the other square. On the right-hand wall inside the tomb are four loculi and the marks for the digging of more, never executed. Work was obviously suspended quite suddenly, but why remains a mystery.

The sides of Jebel Attuf just beyond the Broken Pediment Tomb are dotted with rock façades in tiered rows, as seen in the Outer Siq. Continuing on you come to a fork, at a point that affords a sweeping view of the valley occupied by the city of Petra. Turning left you can quickly reach Kasr el Bint and the nearby refreshment kiosk; if you go right you can round the outermost spurs of Jebel Attuf and the path leads in 20 minutes or so to the mouth of the Outer Siq, near the Theater.

129 center right Wind erosion has given a bizarre appearance to this hypogeum along Wadi Farasa, almost certainly an ancient rock dwelling.

129 bottom The spurs of Jebel Attuf in the lower Wadi Farasa valley are full of tombs — most of the "step" type — aligned in rows.

Petra

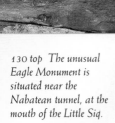

130 top The unusual Eagle Monument is situated near the Nabatean tunnel, at the mouth of the Little Siq.

130 bottom Long stretches of the Little Siq, or Wadi Muthlim, look like a fissure eroded between the sheer high rock walls by water.

131 The sides of the Little Siq are lined with remarkable natural formations and splendid banks of multicolored sandstone.

THE LITTLE SIQ

LEGEND

1) *Tunnel*
2) *Eagle Monument*
3) *Nabatean dam*
4) *Large religious aedicula*
5) *Roman aqueduct*

MOGHAR AL NASSARA

WADI MATAHA

JEBEL EL KHUBTHA

WADI SIDD AL MA'AJIN

WADI MUTHLIM

WADI SHAB QAIS

BAB AS SIQ

N

132 top left and top right The splendid coloring of the rocks makes the Little Siq a particular favorite of photographers.

THE LITTLE SIQ

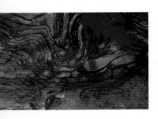

132 bottom left The photograph shows what remains of the barrier built inside the Little Siq. The foundations of a defense wall and what must have been a guard post stand near the rocky spur visible high on the left.

The Little Siq, or Wadi Muthlim, is one of the most spectacular yet least known wonders of Petra. This relative anonymity is due to the objective difficulty involved in the trek along the riverbed and the length of the journey; as a result the following itinerary is for expert hikers, equipped with the proper footwear and plenty of water. We recommend against undertaking the descent of the *wadi* during the rainy season or whenever violent thunderstorms precede the planned excursion, as the gorge may be invaded without prior warning by flash floods.

On the last stretch, where the *wadi* becomes a narrow fracture, great

attention must be paid to falling boulders; this is not uncommon and is often caused by goats grazing on the slopes of Jebel al Khubtha above.

Only the first part of the journey – to the so-called Eagle Monument – can be followed by anyone taking a little care. First leave the main road before the bridge to the Interior Siq; note that some stelae and obelisks, dating from the reign of Malchus II (40-70 AD), are visible on the wall opposite the modern dam. An inscription discovered here bears the Nabatean name of Petra: Reqem.

Following the Tunnel to the Muthlim – to the right of which stands a *"djin"* block, decorated at the top with an Assyrian frieze – presents no particular difficulties, as there is enough light to see any obstacles.

Once on the other side follow the riverbed for about 164 feet; here it is enclosed between two slightly sloping walls dug into the sandstone; then climb to the left.

The surrounding area abounds with Nabatean remains, although they are not easy to see: niches, stelae, obelisks and, above all, the Eagle Monument, a votive niche probably dating from Roman times; in the

132 bottom right
The waters of Wadi
Mousa are deviated
through the 280-
foot-long Nabatean
tunnel into Wadi
Muthlim.

This impressive
hydraulic project is
thought to have been
completed shortly
before Petra was
annexed to the
Roman Empire.

132-133 The Eagle
Monument is carved a
hundred yards from the
mouth of the Nabatean
tunnel. Given the
subject of this bas-
relief, the monument
probably dates from the
period of Roman
domain.

133 top A few yards
from the point where
Wadi Muthlim flows
into the wide Wadi
Mataha valley, the sides
of the gorge are dotted
with niches and baetyli;
inscriptions found
indicate that Dusares, Al
Uzza and "all the gods"
were worshipped here.

middle of the niche stands the figure
of a bird of prey with outspread
wings.

Back on the riverbed the most
adventurous will turn away from the
Tunnel and start to descend Wadi
Muthlim. It takes at least 40 minutes
to reach the edge of the gorge, but
the beauty of the place will inspire
constant stopping. Indeed this
itinerary, which in the near future may
be equipped with steps and handrails,

is particularly spectacular from a
naturalistic and scenographic point of
view, thanks to the glowing colors
and uneven formation of the
surrounding rocks. In addition, the
route does contain some interesting
archaeological discoveries. First, it is
illuminating to observe the
engineering brilliance of the
Nabateans, who managed to exploit
the complex orography of the region
and find a new course for the Wadi

Mousa.

However narrow and difficult, the
gorge constituted a possible route of
access to the city, with the inhabitants
of Petra well aware of the danger. So,
approximately three-quarters of the
way along, where the mountain walls
become increasingly higher and close
to one another, they built an effective
barrier, traces of which are still clearly
visible. Two holes were dug at a
certain height above the river on both

134 top With a large number of aediculae, niches and baetyli dug into the rock walls, the mouth of the Little Siq is an open-air sanctuary, probably linked to the worship of water.

134-135 The Wadi Muthlim gorge – or Little Siq – opens into the wide Wadi Mataha valley right opposite the Moghar al Nassara heights, another area with many rock tombs and cisterns.

135 top left and bottom The spurs of Jebel el-Kubtha lie on the orographic left of Wadi Mataha; numerous rock dwellings and an aqueduct can be seen on the mountainside.

135 center left The most striking rock structure of the open-air sanctuary in Wadi Mataha is this large religious aedicula, carved inside a huge pothole.

sides of the fissure; two protruding stone ledges were fixed to these, and an arch was set on them, beneath a wall which must originally have been about 10 feet high. The span of the arch was then closed by a strong grill, through which the river could pass even when flooded, but which proved an impassable obstacle to invaders.

Moreover, the rocky spur above bears the remains of a wall and a tower, perhaps used by guards. Now that the arch has collapsed and only a part of the barrier remains suspended above one of the ledges, this defense system may seem of little account, but when it was built it must have been of mortal effect. No enemy arriving in this natural bottleneck would have had a chance to report back what he had just discovered.

A few dozen yards farther on, the "Little Siq" becomes a cleft fashioned by the water into fantastic shapes; in some parts no more than 24 inches wide, enclosed between sheer walls that block out the view of the sky. The light that reaches the bottom of the chasm is like that of an aquarium and the scene becomes increasingly impressive.

Suddenly, numerous niches with carvings appear in the multicolored

135 top right The Wadi Mataha gorge is spanned by the beautifully-positioned arch of an aqueduct that brought the water of Wadi Mousa to Petra; the arch probably dates from Roman times.

More determined hikers can prolong this itinerary by turning right at the point where the Little Siq joins Wadi Mataha. Initially, you follow the normally dry bed of Wadi Mataha, passing (on the right) the fissure of Wadi Sidd al-Ma'ajin, a gorge that runs parallel to the Little Siq. Not far ahead, high up, you will notice the daring arch of a Roman aqueduct that used to bring the water collected by the Al Birka reservoir to Petra. Once past the arch, go up Wadi Shab Qais, the right-hand tributary of Wadi Mataha, and in less than two hours you will reach the village of Wadi Mousa, near the Petra Forum Hotel.

135 bottom right One of the votive aediculae carved in the Little Siq is topped with a crescent moon, a symbol often associated with the worship of Al Uzza. A large temple in Petra is known to have been dedicated to this goddess but has not yet been identified.

rock walls, demonstrating that this was considered a holy place. Shortly before the gorge opens in the wide luminous Wadi Mataha valley is a last thrill: two half-columns, surmounted by a massive architrave and framing another two smaller half-columns (this time connected by a curved front), are sculpted within a vast rectangular cavity. The central niche probably contained the image of a god.

Once out of the Little Siq (in an area dotted with rock structures) follow the course of the Wadi Mataha, which bends to the left; you will soon come to the House of Dorotheos, then the tomb of Sextius Florentinus and from here, the center of Petra.

Petra

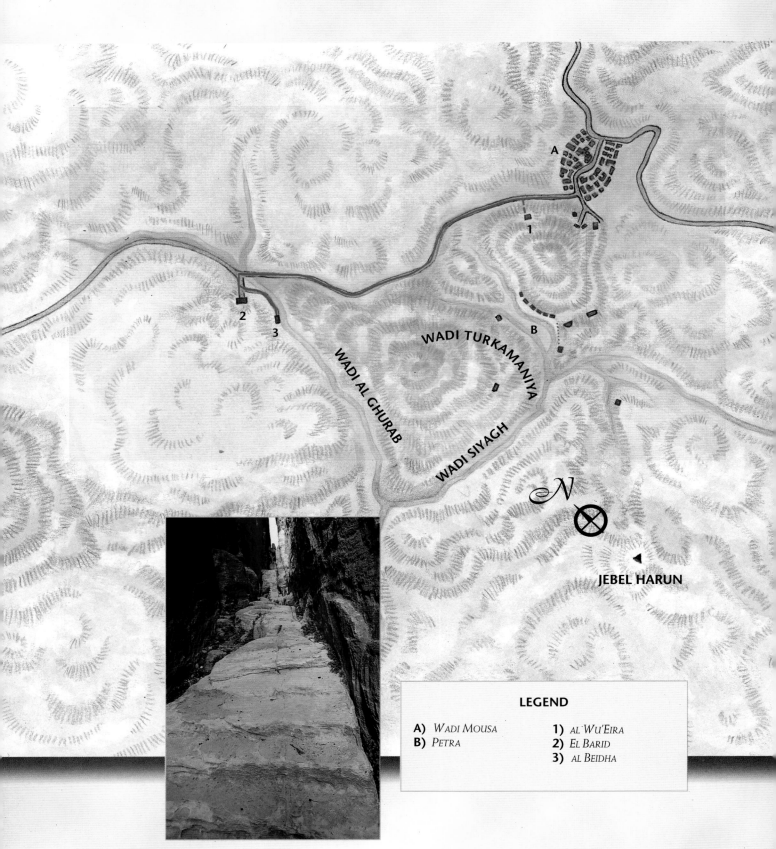

WADI TURKAMANIYA

WADI AL GHURAB

WADI SIYAGH

N

JEBEL HARUN

LEGEND

A) *Wadi Mousa*
B) *Petra*

1) *al Wu'Eira*
2) *El Barid*
3) *al Beidha*

$\mathcal{E}$L BARID (LITTLE PETRA) AND AL BEIDHA

136 Numerous flights of steps cut into the rock have been preserved at el Barid, also known as "Little Petra." Some of these lead to reservoirs and channels, others to small open-air sanctuaries.

137 top This fine porticoed façade with two columns in antis is carved inside the lovely el Barid Siq.

137 bottom Al Beidha is considered one of the oldest settlements in the entire Middle East. Some of the structures discovered here date from the initial phases of the seventh century BC.

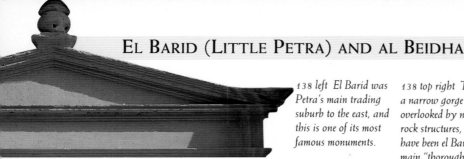

EL BARID (LITTLE PETRA) AND AL BEIDHA

138 left El Barid was Petra's main trading suburb to the east, and this is one of its most famous monuments.

138 top right The Siq, a narrow gorge overlooked by numerous rock structures, must have been el Barid's main "thoroughfare."

139 bottom right With just a few tombs and so many cisterns, triclinia, biclinia, dwellings and hypogea, possibly used to store merchandise, el Barid was, more than anything else, a large emporium.

139 Carved at the entrance to the el Barid Siq - in a similar position to that of the Khasneh — is the elegant pedimented façade of a monument thought to be a temple maybe built during the prosperous reign of Aretas IV (8 BC - 40 AD).

Petra is a vast archaeological area, literally covered with rock monuments, which are often situated some distance from the ancient center. The valleys and peaks of the surrounding mountains are full of unexpected thrills. Within a couple of miles of Colonnade Street, taken as the imaginary geographical center of the area, you will frequently

dedicate half a day or more to a visit to a small but charming village situated a couple of miles from the village of Wadi Mousa, el Barid. This can actually be considered a suburb of Petra and can be reached on foot from the Visitors' Center, along the asphalt road to Shawbak; the scenery is stunning, but the hike takes at least

come across tombs, votive niches, flights of steps, cisterns and channels. The eight itineraries thus far proposed are not intended to be exhaustive, but have been drawn up on the basis of an essentially practical requirement: they cover all the main monuments, are relatively easy to follow, do not take too long, and allow you to form a fairly comprehensive picture of the Nabatean settlement. Those with several days available and who wish to explore the site thoroughly, should buy a detailed map of Petra or engage an authorized guide. Thorough exploration of the area will offer fascinating, often unusual and breathtaking views and groups of tombs hewn into secondary gorges, but you should know that nothing will compare with what has been presented so far. Those who are satisfied with what has already been described can

two hours and so it is best to hire a vehicle – possibly with an escort – or take a taxi (either way, it will take no longer than 15 minutes). The same place can also be reached from the center of Petra by following the Wadi Turkamaniya, but the route is far longer, more difficult and tiring. Before reaching el Barid you can visit the crusader castle of Al Wu'aira; this stands on the left side of the road approximately half a mile from Wadi Mousa, perched in a formidable position, but it is by no means easy to see. Reduced mostly to a heap of ruins, it is nevertheless of some interest. Surrounded on all sides by steep ravines, it can be reached along a path that climbs to an unusual chamber hewn into a solid rocky spur. The original drawbridge that provided access to the fortress has been

replaced with a footbridge. Al Wu'aira, which the Crusaders called Li Vaux Moise, was erected around 1116 at the wish of King Baldwin I of Jerusalem, as part of the system of defense erected to control trade along the road from Cairo to Damascus. Besieged without success by the Muslim armies first in 1144 and then in 1158, it was eventually overrun in 1189, after Saladin had defeated the Christian forces in the battle of Hattin. Al Wu'aira was the last Crusader outpost to surrender. Occupied by an Ayyubite garrison until the early 13th century, it was eventually abandoned.
Turn left at the turn-off for Shawbak; after a few yards on the right you will notice steps cut into the rock. The most curious will stop for a while and climb up to admire the largest known Nabatean cistern in the Petra area.

PART ONE:
A Brief History of Blandford

Approaching Blandford Market-place coming up West Street,
c.1985, with the Town Hall and the Parish Church in sight.

Blandford from the air showing West Street, Salisbury Street and the Market-place, as well as the many lanes, passages and houses leading off the main streets – a typical medieval town plan. (Courtesy Blandford and District Civic Society)

Prehistoric & Historic Blandford

Human beings have populated the British Isles for many thousands of years. Neanderthal man roamed the Welsh hills and southern coastal regions 200 000 years ago, but it was not until comparatively recently that modern humans first appeared. During much of the ice ages of course, Britain was not a good place to be, being largely covered by ice, but at the end of the last ice age a group of people are known to have lived in Somerset, in Gough's Cave cut into the Mendip Hills. These people were hunters and fishermen living about 12 000 years ago. Among their prey they included other people, so they were also cannibals. Shortly after this, a return of the ice forced people out of Britain again, to be replaced by another, unrelated group about 3000 years later.

These were still Stone-Age people, but as the land became warmer they spread out over the whole country. In these early days they would have preferred lowland areas where there was plentiful game and water, and the banks of the Stour at Blandford would have provided rich pickings, especially where the banks rise steeply from the river. Approximately 4000 years ago these people started to develop agriculture and to clear the land for farming.

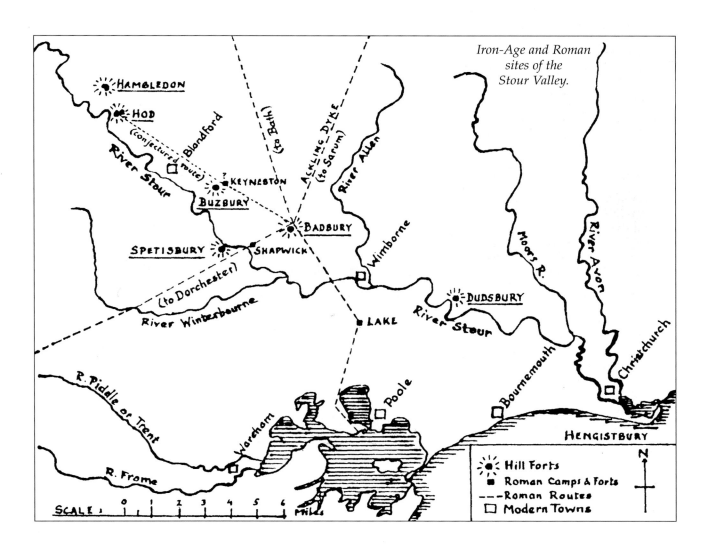

Iron-Age and Roman sites of the Stour Valley.

11

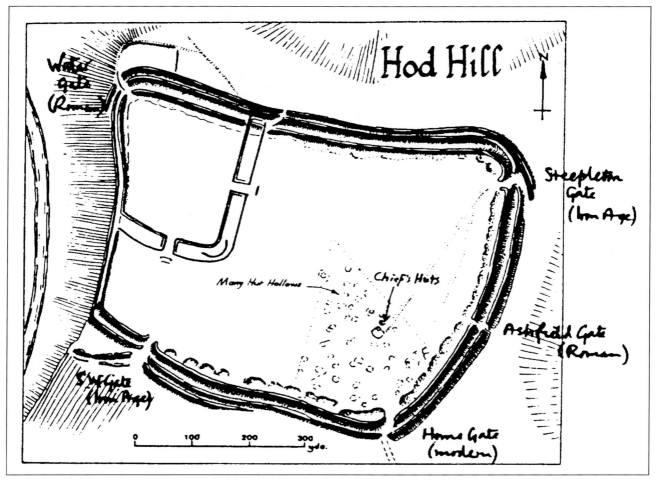

Hod Hill, an Iron-Age hill-fort with a Roman fort in the north-west corner. Hod Hill owes its extraordinary fascination to two special factors – its proximity to the redoubtable Hambledon Hill across the valley, and its unique Roman fort built into the Iron-Age structure. Hod Hill was no doubt made use of by men before the Iron Age. A number of flint instruments were found there by Henry Durden during his many visits, such as a chisel, scraper and arrowhead with serrated edges.

For this they would have moved from the lowlands to upland areas, such as the chalk downs above Blandford where the soil is lighter and the tree cover not so dense and difficult to clear. There is plenty of evidence of human occupation all around Blandford, although there is little from the town itself.

With the development of Iron-Age cultures came also the building of the hill-forts. The hills around Blandford have several of the best preserved hill-forts, notably Hod Hill and Hambledon Hill. It seems likely that these cultural innovations were brought to Britain by immigrant populations, and it is known that by the first century AD, Dorset was part of the territory of the Durotriges, an Iron-Age tribe speaking a form of Celtic language. Life was not pleasant or secure in those days, and the Durotriges were under attack from several different sources. As a result, they took extraordinary measures for their defence as evidenced today in the hill-forts that are so much a feature of the Dorset landscape around Blandford. In AD43 their worst fears were realised

with the invasion of the Romans, and their defences proved totally inadequate against them.

The struggle of the Durotriges against the Romans lasted as long as 15 years, and it seems that the main base of one of the Roman legions was on the banks of the Stour near Wimborne. The attack on Hod Hill seems to have been over relatively quickly, for there is no evidence of hand-to-hand fighting along the walls such as occurred at Maiden Castle near Dorchester. Having taken Hod Hill, the Romans then occupied it for a number of years, building a fort within a fort as a base. There is little evidence to show what events transpired in post-Roman Dorset. The Romans left around AD400, and the Saxon invaders from the East did not arrive in the county for a couple of centuries. It seems likely that the remnants of the Durotriges lapsed into something like their prehistoric past.

From the time of the coming of the Saxons, we have the name Blaen-y-ford, meaning the place of the ford, and after the Norman invasion the

Above: *St Leonard's Chapel.*

Left: *St Leonard's Chapel during restoration.*
(Courtesy Blandford and District Civic Society)

Below: *St Leonard's Chapel interior before restoration.* (Courtesy Blandford and District Civic Society)

Tercentenary celebrations in the Market-place for the granting of the Charter in 1905.

Domesday Book identifies land in the area called Blaneford. The town appears to have developed as a market town with status as a borough (although it did not receive its Royal Charter until 1605). The one medieval building still standing in Blandford is St Leonard's Chapel. The original chapel was built in the early part of the 13th century for use as a hospital for lepers on land that Robert de Beaumont gave to the religious order of St Marie at Fontevrault in France. It is not known who put up the building, although since Robert de Beaumont's brother was a leper and he is known to have built another hospital elsewhere it is likely to have been him rather than the order themselves. In the 15th century the chapel was rebuilt as a hospital and chapel for the poor of the district, and part of this structure is what remains today in fully restored form.

Lords of the Manor

Among the many manorial lands in Dorset given by William the Conqueror to his half brother Count Robert of Mortain after the Conquest, there are nine estates or manors each bearing the name 'Bleneford' or 'Blaneford' mentioned in the Domesday Book of 1086. One entry which may refer to Blandford Forum reads: 'The Count himself [Robert] holds Bleneford. Edmer held it in the time of King Edward the Confessor.' If this does refer to our Blandford, it is probable that the manor would have been on the site that subsequently became Damary Court and is now the Station Court and Damory Court Street area of the town. When Robert died in battle in France, the lordship passed to his son William on whose death in 1106 it reverted to the Crown.

In 1107, King Henry I granted the lordship to Robert de Beaumont, 1st Earl of Leicester, and it stayed with that family for four generations. By 1200 a church had been built and the area around the present Market-place had become a small market town. When the 4th Earl, a crusader, died without a male heir in 1204, his sister Amicia took on the estates until 1207 when she married Simon de Montfort IV, who thereby acquired the lordship. His son, also Simon de Montfort and Earl of Leicester but more famously known as Father of the English Parliament and champion of the Barons, retained the lordship until 1265 when he died in the Battle of Evesham and the estates once more reverted to the Crown.

The estates were then granted by King Henry III to Henry de Lacy who in 1272 was created Earl of Lincoln. Blandford was growing fast by this time, particularly as the result of a bridge replacing the ford by 1268. That stimulated trade and in 1306 Henry de Lacy was granted by Edward I the right to hold another fair day 'in his ville of Blaneford on the vigil of the feast day of the apostles Peter and Paul' (29 June). The lordship remained with the de Lacys until 1331 when Henry died with no male heir, and his estates were granted by Edward III to Henry Bolingbroke, Duke of Lancaster, the son of John of Gaunt and grandson of Edward III. When Henry Bolingbroke ousted Richard II from the throne in 1399 and became King Henry IV, the borough of Blandford Forum became a parcel of the Duchy of Lancaster and as such Crown lands. The present crest of the borough of Blandford was adopted from those of the Duchy of Lancaster with the letters DL placed on either side of the arms (see page 45).

For over 200 years Blandford remained Crown property until on 15 November 1605 James I bestowed a grant of the manor from the Crown to the 'Bailiff and Burgesses of the Borough of Blandford Forum'. They ran the borough until it was ended by the Municipal Corporations Act of 1835 whereby the ratepayers of the town elected the Councillors, Henry White was elected the first Mayor of the borough, and a borough police force was set up. The borough status was lost in 1974.

Coats of arms of the various lords of the manor.

de Beaumont

de Montfort

de Lacy

Lancaster

The Faces of Blandford

Alfred Stevens

So who and what has Blandford produced? Blandford has produced its share of eminent people, and we are going to start with the famous Victorian artist, Alfred Stevens. Alfred Stevens was born at No. 38 Salisbury Street, Blandford, in 1817. He was an internationally famous sculptor and decorative artist but is not well known in Blandford. His father, George Stevens, was a decorator, heraldic painter and joiner. Alfred began painting at a very young age and examples of his early works are exhibited in the Blandford Town Museum. Other works of his are on display in the Dorset County Museum in Dorchester, but most of his drawings are housed at the Tate Gallery in London with some of his portraits at the National Gallery. 'Stevens, with Turner [was] the greatest artist of the nineteenth century'. So wrote a Director of the National Gallery.

His artistic ability was appreciated early on, and at the age of 15 he was sent to Italy with £60 in his pocket to study under the masters. He spent nine happy years there, at first in Naples and later in Rome. One of his sponsors was Pegler, a Blandford clock-maker. On his return he worked mostly in London and soon was much in demand for his portraits and sculptures.

His sculptures brought him fame, and in 1857 he submitted designs for a monument to the Duke of Wellington in St Paul's Cathedral, London. His design was accepted but at less than the estimate he quoted. Nevertheless he undertook the task. His quote was accurate and he found himself funding much of the work from his own pocket. That broke him financially and his fine bronze Wellington memorial, now much admired, was not completed until 1912 when the Government stepped in.

Other famous works of his are the designs for mosaics of the Prophets under the dome of St Paul's, London, the decorative scheme for Dorchester House in Mayfair, and the characteristic seated lions of the British Museum and other public buildings.

John Aubrey & the Bishops

Blandford also produced some famous religious leaders, including two archbishops. Thomas Lindsay and William Wake attended the Free Grammar School in Blandford, which was described by John Aubrey as 'the most eminent school for the education of gentlemen in the west of England'. He attended the school and went on to become well known as historian, antiquary and biographer. Various members of the Pitt family also attended the school, as also did Robert Goldsborough, a distinguished lawyer who emigrated to America and became a member of the Maryland legislature. Thomas Lindsay became Archbishop of Armagh and Primate of the Church of Ireland in 1714, while William Wake became Archbishop of Canterbury the year after. The Wake family claims descent from Hereward the Wake, perhaps a slightly tenuous claim although the christian name of Hereward has been used in the family. While Wake is remembered in Blandford because of his charitable donations to the fire disaster fund and on behalf of the Blue Coat Charity Boys School, Lindsay does not appear to have maintained any contact with Blandford.

A portrait of Alfred Stevens.

John Aubrey also wrote about 'Old Harding' the glass-maker in the 17th century. In 1647 he penned these lines:

Before the reformation, I believe there were no county or great town in England but had glasse painters. Old Harding of Blandford in Dorsetshire, where I went to schoole, was the only country glasse-painter that ever I knew. Upon play dayes I was wont to visit his shop and furnaces. He dyed about 1643, aged about 83 years.

The Hardings' place of business appears to have been on the east side of Salisbury Street, and it seems that their glazing business came to an end with the fire of 1731.

Henry Ward

Another business achieving eminence in Blandford in the 18th–19th centuries was clock-making. Henry Ward also had his business on Salisbury Street in the late-18th century, and early in the following century he is on record as winning various prizes and awards for inventing new clock movements. He was also involved in the telegraph relay system for transmitting messages over long distances. There was one relay station on Blandford Racecourse, now part of the military camp, and Ward invented a system for holding the shutters firmly in place.

Dr William Wake, founder of the Blandford Blue Coat School (1657–1736) and Archbishop of Canterbury.

Archbishop Wake C. of E. School.

Above: *The Bastard brothers' house in East Street opposite the church. The archway led through to workshops which are now the Blandford Town Museum.* (Courtesy Blandford and District Civic Society)

Right: *Thomas Horlock Bastard (1796–1898), founder of the Blandford School.* (Courtesy Blandford Forum Museum Trust)

Below: *Ground-floor room in Coupar House, the work of the Bastards.*

The Bastard Family

The name everyone associates with Blandford and the great fire is the Bastard family. John and William Bastard were in business as architects, builders and joiners at the time of the great fire of 1731. They were experienced and successful in their profession, having, with their father Thomas, played a big part in the Georgian country-house building boom of that period. Thomas had built Charlton Marshall Church and Spetisbury Rectory. With their reputation for good work, they were well placed to undertake planning of the rebuilding of the town after the fire. The Government appointed them as trustees to oversee the proper use of the funding given for the rebuilding. That they did a good job is made evident by the fact that John became Bailiff (and thus Mayor) six times between 1738 and 1759 and William once (1744). John was also Bursar of the Borough which put him in the position of allocating building contracts after the fire.

John was a surveyor and William a draughtsman and they drew up successful plans for the town. Their original design for the new church incorporated a spire but lack of finance caused the church to be re-opened in 1739 with the tower only half built. The funds necessary for building a spire never arrived so after a delay of 20 years the present wooden cupola was constructed instead. Their design for the body of the church was good but stonemasons made the unfortunate mistake of placing the greensand ashlar blocks with the natural planes of weakness vertical instead of horizontal. Preparing the blocks with the planes vertical was easier for the masons, but the result 200 years later is that the stone is beginning to flake off in layers from the outer surface.

The Parish Church of St Peter and St Paul, built in 1739 following the destruction of the old church in the 1731 fire. The tower was completed in 1758.
(Courtesy Blandford Forum Museum Trust)

Their other main achievements were the design and rebuilding of the Town Hall, the Grammar School (now the Old Bank House), the Greyhound Inn, the Red Lion Inn and their own magnificent house opposite the church. They lived only in the East Street half of the house, the other half being constructed as two dwellings that could be rented out. Other contractors must have rebuilt many of the other houses, but no records have survived giving details. To commemorate the completion in 1760 of the rebuilding of the town, John Bastard erected the fire monument/water pump in the Market-place opposite their house.

The Ryves Family

The Ryves are another well-known Blandford family. Most readers will know of the Ryves Almshouses in Blandford's Salisbury Street. George Ryves of Damary Court, Blandford, founded them in 1682 during his term of office as Sheriff of Dorset and principal law officer of the county, but the Ryves family influenced many other aspects of life in the town. They had residences at Damary Court (formerly Dame Marie's Court) and at Ranston (formerly Randolfston in Iwerne Courtney, otherwise known as Shroton). These estates were contiguous and were acquired from the Crown in the 16th century.

The Ryves originated from the South East of France. They came to England as Protestant refugees with considerable wealth and royal support, which made them ideal purchasers of Crown-held estates following the dissolution of the monasteries in the 1530s. The earliest of the Ryves to arrive in Dorset was Robert (1491–1551) who was progenitor of the Ryves family of Blandford and Ranston. His memorial in the old pre-fire Blandford Church was seen in 1644 by Richard Symons, an officer in the King's Army in 1644, who visited Blandford and recorded:

> *Betweene the pillars of the chancel and the North yle stands another plane altar tomb whereon is this description inlayd in brass and this coate only West end: His coat (Of Arms) is also in the north window:*
>
> *Argent, on a bend cotised sable three losenges ermine, Ryves.*
>
> *Here lieth the body of Robert Ryves who departed this life the 11th day of February Anno 1551.*

He probably still lies in the Ryves family vault under the north aisle, which survived the fire. A new memorial has recently (spring 2001) been erected at the same spot in the church by the Ryves Family History Association of America in replacement of the original memorial destroyed in the 1731 blaze.

Damary Court was not within the borough at the time when it was owned by the Ryves, but the estate was mostly east and north of Damory Street as it is today and included parts of Langton Long, Pimperne, Nutford and Stourpaine. Until the 15th century, the Damary Court Estate was a separate manor, which had been given to the Abbess of the Order of Nuns of Dame Marie, Fontevrault near Saumur. It was thus that the name Damary, later Damory, was coined. The income from the manor went towards the maintenance of that order's house at Amesbury. When war broke out with France, the manor was seized by the Crown along with other alien religious houses, and its income diverted for the benefit of Eton College and St George's Chapel, Windsor.

It is believed that the original mansion at Ranston was built by Robert Ryves and remained with the family until 1781 when it was sold to Peter William Baker (who gave his name to Baker Street in London).

Many of Robert Ryves' descendants distinguished themselves as churchmen, lawyers, soldiers and men of business. Particular mention should be made of Dr Bruno Ryves who became Chaplain to King Charles I and Charles II, Dean of Windsor in 1660 and Secretary to the Order of the Garter. He died in 1677 and is buried in St George's Chapel, Windsor. Also of Sir Thomas Ryves who became Master in Chancery in 1618 and Advocate General to Charles I. He died in 1651 and is buried in St Clement Danes, London.

It has been confirmed that the firm of artists' colourmen trading as Reeves, who use the family greyhound as their logo, can trace their ancestry back to Blandford. It is thought that there must be some connection between this logo and the naming of the Greyhound Inn in Blandford, but no proof has yet presented itself of this.

In the 17th century, several of the younger members of the Ryves family went to colonise parts of Virginia in and around what is

Ryves coat of arms.

The Ryves Almshouses, built in 1682 in Salisbury Street.
(Courtesy Blandford and District Civic Society)

now the City of Petersberg. After the American Civil War, the Ryves family erected a memorial church there, which is still called Blandford Church, in memory of the thousands of Confederate soldiers who lost their lives in the fighting that took place during the Siege of Petersberg.

The Ryves family are now located all over the world and many have contributed information to the Ryves (Reaves) Family History Association of America, who are nearing completion of their new book covering the history of the family. The work is supervised by Patrick Reaves, the Association's historian, and will be available in the near future.

The Rose Family

Blandford has also played its part in writing the story of the British Empire. It is well known that the settlement of Australia started with the transportation of convicts during the 18th century. What is less well known is that this was closely followed by immigrants who went there of their own free will and who became the employers of the convicts, many of whom were transported for relatively minor offences. One of the first free settlers to arrive in Australia was Thomas Rose, his wife Jane and their children. Thomas Rose was born in Blandford in 1749 and arrived at Port Jackson on 15 January 1793 with his three children aged 3 to 13 and his 18-year-old niece. They received free passage, free land in New South Wales and an assortment of equipment and food to keep them going for the first couple of years.

The family initially had a smallholding of 120 acres to the west of where Sydney was later built, but they subsequently moved to another farm at Wilberforce. This was not a good move, for they suffered greatly from local flooding at their new home, and it is not clear why they moved in the first place having obviously done very well at their Sydney farm. They were followed to Australia by many other people from the Blandford area, for the Enclosure Acts of the later part of the 18th century produced great hardship for many tenant farmers. By the time Jane Rose died in 1827 and Thomas in 1833, they had raised seven children and at this stage had approximately 50 grandchildren. The family continued to prosper in Australia and is still numerous in North Dorset.

There is an entertaining entry in the *Blandford Schools Millennium Book* by a pupil from the Blandford School relating to Australia:

The Stour River is the lifeline of Blandford. It has always been of some use, either as a transport facility or as entertainment with its annual boat race and duck race, which never fail to gather the crowds. It is a shame how much it is being polluted by the people of Blandford but it is still an outstanding beauty spot. Whether you are feeding the ducks or just taking a stroll, you can always be guaranteed tranquility. I think we should all make a conscious effort to keep it clean because its state is slowly deteriorating in terms of hygiene. Hopefully, we will realise what we are doing to our countryside. There is still a sign on the bridge stating that anyone who damages it will be sent to Australia. Maybe this is an 'old-fashioned' way of stopping vandalism but the Georgians certainly had the right idea. I would like to see the river kept clean because it is what everyone sees when they come into Blandford and they should be impressed with how well we have kept it.

Joel Bough, Year 9, The Blandford School.

The Rogers Family

Shortly after Henry Bolingbroke, Duke of Lancaster, became King Henry IV in 1399, his Manor of Blandford Forum, which was only a relatively small part of the town, became part of the Duchy of Lancaster. His Bryanston manor was passed to John Fitz Roger, having previously been in the possession of the de Boxhull family (before the lack of a male heir put an end to this). The Rogers family remained at Bryanston until the mid-17th century and produced many distinguished Dorset men.

Early records show Sir John Fitz Roger (1385–1441), the last of

Rogers coat of arms.

the family to use the prefix 'Fitz' (meaning son of), nominating as patron successive incumbents to the church at Bryanston in 1415 and 1419. He owned many other manors in Dorset, and in 1430 founded the Dominican Friary at Melcombe Regis. Sir John Rogers (1480–1546) again presented to Bryanston Church in 1509. Married three times, he was Sheriff of Somerset and Dorset in 1521, was a founder-trustee of Milton Abbey Grammar School, and Warden of Cranborne Chase during the reigns of Henry VII and Henry VIII. In his will he is described as 'Lord of the Manors of Little Langton, Gylden Langton, Langton Botelier and Long Blandford'.

The next Sir John Rogers (1502–65) had 16 sons and four daughters by his wife Katrine. He became Recorder of Blandford in 1542, Sheriff of Somerset and Dorset in 1552, and represented the county in Parliament in 1558. His fourth son, Sir Richard Rogers (1527–1604), was the most colourful of the Rogers line. He was a great favourite with Queen Elizabeth and was knighted in 1576. Together with

Interior of the Rogers family vault in Blandford Parish Church.

other members of his family he became involved in the control of smuggling operations off the coast of Lulworth, which at that time was under his control as trustee for a minor. There are numerous stories told of smuggling and piracy implicating Sir Richard, but being Sheriff of Dorset and the chief law enforcement officer for the county at the height of these operations, nothing was ever established against him. He was also involved in disposal of the spoils of piracy, as were Sir Walter Raleigh (at Sherborne) and other Dorset gentlemen of the time. He represented the county in Parliament in 1571–2 as a Knight of the Shire. He could always be relied upon for help in times of need and the Queen enjoyed his support in the form of money, arms and men when required.

Sir John Rogers (1565–1613), second son of Richard, was knighted at Whitehall in 1603 and was a supporter of James I. Richard Rogers (1611–43), second son of John, became Sheriff of Dorset in 1637. He was taken prisoner at the siege of Sherborne Castle, but the circumstances of his death are not clear. There is a record that 'The High Sheriff of Blandford' was hanged in 1643. Another account was that his servant had in his possession £800 with which a pardon was purchased. It was quite common for death sentences to be handed out at this time in order to obtain a substantial reward. He died without any male heir.

The family vault in the church was discovered in October 1970 below the altar rails and found to contain four large lead coffins as well as the remains of many wooden ones. It may be presumed that some of the bones there belong to the above-mentioned family members. The Rogers buried many of their dead in Blandford as they owned a large part of the western, and northern, parts of the town.

What went on at Bryanston between 1643 and c.1689 when the Portman family became Lords of the Manor of Bryanston is a little uncertain, but the troubles of the Civil War point to turbulent times. Richard's cousin, John Rogers, who resided at Langton Long Blandford, maintained the mansion.

The Portman Family

Until the middle of the 17th century, the Bryanston estate was the seat of the Rogers family who had been there for some 300 years, but it came into the Portman family soon after the capture of the rebel Duke of Monmouth by Sir William Portman at Horton in 1685. The Portman family soon had extensive property holdings west of Blandford, as well as the lordship of the Manor of Bryanston, their land reaching to the west side of both West Street and Salisbury Street.

Although Sir William married three times, he had no children and the manor passed to his cousin Henry Seymour, and then in 1735 to William Berkeley who took the name and arms of Portman. William Berkeley's son, Henry William Portman (1739–96), rebuilt the old Rogers' residence, commissioning James Wyatt for the architectural work which was completed in 1778. As a further improvement to his residence he decided that the Blandford–Sherborne road, which passed alongside the house, was too intrusive. He petitioned Parliament successfully in 1755, maintaining that the road, which was the extension of the present Bryanston Street, should be closed and that instead new roads should be built around the estate. New Road is still the name of the thoroughfare which was built around the west side of the estate. On the east and north sides, he extended Milldown Road and built the bridge over the Stour to Durweston in 1795.

Wyatt's house was pulled down in 1896 as the family was not happy with it, but its main gateway

The Portman coat of arms.

still stands. One cause of the discontent was its dampness which was blamed on its proximity to the River Stour, only a few yards away. It was subsequently discovered that the main agent of the dampness was the nature of the sand used in the mortar for its construction. Sea sand, not river sand, had been used, and the encrusting salt not properly washed out before use. Being hygroscopic, the salt drew up moisture from the ground and so made the house damp.

Henry's son Edward Berkeley Portman (1771–1823) became an MP for Dorset for 17 years. His eldest son, also Edward Berkeley Portman (1799–1888), married Lady Emma Lascelles, daughter of the Earl of Harewood, and their concern for the estate workers led to the building in 1866 of Harewood Place in Shorts Lane as retirement homes for them. They also enlarged the estate workers' cottages in Bryanston Street in 1868 and built a mission school in 1889. Edward Berkeley Portman was prominent in public affairs and became Liberal Member of Parliament for Dorset 1823–28, was created a Baron in 1837 and a Viscount in 1873.

Sir William Portman.

Edward Berkeley Portman, created 1st Viscount 1873.

It was his son, William Henry Berkeley Portman, born in 1829, who decided that the Wyatt house had to go. He commissioned Norman Shaw to design and build a new mansion away from the river and up on higher ground that afforded fine views of the estate. It was completed in 1894. However, after the death of the Second Viscount in 1919, the mansion was sold to pay the death duties and it became the Bryanston public school in 1927.

Further heavy liabilities for estate duties consequent on further deaths in the family led to the selling of the Bryanston estate. The Deer Park and most of the rest of the estate were transferred to the Crown, and the estate houses sold into private ownership. During the 250 years or so that the Portman family were at Bryanston, this was not their principal seat; that was at Orchard Portman near Taunton.

The family were generous benefactors to a variety of charities, including the foundation of Blandford Hospital, and were much respected as considerate landlords and employers. There is no truth in the story that they ever owned the Portman Building Society.

Lord Portman. (Courtesy Blandford Forum Museum Trust)

Bryanston House, home of the Portman family in the early-20th century. (Courtesy Blandford and District Civic Society)

Fires at Blandford

Blandford Forum developed a habit early on of suffering disastrous fires. The first was in 1564, when much of central Blandford was destroyed, and there was another in 1579, when it was nearly destroyed. This was followed by the sack of 1644 during the Civil War. There were other fires in 1677 and 1713, by which time there was little remaining in the town of any antiquity. Finally came the great fire of 1731, which started on the afternoon of 4 June at what was then the tallow-chandler's house and is now the King's Arms public house. This fire was almost certainly started by accident, but some of the earlier fires may have been started deliberately.

The King's Arms is situated at the junction of Salisbury Street, Whitecliff Mill Street, The Plocks and Bryanston Street. The fire spread up and down Salisbury Street and then along more than half the length of East Street. It went part of the way up Whitecliff Mill Street and almost the full length of Bryanston Street, leaving only the big house at the end of Bryanston Street, which has since been demolished. The Old House in The Close survived the fire, as did most of the houses at the east end of East Street, because these areas which were burnt down in earlier fires were characterised by houses which were rebuilt with slate roofs which protected them from the fire. The 1713 fire in particular had already burnt the lower end of East Street, and these buildings survived the 1731 fire.

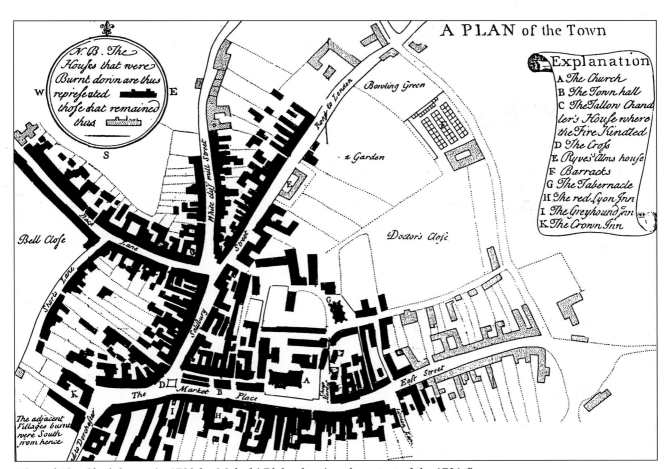

Plan of Blandford drawn in 1732 by Malachi Blake showing the extent of the 1731 fire.
The houses shown in black were all destroyed, and the ones that survived the fire are shown in grey.

A pump was erected 'In remembrance of God's dreadful visitation by fire'. In 1768, John Bastard gave £100 'to keep the pump in repair and supplying the lamp with oil and a man to light the same every night from Michaelmas to Lady Day for ever.' The Bastard brothers, John, Thomas and William, were at this time in business in Blandford as builders and architects, and they played a large part in the reconstruction of the town. John and William supervised the rebuilding of the town (Thomas died a few weeks after the fire), assessing the total cost at £86882.

Artist's impression of Blandford Market-place before the fire of 1731.

Diorama of the 1731 fire (in Blandford Town Museum). (Courtesy Blandford Forum Museum Trust)

East Street built after the 1713 fire which survived the 1731 fire. (Courtesy Blandford Forum Museum Trust)

West Street, built after the 1731 fire, with fine Georgian brickwork, pediment and cornices and Victorian ironwork dating from the time of conversion to shops at ground-floor level. (Courtesy Blandford and District Civic Society)

So much of Blandford was destroyed in 1731 that prompt action was needed to help the town recover. An Act of Parliament was passed to this end, and it placed all available funds, both public and from private donations, in the hands of a group of trustees. This specified that rebuilding should be in brick, with lead, slate or tiles for roofing. A consequence of this act is that there have been no major fires in Blandford since that time.

Two modern accounts of the great fire have been extracted from the *Blandford Schools Millennium Book*, the first of which reads:

The great fire of Blandford happened in 1731. It started on the afternoon of 4 June. The fire first started at the tallow-makers. The tallow-maker was boiling soap when sparks fell from the chimney onto the thatched roof. The wind quickly carried the fire around the town… For rebuilding they received £1000 from King George and £200 from Queen Caroline, £100 from the Prince of Wales and others… They found out that it was better to use slate roofs than thatched roofs and after that they weren't allowed to build houses with thatched roofs because it would burn too easily. Blandford is better now because the roads are wider and it looks nicer, but I think they should have left the railway line there because even if people can't drive, they might still like to go shopping or just look in the shops… Because they took our railway line away, now we have too many cars, which brings us problems… So after the fire they rebuilt the town. Now that we have no railway, who can think of a new idea to replace it?

Marie Butler, Year 4, Blandford St Mary.

The second extract comes from another member of Year 4:

Blazing Blandford, flames burning everything
People running for their lives
Sparks flying everywhere.
The red, orange and yellow flames spreading every-where. Satan's red fingers spreading. Crackle, fizzle, crackle, fizzle, burning fire.
Cries for help coming from every house.
Fire wagons rushing in every direction.
The water pump is just a cold reminder.
Brave men killed whilst trying to save their families.
The fire.
Suddenly: whoosh! – the town was flooded. It covered the lower parts of the town in about half a foot of water. Luckily no one died. Yes, Blandford is an interesting town – it has had both a flood and a fire.

Daniel Daly, Year 4, Archbishop Wake First School.

North wall of Blandford Parish Church showing the old burnt stonework from the 1731 fire. The newer walls and greenstones are in a sad state of decay.
(Courtesy Blandford Forum Museum Trust)

Eagle House, Whitecliff Mill Street, before restoration to its original Georgian façade by removal of the porch. It is now a doctor's surgery.
(Courtesy Blandford and District Civic Society)

The old Free Grammar School (Old Bank House), Church Lane, showing the wall, window and door which survived the 1731 fire.
(Courtesy Blandford and District Civic Society)

Law & Order in Blandford

When the borough of Blandford was incorporated by Royal Charter in 1605, a large part of the town was not included. All the area to the west of West Street and Salisbury Street, and to the north of The Plocks and The Close was in the Warnership of Pimperne. This proved very convenient for local villains, for they could not be arrested if they committed an offence in Blandford if they simply crossed Salisbury Street into Pimperne. Licensing laws in Blandford could also not be enforced in these areas, which increased the problems. They were duly solved in 1637 by an order from the Dorset Assizes on 20 July of that year, but Blandford itself was not greatly extended until 1895, when the western area became incorporated.

Another consequence of the division of what is now Blandford into two different places is that people who lived in Pimperne could not serve on the Town Council in the borough of Blandford. This disqualified many of the most eminent tradespeople, but they then discovered that the boundary actually ran along the fronts of the houses and that if any part of their house crossed the line they could qualify as living in Blandford. As a result there was a rash of bay windows built extending from the fronts of the houses, and this provided the stepping stone for many a career in local politics.

A local custom seemingly popular in Blandford in the 17th and 18th centuries was that of smuggling. Actual evidence for smuggling is extremely sparse,

The former Blandford County Court office in The Plocks. (Courtesy Blandford Forum Museum Trust)

as few cases were ever proved in court, but it seems fairly certain that many Dorset landowners were prime supporters of illegal foreign trading. Their wealth and influence usually provided safety from prosecution but one who was eventually exposed as a secret organiser of piracy and smuggling was the 16th-century Squire of Bryanston, Sir Richard Rogers, owner of much of Blandford, including The Crown. His contraband was transported up the Stour to the inn's own wharf in Crown Meadows and then stored, not only somewhere in The Crown, but even, it is said, in the Rogers' family vault under Blandford Parish Church. Furthermore, Sir Richard was County Sheriff at the time, supposedly responsible for law and order! Two centuries later, 'Slippery Rogers' was a notorious smuggler in the Christchurch area, so named on account of his ability

Smuggler's lantern (held by the Blandford Town Museum).
(Courtesy Blandford Forum Museum Trust)

The 'bond doors' at the Town Museum, formerly the doors to the Excise Customs Warehouse (Bond) in Whitecliff Mill Street. They are the actual doors broken by the smugglers in 1786.
(Courtesy Blandford Forum Museum Trust)

to evade capture in his particularly fast boat. One suspects he may have been a descendant of Sir Richard, with similar nefarious habits.

Another notorious 18th-century smuggler was the shrewd businessman, Isaac Gulliver, who set up a highly profitable contraband supply system from landing-places at Poole and Flaghead Chine to wealthy landowners around Blandford, Salisbury and even as far as Bristol. The trail went first to his purpose-built Howe Lodge, Kinson (now part of Bournemouth) and then via skilfully selected 'safe' houses and carriers to the more-distant customers. Blandford was an important part of that network.

Many of the larger houses around Blandford – Chettle, Cranborne, Eastbury and Stepleton Iwerne, to mention but a few – are suspected of involvement, because of their association with Gulliver's activities and tales passed down from those days. Secret tunnels and hiding-places have been revealed by later demolitions in several houses, and long-blocked-up tunnels have also been found under Blandford properties. In Salisbury Street and East Street, where there were numerous pubs, the tunnels seem to have led down to the river area. These hostelries could probably deal in the smuggled goods within an ostensibly legal business, and Blandford, situated as it was at the important crossroads of the main London–Exeter and Poole–Bristol highways, had many such 'watering-holes' for travellers.

Despite romantic stories, smuggling was largely carried out by ruffians capable of extreme violence. The poorly-supported Preventivemen who were expected to enforce the widely-resented import regulations had an unrewarding and perilous task. In 1778, they thought they had achieved a rare success, having seized a large cache of brandy on the Blandford–Salisbury road near The King's Head, Thorny Down. (Isaac Gulliver had acquired this inn when he married the daughter of its landlord in 1768.) It is said that they took the contraband to the Supervisor of Customs at Blandford who locked it up in the Whitecliff Mill Street bond store. However, later that evening a large party of armed smugglers turned up, forced open the big doors, fought their way in, and, to the cheers of the local townsfolk, grabbed back what they claimed was their property! It seems many Blandford people were sympathetic to, and some involved in, this trade. However, two years later in Blandford Town Hall, an auction was held of '984 gallons of spirits seized from smugglers'. Perhaps in this instance the Revenue Service had actually won!

Nearly every town market-place possessed a building or enclosure in which stray cattle could be impounded and not released until payment of a fine. Blandford was no exception, and the job of minding the strays and collecting the fines was done by the parish constable, who usually delegated the job to a minor official called the pinder. The Blandford pound was on the eastern side of Sheep Market Hill just north of the entrance to the present-day Argos shop. The following is an example from the borough minutes of 24 January 1764:

Writ issued against William Lacy the pig dealer for taking a pig away after the same was in custody of Henry Beale (the pinder), the said pig having been seized for non payment of market toll for the Borough.

The pound was certainly still in existence well into the 20th century, but we have found no records to show how or when it was disposed of.

Pilloried! The town pillory of 1740. (Courtesy Blandford and District Civic Society Photographic Trust)

Blandford Trades

It is sometimes thought that nothing much seems to have happened in Blandford since the great fire of 1731. People talk about this fire almost as if it happened yesterday and assume nothing much else ever took place. Here is an account of Blandford written by a pupil of St Leonard's Middle School for the *Blandford Schools Millennium Book*:

In the beginning there was God and God was bored so he said, 'I'm bored'. He then decided to do something about it. 'I will create paradise and call it Blandford!' said God. So God caught a taxi down to Earth and hovered to a place called Dorset. Unfortunately the people of Dorset said to God, 'You can't create paradise in Dorset!' Maybe they were right but God shunned the people of Dorset and he spake thus unto them 'For doubting God I will make you say 'Ooh, aar' after every sentence'. And from thence forward the people of Dorset said that they were the children of God for they spaketh the language of God.

And so God created Blandford. He created Woolworths and W.H. Smith and said unto them, 'Go forth and have stock', and God created barber shops and said 'Arrive and multiply!' and God said unto the barbers 'Thou shalt be open every day of the week except Wednesdays at 5p.m. when everyone wants their hair cut'. And God created Kwik-Save and said unto them 'Let there be cut prices for the community'.

And God created the Council and needed a day off to cope with what he'd done. Then God said 'Let there be a cinema' and the Council refused planning permission. So God left Blandford as it is and the people of Dorset said 'Ooh aargh!'

Sam Goudie, Year 8, St Leonard's Middle School.

Blandford has always been well stocked with shops and amenities. In the heyday of the individual craftsman you went to the cobbler or leather worker for a pouch; for some metal objects you went to the smith; for a precious object there was the goldsmith; and the weaver provided cloth for those who did not want to weave their own. The town planners of the day ruled that the traders should live in houses on

Ever since medieval times, fairs have been an important feature of commerce. The main function was the buying and selling by farmers of livestock. Sheep Market Hill, The Plocks and The Outhayes remind us of these former activities in town. Fairs were also an important part of the social fabric of the community, times when dancing, singing and entertainments brought people together and provided a break from the drudgery of everyday life.
This picture shows preparations being made for the fair at Coats Farm (where the Post Office now stands), c.1930.

Two sketches used to promote the entertainments of the racing season at Blandford c.1818.
(Courtesy Blandford Forum Museum Trust)

The Georgian Mews are one of the many alleyways leading off East Street down to the River Stour. Today they are home to a number of shops.
(Courtesy Blandford Forum Museum Trust)

the south side of the Market-place with their burgage plots behind them extending down to the river. Thus the raw materials for their trades – timber, stone, metals, etc. – could be conveniently brought by boat, landed directly onto the burgage area and worked in the workshops there. Many of those burgage yards are still there, usually behind an archway, places such as Bere's Yard opposite the church. Many of these tradesmen became the burgesses of the town.

The prosperity of the town was given a boost as a result of the dissolution of the monasteries in the mid-16th century. Monks were replaced by wealthy landowners with big estates, expensive tastes and large shopping lists. By the 18th century, Blandford was prospering as a result of the rise in the coaching industry and booming national prosperity. The evident wealth of Blandford is reflected in the splendour of the Georgian houses built at that time, despite the setback of the great fire of 1731. The annual horse races and associated events brought considerable trade to Blandford. By the 20th century, the breadth of expertise available in Blandford was surprisingly comprehensive. Blandford had its own iron foundry, and at one stage had over ten clock- and watch-makers.

Some of the more notable trades performed in Blandford should be mentioned. Coach-building and maintenance was in its time a big industry here

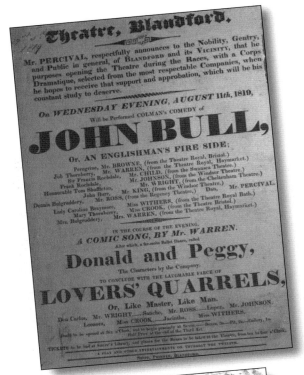

Left: *Notice for a theatre to be staged during the races, 1819.*

Below left: *A notice for the Blandford Races, 1894.* (Courtesy Blandford Forum Museum Trust)

Below: *The Westcote clock, entirely handmade (held in the Town Museum).* (Courtesy Blandford Forum Museum Trust)

and the former Coachmakers Arms in Damory Street reminds us of that. The woollen trade was the staple of Dorset, and Blandford was a beneficiary, a fact which is underlined by the presence of Sheep Market Hill. Wool-stapling was a major occupation locally until the last century.

Some trades particular to Blandford included glass-making and painting, button-making, lace-making and gloving. A trade for which Blandford became famous in the 18th century was that of the nurseryman. John Galpine had an extensive garden nursery on the north side of town, where, according to his 1782 catalogue, he grew 'most useful and ornamental hardy trees, shrubs, plants, etc., also herbaceous plants, fruit-trees, garden seeds, flower roots, flowering shrubs, etc.'

Shops were uncommon until Victorian times, and when the ground floors of the houses surrounding the Market-place were converted to shops, the new shopkeepers were viewed with suspicion. The townspeople had previously bought their food direct from the farmer at market and their other requirements from the relevant craftsperson. Although some items such as sugar and tea had to be brought in from outside, the shopkeeper was seen as an interloper in the system as he brought in goods formerly manufactured in the town – a potentially damaging situation for local traders and burghers.

Merchants' houses, now shops in West Street. (Courtesy Blandford and District Civic Society)

Hall & Woodhouse. The new Hall & Woodhouse brewery built in 1900. It replaced Hector's Brewery on an adjacent site that was burnt down earlier that year. The two pyramidal towers have now gone.

One of the three Foden steam wagons named 'Fox', 'Badger' and 'Hare', used by Hall & Woodhouse for deliveries from 1912 until 1933. The one shown is the 'Fox' with driver Charlie Foyle (left) and Ephraim Harris (right). (Courtesy Blandford Forum Museum Trust)

The drinks industry serves as a good example. In the 16th and 17th centuries, most households brewed their own ales. In the 18th century, pubs and inns brewing their own ales became commonplace. By Victorian times, the large breweries were appearing and by the 20th century the trade was reduced to one large brewery, that of Hall & Woodhouse. Today of course it serves much of southern England and thus its success has in fact been a boon as a source of employment in Blandford.

Hall & Woodhouse actually began in Ansty in 1777 under the leadership of Charles Hall (his younger brother, Thomas, continued brewing in Dewlish at their father's brewery). In 1847 Robert Hall (the founder's son) brought G.E.I. Woodhouse into the business and was very impressed with him. Perhaps because he was a batchelor and childless, he began to look upon the industrious young man as the son he didn't have. G.E.I. Woodhouse became a partner, married Robert Hall's niece, and ultimately received the bulk of Robert's share in the brewery. The Woodhouse family became the sole holders after Robert's death in 1858 and no Hall has been active in the company since then.

It was at this time that the company acquired the tenancy of Hector's Brewery in Blandford St Mary. Brewing had been taking place on the site or near it since at least 1789. At that time a tenant brewer, William Clapcott, had leased it from Lord Camelford and established a brewing, wines and spirits business. Later, a brewer named Henry Snell leased the site and built his home nearby, The Old Ford House, which still stands. John Hector leased the site in 1826 (hence the name 'Hector's Brewery') and it was briefly occupied by the Neame family, England's family brewing counterpart to Hall & Woodhouse in the South West.

A younger son of G.E.I. Woodhouse, Alfred, took over 'The Brewery', as it became known, while the eldest, George Edward (G.E.), maintained the Ansty operation. A letter, the first since their marriage, was sent from Alfred to his wife Florence on an occasion that is very familiar to all of us today, that of a full flooding of the Stour. Alfred wrote from The Brewery to his wife in their home at Fields Oak in Blandford:

Brewery Office. The Knight Keeping his vigil to his Ladylove.

Greetings. Look out the last thing behind where the cellar steps are and if the water still rises take up the carpets at once, I will come at once, the dining room will not be much trouble as none of the furniture is placed upon it. The water is still rising.

Yr. Affect. Husband Alfred.

The Flood Wall of Blandford, built by the NRA, c.1995. (Courtesy Blandford and District Civic Society)

Sheep Market Hill, 1977. Blandford has always been a market town, and Saturday has been market day ever since it was so decreed by King John in 1216. Until Victorian times, almost everything required to run house and home in Blandford could be obtained from one local source or another. Records show that, even in the 14th century, most people came to town either for food brought there on market day by the farmer-producer, for items made by trades-men in their workshops, or to the miller. The only recorded mill was that at Whitecliff on the Shaftesbury Road.

The crises facing residents of Blandford's past remain crises for many of us today!

Brother Frank succeeded Alfred as the director from 1898 to 1952, while his eldest brother, G.E. Woodhouse, remained at Ansty until 1916. Ansty remained an adjunct to 'The Brewery' until 1937 and is today the Ansty Village Hall. The 'Badger', symbol of Badger Beer, was becoming well known in the county and in neighbouring counties as well.

In August of 1900 a fire demolished most of the original brewery, although vestiges still remain. There had been recognition of the need for a new brewery, and planning as well as construction had been taking place since 1894 (a new malthouse was constructed in 1895). Frank Woodhouse reported seeing no sign of a fire as he locked up the premises that night in August and walked the short distance home to his house next door. It was due to his quick action later, however, when the alarm was raised, that most of the casks, carts and wagons were saved from the conflagration. Fortunately, the horses were safely ensconced in the untouched new stables nearby. The fire had resulted from a defective flue near the hop and cork room, but the damage was limited due to the prompt action of local residents and the availability of water close by from the River Stour.

Due to the fact that much of the new brewery was untouched and so much was successfully salvaged, along with the fact that Ansty was still in operation, business continued with little obstacle. The losses of the old buildings were covered by insurance and construction continued on the new brewery, so that between the fire and the first brew on the new premises in October 1900, there passed only about two months. The Brewery today stands as it did at the turn of the century. New buildings have been added over the years as the business has expanded, first to include aerated waters (which accompanied the move to Hector's Brewery) and, more recently, soft drinks.

In 1901, Hall & Woodhouse became involved in a lawsuit over the use of the Badger symbol. While the company had used the symbol for more that 25 years (since 1875), a manufacturer of mineral waters in Yorkshire had in 1888 registered the symbol as his trademark. Hall & Woodhouse subsequently had to apply to the High Court to assert their right to use the trademark. But the matter was not settled until 1929 when the owner of the mineral water company, Mr Verity, sold his trademark to Hall & Woodhouse for £52.10s.0d. The 'Badger', while changing posture and appearance slightly over the years, has remained the hallmark for Dorset's Best Badger Beer.

The Town Museum

Blandford's first museum was in a room above Durdens the grocers on the corner of the Market-place and Salisbury Street. It housed the large collection of antiquities which Henry Durden assembled during the 19th century from the locality. A visitor in 1887 recorded that 'it was fitted out with cases richly stored and nicely arranged. We spent about an hour which after all only gave us a glance at the numerous treasures collected'. On Mr Durden's death in 1892 he left the entire collection to the British Museum in his will and it took four days to pack up and move. This was a great loss to Blandford, and it was not until 1974 that the idea of a new museum for Blandford began to receive interest.

Local Government reorganisation meant that the town lost its borough status and this raised the consciousness of its interesting past. Stanley Lawes speaking at his Mayor-making ceremony that year expressed his wish to see the foundation of a museum, and his words were not wasted on John and Susan Tupper who kept The Sapling in East Street. They had long been hoping that this would be a reality and promptly set to work to make it so.

In 1975 Blandford Forum Museum Trust was formed with John in the Chair and Sue as Secretary. They promptly engaged the support of such heavyweights in local politics as Revd Ray Balmer, Cyril Hill, Gwen Lane, Agnes Williams, David Wright, Charles Lavington (the former Borough Clerk) and Barbara Solly of Langton among others. There were three problems – no premises, no money and precious little to display (and some of that, stored in the Tuppers' house, was damaged by the floods of 1979). An attempt to get Dray George Trust money (held by the Town Council for a riverside garden) released to support a museum was unsuccessful, while no grants were obtainable until premises could be found.

A solution presented itself in 1981. In January a lease was signed to rent from the William Williams Trust the old stables and the garden in Beres Yard,

believed to have once belonged to the Bastard family. It was also the year that Blandford celebrated the 250th anniversary of its great fire, raising further interest in the town's history. North Dorset District and Town Councils, increasingly aware of the value of tourism, began to give grant aid and with fine timing Ben Cox arrived in Blandford from Evesham where he had started – and for 30 years had been Curator of – the Almonry Museum.

One of the many fund-raising events held to get the museum going.

SUPPORT THE PRESERVATION
OF THE HISTORY OF
BLANDFORD FORUM
BUY A TICKET IN THE
BLANDFORD FORUM MUSEUM TRUST

LOTTERY

GRAND DRAW BY

MR. JACK HARGREAVES (of TV fame)

ON

SATURDAY 6th MARCH, 3.00 p.m.
1982
AT

BLANDFORD MUSEUM PREMISES, BERE'S YARD

★ ★

FIRST PRIZE
PORTABLE BLACK AND WHITE TV
+ MANY MORE CONSOLATION PRIZES

★ ★ ★ ★ ★ ★ ★ ★ ★ ★ ★ ★ ★ ★ ★ ★ ★ ★ ★ ★

TICKETS 10p EACH

AVAILABLE FROM
LOCAL TRADERS DISPLAYING
'TICKETS ON SALE HERE' POSTERS

ORGANISER: P. Watts, c/o Legrand Brothers, 26/28 Market Place, Blandford. Tel: 51313
PRINTED BY: The Minster Press, 5 Mill Lane, Wimborne, Dorset, BH21 1JQ. Tel: (0202) 882277
Registered with the N.D.D.C. under the lotteries and amusements act 1976

Starting work on the site of Blandford's future museum.

Sir Anthony Jolliffe, GBE, former Lord Mayor of London and President of the Society of Dorset Men, declares the museum open.

Councillor Martin Brickell, Mayor of Blandford, makes his speech at the museum opening.

*The museum's generator being inspected by (left to right): Mrs Susan Tupper,
Jim Langridge (Town Crier), Lady Jolliffe, Sir Anthony Jolliffe, Ben Cox.*

Ben was swiftly appointed as the first Curator of Blandford Museum and began to research the town's history, producing a series of publications, which provided an important source of income to the Trust. Meanwhile, based on plans drawn up by John Turnbull, work began on restoring the dilapidated building. The Tuppers turned their energies to begging and borrowing materials (the stairs came from the old South Western Farmers shop, tiles were found in New Milton), display cases and exhibits. However, progress could not be sustained by adequate funds until in a bold move by the Treasurer, David Lang; a loan from Barclays Bank was negotiated in order to complete the work.

Following a fortnight's opening in 1983 the museum was partially open during the summer of 1984. In April 1985 it was formally opened by Sir Anthony Jolliffe, the President of the Society of Dorset Men and a former Lord Mayor of London. However, some problems still remained. The loan had to be serviced and repaid, which proved beyond the income generated by admissions. There were some disagreements – not least concerning the name of the museum. It had originally been called the Old Coach House Museum and, as so often happens in voluntary organisations, some of those who worked hardest for the facility were intractable when

decisions went against them in Committee. There also remained the question of what to do with the garden, for which the plans had always been to create a Georgian area. It was cleared and for a while held an additional attraction in Revd Valentine Fletcher's collection of chimney pots, but resources could not be stretched far enough and the lease on the garden was surrendered.

All turned out well in the end very largely thanks to the good fortune which brought Ben Cox to the curatorship. His steady, serene and methodical approach was the museum's greatest asset and he had a good team in support – Jane Haines' expertise with costume, Eric Schmidt's work on military matters, the Pountneys and Anne Hosford (who served as Secretary when the Tuppers, their dream realised, retired from an active role in the Trust) being among many who helped in the work of the museum. It played a wider role in the community by providing an exhibition site for local artists in the Alfred Stevens Room, by organising talks on local history and by mounting displays to mark special events.

Ben Cox retired from the post of Curator in 1997 although not from active involvement and was succeeded by Dr Nigel Yates, formerly of Kent County Archive Service. It was clear that, to meet enhanced

Ben Cox completing building work at the museum.

criteria to ensure formal registration standard, an upgrade to the museum was now necessary. Dr Yates drew up plans for major work and an application for Lottery funding was lodged, the museum remaining closed through 1999 for the purpose. The application was not successful but a great deal of improvement work was nevertheless undertaken during the following two winters by a band of volunteers guided by the building skills of John Barnes.

Blandford's good fortune in attracting the right talents at the right time meant that, when Dr Yates left the area, the Trust was able to appoint Dr Peter Andrews as Curator. He came to the museum from his post at the Natural History Museum in London, where he researched human origins, and together with his Assistant Curator, geologist Dr Michael Le Bas, they were able to bring fresh skills and new ideas to take the museum forward and still with a strong team in support. Long may it continue to thrive.

Blandford Wines, formerly Durdens, on the corner of the Market-place.
This is one of the two Georgian buildings especially built as a shop.
(Courtesy Blandford and District Civic Society)

Twinning & Town Administration

Our Twinned Towns

Mortain is an historic Normandy town, about 90 miles due south of Cherbourg. Built on a hillside, it dominates the wooded gorges of the River Cance, which together with its tributary provide some of the most beautiful waterfalls in the west of France. From the summit, at 323 metres one of the highest points in Normandy, you can see a great vista stretching from Domfront to the bay of Mont St Michel.

Mortain was the citadel of Count Robert, half brother to William the Conqueror. Blandford Forum formed part of the lands given by William to the Count, and so this twinning re-establishes a centuries-old link between the two towns.

Mortain has been besieged many times throughout its turbulent history. In 1944 the town was the point from which the German counter attacking forces retreated towards Avranches. Much of the town was destroyed in the bombardment, but it has been delightfully rebuilt. The 12th- and 13th-century Church of St Evroult escaped damage during the First and Second World Wars, and is a precious storehouse of Mortain's long history.

Mortain is also twinned with the German town of Thannhausen – a great symbol of reconciliation and friendship between the ordinary folk of their two nations – Vive le jumelage! The official twinning with Mortain was held on 22 March 1986.

Preetz is a lovely town in the far north of Germany, ten miles from Kiel, and not far from the Danish border. It has a population of about 15 000 and is built on the shores of two of Schleswig Holstein's many lakes. It is within easy reach of both the North Sea and the Baltic coastlines.

The Blandford and Preetz Friendship Society was formed in 1962 following a visit from a school choir from Germany to Blandford Parish Church the previous year. Since 1979 Blandford Forum has been twinned with Preetz. The official twinning set the seal on a long-standing friendship between citizens of the two towns. Exchanges of students have continued ever since, with the society subsidising the cost of travel, and students staying with families. Visits of adults are also arranged each year, and many long-lasting family friendships have been forged. Membership of the society is open to all those interested in visiting the area and fostering international friendship. The official twinning with Preetz was held during September 1979.

Official crests of Blandford's twin towns, Mortain in France and Preetz in Germany.

Mortain Bridge in Blandford Forum, 2001.

Trudy, Jessica and Andy Vick with their dog Buster at Preetz Bridge, 2001.

Honorary Freemen, Town of Blandford Forum

J.T. Counter, VC	19 June 1918	Royal Corps of Signals	13 October 1972
Lady Baden Powell	17 April 1929	The Devonshire & Dorset	
Alderman Miss E.G.		Regiment	16 June 1983
Castleman-Smith	20 November 1935	Gwendoline Florence Lane	5 March 1988
W.H. Wilson Esq.	14 June 1949	Agnes Audrey Williams	5 March 1988
W.J. Newman Esq.	8 December 1953	Dr David Harries Davies	13 April 1991
The Dorset Regiment	18 November 1955	Reverend Raymond Oliver	
Alderman B.C. Hunt	1 November 1956	Balmer	11 September 1995
C.K. Lavington	14 October 1970	Cyril E. Hill	12 May 2000

It is also understood that men who fought in the Boer War, 1899–1902, were also given Freedom of the Borough.

Blandford Forum Town Seal.

John Iles Barnes, eight times Mayor of Blandford, 1903–10.
(Courtesy Blandford Forum Museum Trust)

Mayors of Blandford

1900	Albert Henry Hillyer		1953	Ella Gertrude Castleman-Smith
1901	Philip Abraham Barnes		1954	Joseph Lazarus Carter
1902	Alfred Charles Woodhouse		1955	Bertie Cecil Hunt
1903	John Iles Barnes		1956	John Tricket
1904	John Iles Barnes		1957	Richard John Wesley King
1905	John Iles Barnes		1957	George Robert John Haskett
1906	John Iles Barnes		1958	Agnes Audrey Williams
1907	John Iles Barnes		1959	Trevor Winston Fowler
1908	John Iles Barnes		1960	Edward George Riggs
1909	John Iles Barnes		1961	Joseph Lazarus Carter
1910	John Iles Barnes		1962	Bertie Cecil Hunt
1911	Edward Derham		1963	Gwendoline Florence Lane
1912	James John Ball		1964	George Robert John Haskell
1913	Sidney James Norman		1965	Wilfrid Lewis Penny
1914	Sidney James Norman		1966	Agnes Audrey Williams
1915	Joseph John Lamperd		1967	Thomas Latham Hughes
1916	Joseph John Lamperd		1968	Gordon Olaf Fry
1917	Joseph John Lamperd		1969	John Trickett
1918	Joseph John Lamperd		1970	Gwendoline Florence Lane
1919	Louis Bodley Bunce		1971	Arthur William Gordon Adams
1920	Louis Bodley Bunce		1972	Arthur Noel Lane
1921	Alexander John Hicks		1973	Albert Powis
1922	Alexander John Hicks			
1923	Alfred Hobbs			**Blandford Town Council**
1924	Alfred Hobbs			**Local Government Act 1972**
1925	James Thomas Rankin			
1926	Harold Sealy Woodhouse		1974	Stanley E. Lawes
1927	Harold Sealy Woodhouse		1975	Dr David Harries Davies
1928	Waller James Newman		1976	Dr David Harries Davies
1929	Alexander John Hicks		1977	Arthur W.G. Adams
1930	Alexander John Hicks		1978	Gladys May Cole
1931	Ella Gertrude Castleman-Smith		1979	Revd Raymond O. Balmer
1932	Ella Gertrude Castleman-Smith		1980	Gwendoline Florence Lane
1933	Ella Gertrude Castleman-Smith		1981	Dr David Harries Davies
1934	Ella Gertrude Castleman-Smith		1982	Revd Raymond O. Balmer
1935	Bertie Cecil Hunt		1983	Gwendoline Florence Lane
1936	Bertie Cecil Hunt		1984	Martin Jeffrey Brickell
1937	Charles Sumner Tripp		1985	David Charles Kinsey Wright
1938	Charles Sumner Tripp		1986	Cyril Enoch Hill
1939	John Edward Conyers		1987	Cyril Enoch Hill
1940	John Edward Conyers		1988	Haydn Roger White
1941	Algernon John Ewart Blandford		1989	Revd Raymond O. Balmer
1942	Algernon John Ewart Blandford		1990	John William Tumbull
1943	Algernon John Ewart Blandford		1991	John David Barnes
1944	Dennis Samuel Cuff		1992	Joseph Roger Hickish
1945	Dennis Samuel Cuff		1993	Deborah Helen Bore
1946	Bertie Cecil Hunt		1994	Frankie Maurice Lane
1947	Bertie Cecil Hunt		1995	Haydn Roger White
1948	Bertie Cecil Hunt		1996	Cyril Enoch Hill
1949	Percy John Lucas		1997	Carole A. Sharp
1950	Ethel May Biddulph		1998	Peter J. Warrington
1951	Ethel May Biddulph		1999	Haydn Roger White
1952	Charles Bernard Faulkener		2000	Rosemary Holmes

Town Administration

Blandford Forum Town Council as the parish authority for the town of Blandford Forum is the fourth tier of government after Parliament, the County Council and the District Council. The Town Council's legal powers are granted and regulated by various Government Acts.

Before the 1974 local government reorganisation Blandford was a Borough Council, its Borough Charter having been granted in 1605. It was subsequently created a municipal corporation under the Municipal Corporations Act of 1835. When North Dorset District Council was created in 1974 many of the town's powers and responsibilities were relinquished and the town lost its borough status although it retained the right to elect a Mayor.

The borough's population around the turn of the 18th century was approximately 1000 and its boundaries were roughly formed by West Street, Salisbury Street, Damory Street and East Street. Over the next two centuries the growth of the town meant that it had to expand into the adjoining parishes of Pimperne, Bryanston and Langton Long, and these extensions to the town's boundaries have resulted in a population in 2000 of approximately 8700.

At the time of the municipal corporation there were four aldermen and a dozen councillors from whom a Mayor was chosen annually. The councillors were elected by the townspeople who had the right to vote and the councillors then selected the aldermen. Nowadays there are 16 councillors elected for four years with the Mayor and Chairman of Council being elected annually by fellow councillors. Town Councillors are unpaid, and, with the exception of the Mayor, do not receive any attendance allowance or payments for their duties, which they undertake on a purely voluntary basis.

The administration of the Town Council is the responsibility of the Town Clerk who ensures that the instructions of the Council are carried out. The Council's staff under the line management of the Town Clerk deal with the day-to-day management of the Council's buildings and properties, the financial, administrative and support services for Councillors, the venues booking service and secretarial support for the Mayor and organisation of the town's civic events.

The Council usually meets three times per month and all meetings are open to the public. There is a 15-minute public discussion period at the start of each meeting when members of the public can raise any concerns or put questions to the Council. Agendas for each meeting are posted on the Council's website and notice boards and minutes of meetings detailing the decisions made are available on the website, at the Library or the Town Clerk's Office.

The Town Council supplements the provision of local government services in Blandford and provides a range of social and recreational facilities including sports pitches and pavilions, children's play areas, Woodhouse Gardens and pavilion, the civic buildings of the Corn Exchange complex and Town Clerk's office, the Cemetery and ancillary buildings. Other matters dealt with by the Council relate to the town and its environs including the supply and maintenance of town signs, floral displays and planting programmes, town benches, notice boards, web sites, Christmas lighting display, etc. The Council also has a statutory right to comment on planning applications.

In addition the Town Council represents the town with other national and statutory bodies and acts as a consultee and lobbying force with both the County and District Councils, and both regional and national government, putting forward the wishes and needs of the local community. Dorset County Council, which covers the whole of the county except Bournemouth and Poole, and whose main responsibilities include education, social services, highways, fire and rescue, strategic planning and libraries, consult with the Town Council on such subjects as the County Structure Plan, the Local Transport Plan and the Mineral and Waste Local Plan. North Dorset District Council, which is mainly responsible for development control, housing, environmental health, refuse collection, economic development, tourism and major recreational facilities such as the Blandford Leisure Centre, also consults with the Town Council on the District Wide Local Plan, the Economic Development Strategy, etc.

Other than receipts from the hire of its facilities the only income the Council receives is a portion of the Council Tax paid by residents. The Town Council does not receive any revenue support from central government, unlike the County and District Councils; neither does it receive any funding from local businesses and retailers via their payment of the non-domestic rate.

The Council Tax paid by Blandford Forum households includes the spending requirements of Dorset County Council including the Fire Service, North Dorset District Council, Dorset Police and the Town Council.

Each year the Town Council calculates the money it needs to raise to provide its services. The income that it expects to receive from fees and charges such as the hire of sports facilities, lettings of the various halls, etc., is deducted and this leaves the amount required to fund the services and any capital projects which are planned for the year ahead. This sum, called the precept, is the amount levied on the District Council which is collected by them as a proportion of the total council tax paid by Blandford's households. In the financial year commencing 1 April 2000, the Council's precept totalled £237055. For those living in an 'average' Band-D house, a contribution of £77.10 out of a total council tax bill of £898.66 will have been made to Blandford Forum Town Council.

Members of Blandford Forum Town Council 2000–01

Left to right: back row; Cllr Mrs Lynn Lindsay, Cllr Mrs Esme Butler, Cllr Peter Randall,
Mace-Bearer Mr David Jardine, Cllr Frank Webber, Cllr Mrs Dot Powell, Cllr Harold Galpin, Cllr Miss Sara Loch
Left to right: front row; Cllr Gerry Chapman, Cllr Mrs Carole Sharp, Cllr Mrs Sheila Chapman,
The Mayor Cllr Mrs Rosemary Holmes, Cllr John Tanner, Cllr Haydn White

Inns & Hostelries

Blandford has a long history of hostelries. In 1390/1 a dozen Blandford men and one woman were taken to court for brewing and selling ale contrary to regulations, so evidently drinking houses were in existence then. The earliest record of an inn in Blandford is The Crown in West Street in 1465. By 1547 there were seven 'licensed tapsters' (innkeepers) in the town, and by 1700 there were about 20. Just after the fire of 1731, the number rose to 30, perhaps to quench the thirst of the many workers involved in rebuilding the town. The records suggest that many hostelries led to disorders, whereupon some of the townspeople petitioned the magistrates to reduce the number to 20 and provided a suggested list.

The coming of the railway in the 1860s caused another surge in the number of inns, seven being built in the vicinity of the railway station, taking the total to 29. Now it is down to less than half that number.

Inns played a vital role in the health of the town. In the days before tea was readily available, ale and beer were the only safe drinks, as river water and well water were liable to be contaminated, particularly in the larger towns. Drains and sewers arrived in Blandford only in the late-19th and early-20th century.

Inns also played a significant role in the economic prosperity of the town. In the 18th century, trade was expanding in England and transport of goods was facilitated with the development of tolls on roads that brought them into reasonable repair for the first time. Furthermore, Blandford lay mid-way

Laying the sewers in East Street during the 1920s. The old cinema is the white building on the left, now the site of Argos. (Courtesy Blandford Forum Museum Trust)

The Greyhound Inn built in 1734 and refronted in 1766. (Courtesy Blandford Forum Museum Trust)

Entering Blandford over the bridge with The Crown Inn Hotel on the left and former Assembly Rooms on the right. (Courtesy Blandford and District Civic Society)

Left: *A coachman from The Crown Hotel, who met passengers off the trains who were staying at the hotel.*

Inset: *Milestone against the wall in the garden of The Crown.* (Courtesy Blandford Forum Museum Trust)

line with Salisbury Street. During the coaching era, the Greyhound Inn was a much more splendid establishment. The present Greyhound building which fronts on to the Market-place was the main site of the inn. When it was rebuilt just after the 1731 fire, the building was modest, but by 1766 when the coaching industry was growing rapidly, it was re-fronted with the addition of the four massive Corinthian pilasters, the pediment above and the window sills decorated with bunches of grapes and bacchanalian figures sculptured in stone to indicate that it was a wine house appropriate for the 'well-to-do'. Their servants would have been directed to the rear of the inn, the present Greyhound Inn, where beer and ale could be found.

The other main inns of the town were the Red Lion and the Bell Inn. The Red Lion Inn building still stands but is now private dwellings. In its heyday in the mid-18th century it was famous for its cockfighting, but by 1786 it had been declared bankrupt. Of the Bell Inn at the bottom of Salisbury Street very little remains: only the archway facing on to the road, and a brick-and-flint building half way up the yard on the left-hand side that is now partly used as a car-port and partly as the offices for a firm of quantity surveyors.

Another inn famous for its cockfights was the Cock and George in West Street, but when in the 1840s the sport became illegal, it changed its name to The Crown and Anchor. The building dates from the 18th century but it was refronted in 1863 after a fire.

Other inns that spanned the 18th to 20th centuries quenching the thirst of Blandfordians are The Half Moon in Whitecliff Mill Street, The Kings Arms on the corner of Bryanston Street, the Three Choughs in West Street, the White Hart at 42 East Street (now the Dolphin), the White Bear at 53 East

between London and Exeter, which was the gateway to the West and therefore well positioned for the overnight stop of travellers. An increase in trade meant more coaches and wagons, and Blandford became a centre for their repair. The repair trade brought much employment to the town, including wheelwrights, smiths and harness makers.

The two most notable inns in Blandford were The Crown and The Greyhound. The Crown, occupying the prime position at Blandford, is entered over the bridge. Before the 1731 fire, it was a fine old galleried inn. The present Georgian-style building is not entirely that built after the 1731 fire because there was a subsequent fire which led to further rebuilding in 1937. The Greyhound Inn is perhaps older as it occupies the crucial site at the intersection of the Market-place with the old road from Dorchester that crosses the Stour at the ford. That road is now merely the passageway between Safeways and the present Greyhound pub, and in

The former Red Lion Inn, now apartments. The archway led to houses, workshops, gardens, yards and the River Stour. (Courtesy Blandford and District Civic Society)

The Crown and Anchor Inn, West Street. (Courtesy Blandford and District Civic Society)

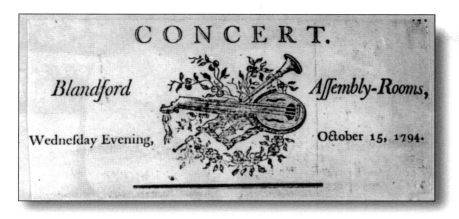

Notice for a concert at the Assembly Rooms, 15 October 1794.

Street (which later became The Star but which is now a shop) and The New Inn at 30 East Street (which disappeared when that area was developed some years ago). A Blue Boar Inn was built behind the Town Hall after the great fire but after 100 years' service closed in 1840 to make space for building the first Corn Exchange. Within a few years, the Blue Boar re-opened its bar at 10 East Street before closing over a century later in 1970.

Blandford's old Red Lion Inn and the Greyhound were two of the most handsome Georgian buildings in the town, although over the years neither establishment has retained the original frontage on to the Market-place. Today the Greyhound occupies premises in Greyhound Yard close to Safeways, reached through the adjacent archway. The Red Lion fell on hard times and is now no longer in existence as a public house though the red lion rampant (no longer red) still occupies the pediment near the top of the building. Both inns and a dwelling were rebuilt by the brothers William and John Bastard, along the south side of the Market-place after the 1731 fire but in a much grander style than their predecessors, and they lend distinction to the town's Georgian features.

In the 1770s the landlord of the Red Lion was declared bankrupt, and all the contents of the inn were auctioned off. The Inventory for this sale has survived and is kept at the County Record Office in Dorchester. In its pages we are taken through all of the rooms of the inn, public and private, into the stables, coach house, brewhouse, etc. The Red Lion, the Greyhound and The Crown served, between them, the annual influx of fashionable and wealthy visitors to the local races. Perhaps there was not enough trade to sustain all three through-out the year, although Blandford was on the London–Dorchester–Exeter stage route. The races brought many wealthy visitors to the town, and entertainments were laid on for them at the Assembly Rooms in West Street. The most notable of these was a concert given during the 1770s by

the so-called English Bach, the youngest son of the great J.S. Bach – Johann Christian – who left his native Germany to make his home in London.

Proprietor of the Red Lion John Biles has left us an interesting inventory dated 1772 compiled on the advent of his bankruptcy. But who was John Biles? Was he a local man? We discover in the Parish Registers that there were other people of the same name living in the town, and it is probable that this John Biles was related to them. We do not know how many people he employed, or what his weekly takings were, and we can only draw our own conclusions as to his success as an inn landlord; we are told he could not pay his rent. All that remains is this tantalising inventory. It is ironic that we might know nothing about the old Red Lion had Mr Biles' business prospered.

The inventory is handwritten on 14 sheets of paper 15½ inches in length. The appraisers Edward Percy and Thomas Fry listed the contents room by room, so we know how many bedchambers there were and what furniture was in them and what was in the public rooms (including the bar), while the domestic concerns of the inn even tell us the number of tablecloths and napkins. The appraisers valued the total contents at £955.18s. but the sale realised under £900. In those days the inn occupied the full Market-place frontage, with the exception of the two shop premises on the ground floor, which were let to Pitman and Applin. The owner of the property was Isaac Webb Horlock, apothecary, to whom Mr Biles owed £92 in rent.

We turn now to the document itself. There were 17 bedchambers, from the best to the plainest, including the double-bedded garret. The four superior chambers each contained an oak four-poster bed. For instance, for the 'Crimson Cheney Bedchamber' the entry runs as follows: '1 Oak 4 post Bedstead & Sacking compleat with crimson cheney Furniture compleat, £8.0s.0d., 1 Feather bed. Bolster and Pillow, £4.' In the 'Yellow Check Bedchamber' meanwhile we find: '1 Oak 4 post Bedstead & Sacking with yellow Check Furniture, £4, 1 Check Mattrass & 3 Blankets & 1 Yellow Sattan Quilt, 1 Goose feather Bed, bolster & 2 Pillows, £7.80.' It is interesting that 'the paper of the room' was included – valued at 10 shillings in one instance. Was it removable?

Bathrooms and WCs are conspicuous by their absence as was running water though guests might have a bowl and washstand, and hot water would be

Inns of 1940 & 2000

Before the Second World War, those who wanted a pint and a chat were spoilt for choice. With 22 public houses in the town a 'pub crawl' really had some meaning. One wonders how many different brews were available at that time? In 2000 there were only 11 of the original pubs still trading and with Nelsons Wine Bar in Salisbury Street, there are now a dozen public houses in the town.

Inns in 1940

The Wheatsheaf Inn	Albert Street
The Badger Hotel	Salisbury Street
Rose & Crown	Dorset Place
White Horse	Orchard Street
Coachmaker Arms	Damory Street
Railway Hotel	Oakfield Street
Railway Inn	Damory Court Street
Damory Inn	Damory Court Street
Blue Boar	East Street
New Inn	East Street
White Hart	East Street
Star Inn	East Street
Red Lion Inn	Market Place
Greyhound Inn	Market Place
Three Choughs	West Street
Crown Hotel	West Street
Crown Vaults	West Street
Crown & Anchor	West Street
George Inn	Salisbury Street
Kings Arms	Whitecliff Mill Street
Half Moon	Whitecliff Mill Street
Stour Inn	Blandford St Mary

Inns in 2000

The Wheatsheaf Inn	Albert Street
Railway Hotel	Oakfield Street
White Hart (Dolphin)	East Street
Greyhound Inn	Market-place
Three Choughs	West Street
Crown Hotel	West Street
Crown & Anchor	West Street
Kings Arms	Whitecliff Mill Street
Half Moon	Whitecliff Mill Street
Stour Inn	Blandford St Mary
Damory Inn	Damory Court Street
Nelsons Wine Bar	Salisbury Street
Damory Arms Hotel	Salisbury Road (Closed in 2001)

Off-licences in 1940

Chaman & Richards	The Plocks
Marshes	Bryanston Street

brought by the servants. As for warmth, every bedchamber had its fireplace complete with fire irons, dogs, etc. We are in the realms of Georgette Heyer when we read of a chaise for hire, valued at £70; the horses in the stable comprised '2 black, 2 grey, 2 black old horses, 1 stout black gelding, 1 chestnut gelding and a black pony'. These plus stable gear made £69.13s. in the sale.

The 'Public Rooms' comprised 'the Bar, three parlours, two dining rooms, and a drawing room where there were two Wilton bedside carpets'. The word 'rug' does not appear in the inventory but 'matting' is mentioned for all three parlours, plus the paper of the room, and bell and cranks. The kitchen, pantry and bar are listed first, and contain many items which would be found only in museums today. What, for instance, is a 'Copper Fountain'? The cuckold or cookhold hung in the chimney for suspending a cooking pot over the kitchen fire. We are not quite sure about the 'Footman almost new' in the bar.

Finally, the big question – what was the cost of a pint of beer in those days? The cellars were well stocked (containing beer, rum, port, claret, cider and French brandy) and a few rough calculations show that beer worked out at 5p (12 old pence) per gallon, rum 1 old penny a pint, port and claret 8 new pence a bottle, white wine six old pence per gallon. Madeira was 30p a bottle and cider 3 old pence a bottle. What are we to make of the amount of port in the cellar (27 dozen bottles)? Either the landlord needed to keep a big stock of it, or it was a mistaken purchase. We shall never know the answer, but how fortunate it is that this inventory survived as a unique piece of local history.

The Red Lion continued as an inn, but never recovered its old standing; only in the last few years has the pub closed for good. The inventory mentions 'Brookmans Lane' which was probably the old name for Red Lion Yard and beyond.

The Crown Inn dates back to the 15th century, although the present building was almost completely rebuilt after the 1731 fire. The earliest reference to an inn on the site appears to be in 1465 through a grant made to 'a tenement or hospice called le Crowne in Blanford', although it could have been earlier when the Blandford bridge was first built. This would have greatly increased the traffic through the town, and its position close to the bridge would have given it great strategic advantage in catering for travellers. References to it in later years show that The Crown continued as an inn right up to the present, and as roads improved it became an important staging post on the London–Exeter road.

The Half Moon Inn, Whitecliff Mill Street. (Courtesy Blandford and District Civic Society)

The Crown also was involved in other activities. It is said that contraband was stored under the floor (as well as in the Rogers' vault in the Parish Church) as a result of the activities of Sir Richard Rogers, a favourite of Queen Elizabeth I. He combined the duties of County Sheriff with piracy and control of the smuggling trade along the Dorset coast, and it seems that he made use of The Crown's own wharf in the Crown Meadow to land smuggled goods brought up the river.

The Crown was almost totally destroyed by the 1731 fire. Before the disaster, the pub was a fine old galleried inn of the kind so well described by Charles Dickens, but it was not rebuilt in the same form. The front, middle and back buildings were rebuilt at a cost of £484, and the galleries that were probably previously in existence and the stables also had to be replaced, with additional cost. It was owned at this time by the Pitt family, well known subsequently from two eminent prime ministers, and later it came to the Portman family and eventually to Hall & Woodhouse. It was rebuilt in 1937/38 in its present form, but the photo (page 50) shows the old Georgian façade as it was rebuilt after the fire.

The Old Maltings, Bryanston Street, shortly before demolition. This is now the site of Ryan House retirement apartments.
(Courtesy Blandford Forum Museum Trust)

King's Arms Hotel, 1930, with Marsh's Brewery behind.

PART TWO:
Memories of Blandford

*The May 1945 Charles Street party held to celebrate the end of
the Second World War. The owner of this photograph,
Myra Adams, was nine years old at the time and is pictured
with her sister Marcia eating a very rare orange.*

An alleyway off East Street. (Courtesy Blandford and District Civic Society)

Blandford in Business

Since the age of the supermarket the little grocery shops have all but disappeared. The town has many more shops now in 2001 and serves a much larger community. A number of the older shops are still trading, among them Arthur Conyers in West Street, Jeans in the Market-place and James' Newsagents in The Plocks. What is significant about these shops is that they were family businesses that have been passed on down through the generations.

The adverts on the following pages are from the Blandford Forum Official Guide, 1946.

Confectioner and Ice
Cream Manufacturer

AWARDED DIPLOMAS
1938 and 1939

Ice Cream Block

E. H. JEANS

22 Market Place
BLANDFORD

*PARTIES
DANCES
AND FETES
ATTENDED*

R.A.C   A.A.

DEALER IN ALL CLASSES OF MOTOR VEHICLES

ARTHUR CONYERS
AND SONS
1, 3 & 5 West St., Blandford
Telephone 7   Telegrams : "Conyers"

OLD ESTABLISHED PRACTICAL GUNMAKERS

CARTRIDGE MANUFACTURERS AND FISHING TACKLE DEALERS

GUNS, RIFLES AND SMALL ARMS REPAIRED, ALTERED OR BUILT TO CUSTOMERS' REQUIREMENTS

Member of British Field Sports Society

Blandford & Son
(FURNISHERS) LTD.

Complete House Furnishers
Cabinet Makers-Upholsterers
Bedding Specialists-Removals
and Warehousing Arranged
Funeral Directors

BLANDFORD   Telephone 106

Ensor & Southcombe Glove manufacturers at Eagle House, Whitecliff Mill Street, 1947. Left to right, back: Eve Pitman, Val Jones, Marianne Fenn, Nelly Lane, Jean Hodinet; middle: May Vacher, Terri Young, Edith Marsh; front: Queenie Young, Winnie Henley, Elsie Armstrong, Eva Hardy, Dolly Armstrong. Elsie Goddard (née Armstrong) remembers the factory fondly. There were two rooms where men's gloves were made. The Chant family ran the factory and Mr Chant cut the gloves while his wife ran the men's room and his daughter Lilian ran the ladies' room. At the rear of the building there were tennis courts, orchards and gardens.

*Mr Chant with the girls at Ensor & Southcombe Glove Factory,
1954. Rosemary Dean is fifth from the back left but the names
of the others are unknown.*

*Ensor & Southcombe, Christmas Party, 1954. Rosemary Dean is in the second
row in the middle, sitting on the lap of Wilf Christopher who was to become her husband.*

Mac Fisheries, 71 East Street, Blandford. Left to right: J. Pitman, Sid Pitman, Gilbert Neale, *Bill Butler. The boys were kept busy on their bikes with all the home deliveries.*

Left to right: *Bert Pitman, Sid Pitman, Doug Pitman.*

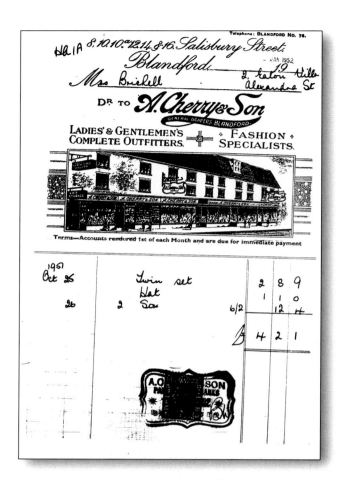

Invoice from A. Cherry & Son to Mrs Brickell whose husband ran the local auction rooms.

Salisbury Street before Woolworths was built.
This picture was taken in July 1966.

Church Lane car park at the back of Salisbury
Street where Woolworths now stands.

Loader's cycle shop, Okefield Street, c.1914.

A Short History of D & H Cuff (Hauliers)
by Richard Cuff

Dennis Cuff (twice Mayor of Blandford) and Harry Cuff (D & H) were born in Bishops Caundle near Sherborne in 1896 and 1899 respectively, of a family of nine children. Their father, Sam Cuff, was a farmer, family butcher and cattle haulier. After active service in the First World War, the two bothers moved to Blandford – Dennis working in farming and Harry with Sturminster Newton and District Farmers. In 1922 two AEC model 501 lorries were purchased from the depot in Slough where these ex First World War Army vehicles were rebuilt for civilian use, and the firm of D & H Cuff came into being.

During the 1930s regular contracts were obtained with H & G Simonds the Reading brewers who had a depot at the old Marsh brewery in Bryanston Street, and this entailed keeping the depot supplied with all types of beer from their Bristol brewery. A 6-ton Glasgow-made Albion lorry was purchased for this run as it weighed in at less than 2½ tons not loaded, and could travel at 30 mph (any vehicle over this weight was restricted to a top speed of 20 mph). This lorry was driven for many years by Geoff Day, who emigrated to Canada after the war.

An AEC Matador and trailer were used by the Devenish brewery of Weymouth to run beer from their Weymouth brewery to their Exeter depot on a daily basis, and another well-known local man Iram Gosney was on this run for many years before joining the local brewery Hall & Woodhouse after nationalisation.

Seasonal work was undertaken for Hall & Woodhouse, other regular customers being Dorset Farmers, Blandford and Webb, and United Dairies at Bailey Gate (cheese and whey products). Many of the houses in Blandford are built with Bridgewater bricks and this was another regular return load from the Bristol area for D & H. For many years all the milk for the Malmesbury and Parsons dairy in Boscombe was hauled from the Tarrant Valley by the Cuffs, starting at Hoopers at Tarrant Hinton and calling at six farms. The last pick up was at Hardings Farm at Tarrant Keynston, the driver being Jack West. This was a useful milk cheque for the firm as it was a 356-day-a-year job.

From the beginning both brothers insisted on a high standard of maintenance and the fleet was famous throughout the South for its immaculate paintwork (red chassis and wheels, mid-brunswick-green bodywork, black wings and yellow sign writing).

This lorry was on solid tyres and had a Tyler petrol engine with a 5- or 6-ton carrying capacity. In due course several more of this make were acquired, and the fleet had grown to five when in 1927 the first new lorry was ordered from the works, it being an AEC (Associated Daimler) model 509. AEC were the builders of London buses and for a short time were joined to Daimler, but the union was not successful and they went their separate ways after two years.

The brothers shared all tasks in connection with the business, which was basically haulage for the agricultural community, but with five vehicles a regular service between Blandford and Bristol, Southampton and London was soon established. Farm and dairy produce of all kinds were taken to the ports, with cattle feed, grain, fertilisers and barley for brewing being transported on the return run.

A 1932 Morris Commercial 'Leader' 6-tonner with Mr Rowland Smith the driver.

MEMBERS OF

D. & H. CUFF

MOTOR ENGINEERS AND HAULAGE CONTRACTORS

DAMORY COURT STREET, BLANDFORD
DORSET

TELEGRAMS :
CUFF, HAULIER
BLANDFORD

GARAGE :
DAMORY STREET
BLANDFORD

FURNITURE
REMOVERS

PHONE :
BLANDFORD 105

D & H Cuff's letterhead.

Other than the men previously mentioned, were employees Bert 'Dusty' Miller, Bert Wareham, Rowland Smith (who used to drive steamers for Hine Brothers at Gillingham), Johny Thomson, Bob Ingram and Frank Ingram. Sadly all of these men are now gone, and nearly all of them were away on active service during the Second World War.

After the war the Damory Court Street premises were improved upon and a full-time fitter employed. Several new Bedford 5-tonners were purchased from Selbys of Parkstone, mainly for local work. The first eight-wheel 15-tonner AEC Mammoth Major was ordered for long-distance haulage. Sharps Yard at St Leonards Avenue (now the fire station) was used for overflow parking.

On de-nationalisation in 1956 Dennis Cuff struggled back into the haulage business as Blandford Transport and was able to employ three old friends – Bert Miller, Bert Wareham and Mitch Mitchell from Sturminster Newton. Sadly Dennis passed away in 1959 and the fleet of five vehicles was taken over by Harry Perry of Wareham Transport. So ended a chapter in the history of Blandford and one which was typical also of so much of the road transport industry of the time.

Telephone : BLANDFORD 105
Telegrams : Cuff, Haulier, Blandford

D. & H. CUFF, LTD.

ROAD TRANSPORT CONTRACTORS

FURNITURE REMOVERS

OFFICES AND GARAGE

Damory Court Street, Blandford

Vehicles from 5 to 15 Tons   -   Any Distance

The Development of Cowards Farm

(Now known as the Damory Down Estate)

Cowards Farm was probably one of the largest single areas to be added to Blandford at one time and during the period 1960 to 1990 this area was developed by a national housebuilder into the estate we know today.

In 1946, just after the war, Herbert Holland and his wife and son Owen sold their farm at Manston in the Blackmore Vale and purchased Cowards Farm on the outskirts of Blandford. They ran a mixed farm with pigs, poultry, a dairy and a substantial acreage of arable. In 1960 Owen married Marlene Churchill, a daughter of Ralph Churchill who ran a butcher's shop at 59 Salisbury Street in the 1950s and '60s. They have three daughters and six grandchildren.

In the early 1960s Blandford was ready to expand and was anxious to attract industry to the area. Cowards Farm was earmarked for development which was to include an industrial estate, now known as the Holland Way Industrial Estate.

In the late 1960s Owen had taken up interests other than farming and Herbert decided to retire to a bungalow which he built on his remaining farm-land at Shaftesbury Lane and which he named Holmlea. Both Herbert and his wife died some years ago and the family company of Holland Estates Ltd is now managed by Martin Street, Owen's son-in-law. The site of Holmlea has recently been redeveloped and the name has been retained.

Owen is now well past normal retirement age but still maintains involvement in Holland Estates and the engineering company at Holland Way Industrial Estate which designs and manufactures airport apron passenger and cargo handling equipment which is exported all over the world.

Opposite page top: *This aerial photo of Cowards Farm yard and buildings was taken in 1957. Except for the farmhouse and an adjacent bungalow the whole area was transformed by Holland Estates Ltd between 1984 and 1999 into a residential development known as Old Farm Gardens. The latest redevelopment on this site was for eight residential units known as Holmlea and these were built on the site previously occupied by the retirement bungalow of Mr and Mrs Herbert Holland. (This site is marked 'B' on the Cowards Farm plan.)*

The late Mr Herbert G. Holland who farmed Cowards Farm from 1946 until he commenced its residential and industrial development in the 1960s.

*Ploughing at Cowards Farm, early 1950s. The clump of trees ahead of the
tractor is nearly in the centre of what is now known as Damory Down Estate.*

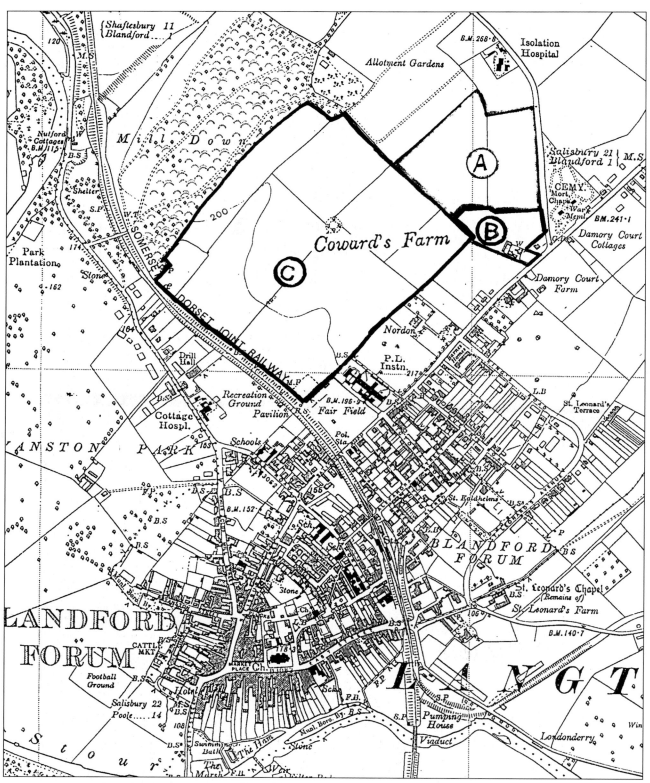

Key to plan of Ordnance Survey showing Cowards Farm and Blandford of the 1930s and '40s. Area A relates to industrial development known as Holland Way Industrial Estate with several industrial units directly off Shaftesbury Lane. Area B relates to residential areas known as 'Old Farm Gardens' and also 'Holmlea'. Area C on the plan relates to more or less all of the residential development known as 'Damory Down'.

A 1997 aerial view of the Cowards Farm development (outlined centre).

Right: *The cow in this picture taken some time in the 1950s is lying somewhere near where the Holland Way road now passes through the Damory Down Estate. Nordon House, which is the NDDC offices, can be seen in the background.*

Below: *Milking time at Cowards Farm, early 1950s. This portable milking machine was self contained and was moved to suit the herd's grazing locations.*

Kenny Haim and Alan Stayner (Beaver) sitting on the boot of Geoff Holland's car in the Three Choughs car park, 1972.

Well Remembered People of Blandford Past & Present

Aggie and Emmie, who were sisters, lived with their father in one of the East Street yards. They were a familiar sight in Blandford, trudging around with their old pram, which they used for collecting wood. Their father, Freddie Clapham, worked for Alex J. Hicks as a sandwich man which meant he also trudged around Blandford like his daughters. To look at them you would have thought that they were down and outs, but they would shop regularly at the grocer's shop owned by Mr and Mrs Parr (now Douglas King) in East Street. They would buy best red salmon and dairy butter, not the cheaper alternatives.

Happy Allen had a wooden leg and lived in one of the Ryves Almshouses. His daily walk would be to the Market-place to feed the pigeons, much to the disgust of the local vicar. Well known as the outside porter at Blandford Railway Station, Henry was never without his sack trucks, and would escort visitors to the town to the Crown Hotel. His first words to any local would be 'give us a fag mush'. Chippy Sutherland was very popular and kept a doss house on the corner of The Close and Damory Street next to the Coachmakers Arms. Old Jim, a vagrant who used to frequent Fairfield Road, would knock regularly at houses for a can of tea and something to eat.

Mrs May (who had two well-endowed daughters) ran a café in Salisbury Street, now the site of Granada TV. Mrs May would escort her daughters to the local Saturday-night dance where the local boys and soldiers would queue to greet them. Then there was John Paulley, former PE teacher of Blandford Grammar School and Blandford Upper School. Even since his retirement he has been actively involved in promoting sport within the town, and is still a Governor of Blandford School. His involvement has spanned over 50 years.

Joe Carter, who had a shoe shop on the corner of Damory Street, was probably the first shopkeeper in Blandford to offer shoes on the 'never never'. By the time you had paid for a pair it was time to choose another. Jim Langridge, a local Town Crier, now lives in Barnes Homes. Dougie and Rosa Downes were caretakers of the Corn Exchange for many years, and they would follow you into the respective toilets to ensure no mess or vandalism took place. Any messing around and Rosa would soon shoo you out. Dougie, it is assumed, did the same! He was also the Mace Bearer for Blandford.

Marianne Bourne, dubbed Blandford's 'Guardian Angel', was for over 20 years the ruler supreme in the open-air swimming pool. She commanded the greatest respect from every child who came into the pool and was affectionately known to all as 'Ma' or 'Mrs B'.

Ted Ingram was the car-park attendant for the Marsh and Ham. Ted used to sit in a little wooden hut in the middle of the car-park entrance and collect the money. He had a little electric fire to keep him warm in winter, and the only time you saw him move was to run across to the toilets; it was funny to watch him as he would dart across like a little rabbit!

Mr Parker of Parker & Sons would bring a mobile shop around the streets of Blandford. The most important product on board would be the paraffin which most households used for their stoves. Dr David Davies was not only a doctor, but someone you could always talk to; nothing was ever too much trouble for him and he became a friend to all those he cared for.

With the help of the curate Mr Harding, Canon Geoffrey Goodall and his wife turned their cellar into a meeting place for those who attended the Church of St Peter and St Paul. The club was called the Fellowship of the Upper Room – FUR for short. Their back door was always open because it was the only entrance to the cellars.

Mrs Betty Penny created the Cavalcade of Costume and spent many years collecting period costumes and travelling the length and breadth of the country with her collection. The costumes were modelled by local children and adults. The Cavalcade of Costume is now permanently housed in Lime Tree House at the top of Church Lane.

Mrs Gwen Lane, a former Mayor of Blandford, was well known for her hospitality in regularly taking children who attended Sunday School home for special teas. She is also remembered for helping the needy of the town.

For over 50 years the name of TGWU's Ernie Amey has appeared in the local press because of a lifetime dedicated to helping fellow trade unionists.

When his father started work the wage he earned was only 6d. a day. Mr Ernie Amey was born into a lovely looking cottage but it had no electricity, bathroom or inside toilet. Leaving school at the age of 12 he started work at the same farm as his father, getting up at the crack of dawn to milk the cows and finishing late in the evening – and putting in a 60–70-hour week.

In 1945, concerned about the poor wages and conditions offered to farmworkers in Dorset, Mr Amey joined the then Farmworkers' Union. Since that time he has fought for well over a £1 million in compensation for accidents suffered by members. And his interests also include helping the wider community. A nurse from abroad was able to stay on in England after she contacted Mr Amey who helped in the provision of a visa and in 1985 the Blandford & District Trades Council raised £1000 to help construct a ramp to the Blandford Library.

This is a picture of a compensation cheque being presented by Mr Ernie Amey.

The Bellows Family

L. Bellows and J. Jay, 1946.

Blandford Cycling Club, 1948.
Left to right: *Les Bellows, Dennis Belbin,
Cyril Plumber, Geoff James.*

*The Mayor Mrs Gwen Lane at the celebration of Reg
and Bessie Bellows' 50th wedding anniversary, 1972.*

Blandford Cycling Club, 1949.
Left to right: *Les Bellows, Ronnie Silk, Peter Crewe.*

Scout Bazaar, Corn Exchange, 1965.
Left to right: *Sandra Cullum, Pat Bellows, Les Bellows.*

*Les Bellows with his cycling awards, 1949–50.
In 12 hours he cycled 238.75 miles
and in 24 hours 407.375 miles.*

Personal Recollections

A View of Blandford
Jim Langridge

Blandford Forum was, in the 1920s, a municipal borough, parish, market and union town, head of a County Court district, and petty sessional court, and was situated near an ancient ford on the River Stour. It was destroyed by fire in 1731, but rebuilt in the Georgian style of that time, and is renowned as a Georgian town of fine repute. Having been consumed by fire, the Parish Church was rebuilt during the period between 1732 and 1739 at a cost of £3200, and re-opened on 8 April 1739. The Congregational Church was founded in 1662, rebuilt in 1867, and renovated in 1894 at a cost of £455, with seating for 450.

A primitive Methodist church in Albert Street, erected in 1877, seated 300, a Sunday school having been built in 1849. Originally built in 1830, the Wesleyan chapel in The Close seats 250, and has been restored at various times.

Now the Art Gallery, the open Brethrens' meeting room in East Street seats 250 also, and was erected in 1882.

Blandford Secondary School in Damory Street was founded and endowed by Thomas Horlock Bastard of Charlton Manor. In 1729 Archbishop Wake founded the school which bears his name in Park Road and was known as the Elementary School.

There were approximately 200 businesses in the town, 16 public houses and six clubs during the 1920s. In 1920 itself the office of Town Crier was held by Thomas Inkpen.

The Palace Theatre, c.1930s.

Sid Pitman stands proudly outside his shop, showing off his wonderful display of fresh fish and poultry.

Blandford's majorette troop in the early 1960s. Included are: S. Barrett, M. Chinnock, B. Preston, J. Tait, D. Powis, M. Wright, M. Cave, S. Payne, S. Marcow, V. Ingram, R. Cooper, V. Legg, M. Wareham, Marcia ?, W. Davis, G. Gainsford, J. Morgan, P. Taylor, K. Dutfield, A. Boyl. (Courtesy Mrs Myra Adams)

Blandford Carnival, c.1960.

Blandford 1960s–'70s

When I came to Blandford in 1958, I journeyed to town daily from my cottage in Stourpaine, for my job with the Hants and Dorset Bus Company. Buses at that time were frequent, with hourly services between Weymouth and Salisbury, and Shaftesbury and Bournemouth. Fares were similar too; being around 6s. and 9d. for either journey (approximately 34p!). After 2½ years on the 24 route between Bournemouth and Shaftesbury, I decided to return to my profession, namely hairdressing, and took over the premises at 15–17 in East Street, known as the Forum Hairdressers. During the years which followed many changes took place. Blandford Borough became a town, losing its prestige together with much civic pride which the older inhabitants had nurtured over the years. Fortunately, the Mayoralty was held on to, but even that has lost some of its dignity, now that the post is 'Town Mayor'.

Many a small shopkeeper has disappeared. In the Market-place there were 17 retail shops. Shopping was a pleasure, indeed most requirements could be obtained in the three streets – West Street, East Street and the Market-place. On market days,

Thursdays and Saturdays, the town became crowded with shoppers from outside villages; now there are supermarkets and the like without a friendly greeting or a 'Can I help you?' These days it's serve yourself and pay at the desk.

What of entertainment? At that time there were two cinemas, the Palace and the Ritz. After an absence of nine years, Blandford's annual carnival was revived in 1972, and is still going strong and raising funds for local charities. In 1982, having been in abeyance since 1939 (bell-ringing being forbidden for the years of the Second World War), the office of Town Crier was revived, Mr Jim Langridge being appointed to the position. Besides his travels within England, he travelled abroad, proclaiming the many [delights] of the town and the countryside of Dorset. He became a well-known figure with his bell and regalia, and organised the first Town Crier's contest, which subsequently became the South of England Town Criers' contest held annually each May. It is now held as part of the Georgian Fayre, on which day the main streets are closed to traffic. The town is filled with fun-fair rides, stalls, entertainers, bands and thousands of people – a sight worth seeing.

Wartime Memories

Doris Payne (née Steel), now of Ryan Court

It was in March 1940 that my father became licensee of the New Inn in East Street Blandford, which is now Douglas King Insurance Services. My three brothers had joined the Army and two sisters lived away from home. My younger sister was still at school.

During those wartime evenings, my parents, sister and I worked hard to cope with the needs of the customers. At times we were so busy that every drinking glass was in use. And when supplies ran short we had to ration the beer and cigarettes. There was rarely any trouble with the soldiers from the nearby Army camp, and if there was the local regulars would help us by diffusing the situation. Events of the war and arrivals at the camp were reflected within the pub. Among our customers were men who had faced real dangers, including the Dunkirk survivors. Unknown dangers lay ahead and many did not survive.

My brothers and sisters visited when leave permitted. It meant a lot to servicemen away from home that we were a family and shared our home with them; this was our way of adapting to make the best of wartime life.

In April 1940 I started work at the Red House, Salisbury Street, for the solicitor W.H. Wilson who was also the Town Clerk for the borough. The office now is the optician's, Melson Wingate. When the wartime paperwork escalated more space was needed and other premises were found. The office then moved to 61 Salisbury Street and I transferred there as receptionist, secretary, and book-keeper.

Satisfactory billets had to be found without delay for people who had lost many possessions in the bombing raids on London. Empty houses not used were furnished for use by small families. Ryves Almshouses became small family homes. Later it was decided that the proximity of the camp made the town unsuitable as a reception area for evacuees. Alderman B.C. Hunt was the Billeting Officer and British Restaurant Officer; in the office we kept the orders, records and accounts for the British Restaurant.

To maintain supplies and provisions in those days of rationing, forms had to be sent to the Ministry of Food, showing the number of meals and cups of tea supplied in the restaurant. For a time, above the restaurant, the rooms were fitted out to accommodate workmen employed in essential building work at Tarrant Rushton Airfield. The site of the restaurant is now Jocks Barber's Shop.

Outside the NAAFI in Orchard Street, 1946. Left to right, back: Josie Neal, Velma Bellows, Ken Thoroughgood, Sylvia Dugdale, Violet Hall; middle: Cissie Caines, Una Gibbs, Mr Thoroughgood, Josie Hardy, Fred Oswaldstone; front: Florrie Hayter, Ethel Pucket, Pat Cullum, 'Flash Lane', Janet Marsh, Betty Bolash, Mary Hall.

The New Inn (1720–1956) at 30 East Street, Blandford, which was originally built by John Bush of Blandford, innholder, on a piece of land that, prior to the fire of 1713, was the site of the house belonging to John Skinner.

Entertainment in the town was plentiful, with two cinemas, regular dances, and many public houses.

We left the New Inn in 1943 and I married my soldier husband in the same year. I continued to work for the Borough Council until the birth of my daughter in 1944. Soon after my husband was sent to Burma for 15 months – the eventful wartime years touched so many.

The following is a poem by Doris Payne, 6 July 1978, on the occasion of the demolition of the railway bridge and before the new bypass.

HOLIDAY ROUTE THEN AND NOW

All Holiday makers in Dorset so dear
Are likely to pass through Blandford.
Those who travelled for many a year
Just loved the name of Blandford.

Southwards, on trains they sped, via Bath,
Through splendour of Mendip range,
Blackmore Vale and the Stour Valley,
To reach our Georgian town.

Past hospital and playing field,
To pause in our lovely station,
Where it said 'Alight here for Bryanston School',
The great house standing up among trees.

From the bridge, they'd see roofs of East Street,
then look back, where sun shone on church tower.
On the brewery side the river has ever
Meandered, just hugging our town.

Then, through leafy trees and grassy banks
They'd speed on enjoying the views, perhaps
Changing trains by a golf course,
Poole Harbour or Bournemouth Bay.

And how is it now, by car, to get through?
On a summer weekend, it's no fun.
They must curse at the little there is to be seen
As they wait between roadside houses.

In the future they'll go another way round,
Or fix a time for travel, off-peak,
Eager they'll be to leave Blandford behind,
A black mark in the county of Dorset.

Never a wave from a carriage again,
Summer weekends are no fun.
Never a wave from a carriage again,
Because the trains don't run.

The programme of the Matinee Dancing Display put on by the pupils of Mary Lethbridge in aid of the welcome-home fund. (Courtesy Mrs Myra Adams)

Notes from a Blandford Diary

Thomas Tanner

1911

9th August   Three ladies (one a Mrs Hume from Bournemouth) spoke from an open car in the market-place on votes for women. Several drunken men in the crowd would not let them speak and started pelting them with rotten fruit. When matters seemed to be getting out of hand members of the Adult School escorted the women who had arrived by train back to the railway station for their safety. The police did nothing to help these ladies.

14th September   Bought a pair of overalls for four shillings and six pence at Sandersons and a pair of cloth trousers at Mr Hicks for five shillings. At the butchers beef is four and a halfpenny per pound.

Oct 1st   Bought a pair of trousers for two pounds and seven and six pence, the trousers were replaced as they were made of shoddy material. A guest visitor came to the Adult School and talked on living a natural life, during his time in Blandford he lived in a tent in the park.

1912

General Booth died when he came to Blandford. He had spoken to a great crowd in the Market-place.
18th January   Four foot of snow covered all of Blandford.

Feb 29th   The national coal strike has started, my father has smashed up some chalk, damped it down and mixed it with the little amount of coal we have left. This helped keep our fire going a bit longer.

March 3rd   Everything they say is costing more. Coal is now up to two shillings and nine pence a hundredweight and whisky seven and six a quart, thanks to Lloyd George. Earlier it was four shillings and sixpence a quart in the wine stores. Up to this date I have kept the pledge of total abstinence so it's no bother to me except I like to rub it in to my limbs for rheumatics and into the gums for toothache.

March 21st   A large number of people are leaving here for Canada. Many people say that at present it seems impossible for working folk to eat and live in a reasonable way, to get a home together and save a little for old age. Albert Miller who works at the brewery from 6.00a.m. to 6.00p.m. gets eleven shillings a week, under gardeners from eleven shillings to twelve shillings and six pence per week. The top rate for tradesmen is from four to six pence per hour.

March 28th   The Suffragette Bill has been thrown out of the Commons. A lot of people says that it may be a good thing for they say it may break up so many homes and bring man's complete ruin as Eve appears to have accomplished in the Garden on Eden. One man told me that rather than be ruled by women (who are in a majority) he would prefer to become a monk.

1913

30th July   I marched to the Downs with the local Red Cross party to take part in sham fights, our job was to pick up the fallen and take the casualties to a temporary hospital. After this we were marched to the town bringing the wounded in wagons to the principal hospital in Bryanston Park. During the evening they held a torchlight tattoo. Our workers formed the fence around the square. Personally I had nothing to eat from 6.30a.m. until 9.30a.m. the next morning.

22nd   An Army airship passed over Blandford.

23rd   Had a tooth out and paid up eighteen shillings.

22nd December   Went to a Dr Fowler and was X-rayed. I was squeezed as in a press on a table, the picture being taken through a square hole in the centre with a drawer where the plate was inserted. As they had to make their own electricity there were tremendous bangs when the apparatus was started up. I was told to hold my breath as long as possible. This cost me five guineas.

Thomas Tanner, 1887–1968.

1914

Jan 8th Talk given at the Adult School on the need for Blandford to have a sewerage system.

June 18th Great thunderstorm, two houses were struck by lightning in Queens Road. Also sixty sheep killed at Thornicombe, the flagpole in the Recreation Ground destroyed, as were many trees opposite the cemetery at the junction of the two roads and many other places.

August My father says he will not be drinking intoxicating beverage in the future because of the war.

11th October Toiled up to the Downs to see the huts being erected, the following Thursday the men struck work for an extra one penny per hour. This was not granted. Carpenters are now getting nine and a half pence an hour that is three to three and a half pence more than in Blandford. The Germans have reached the coast of Belgian near Ostend.

24th October A magistrate at Stratford said there had been a great increase in drunkenness among women since the war started and they might have to be banned from public houses.

1915 January Members of the Naval division are being billeted in Blandford, the government is paying twenty-three shillings and seven and halfpenny for two men.

April 5th Meningitis has broken out in Blandford, people are saying it has been brought back from India and the East by the troops... [and] call [it] spotted fever.

1916

The townsfolk have petitioned the military authority to stop the bands playing the dead march, etc. from the upper Salisbury Road to the railway station when they take the soldiers that have died at the camp to the station for transport to their various towns to be buried. The folk on this route say the almost nightly playing of the bands and the slow tramping of the troops gets on their nerves and wakes them up from their sleep.

December There are continuous frosts, the river is frozen from the boundary stone for as far as I can see.

January War bread number two produced – it is supposed to be 81% whole wheat and 10% other cereal mixed in with potatoes. It costs eleven pence or a shilling; it is hard and rough staff indeed.

March 7th The war is getting on everyone's nerves. It's the usual thing when I return home from work in the late evenings to pass soldiers lying dead drunk in the gutters of East Street, Church and School Lanes.

September 29th Strikes have broken out in Blandford. Went to see the new railway to the camp on the Downs and also saw the stream navvy working. What a waste of money owing to the gradient and the probable closing of the camp.

The Municipal Borough of Blandford Forum had a population of males 1523 and females 1672. In total 283 died. To use the town cost four shillings and six pence.

1927

May 7th I bought my Singer Junior car, its delivery to Blandford cost three pounds and five shillings, the car one hundred and forty eight pounds the licence eight pounds, insurance eight pounds and nineteen shillings and six pence, membership of the Automobile Association one pound and sixteen shillings, driver's licence five shillings, learning one pound and five shillings. Petrol was one shilling and two and halfpenny per gallon and oil six shillings and eight pence a gallon.

Left to right, back row: *Mary, Rosalie, Herbert and Pearl Wort with Roy in front standing outside their home, 2 Field View, Alexandra Street, May 1937. Roy still lives in the house and is well known in the town for his work in Mr Gent's Dental Surgery. If you had a problem with your dentures, then Roy was the man to see.*

Growing up in Blandford
Jack Manson

First and foremost I was born and bred in Blandford, and therefore I am allowed to be called a 'Blandfordian'. My days at school were during the 1930s, when I attended the Infants School in Damory Street, then moving on to the Blandford Boys' School in Park Road at the age of seven until I was fourteen years old, which was the age of leaving and out to work. During those days we had a headmaster by the name of Mr Collins, a good chap who went off to the Dorset County Education Department; he was replaced by Mr Perry, who loved sport and took a swim in the river in all weathers.

Whilst in my very early days at school, there was an air disaster of the airship R101. The school was assembled in front of the flagpole in the school yard for a service when the news broke.

Blandford in days gone by was a very busy town, especially on a Thursday and Saturday with the market. The country people came into town; it was the highlight of the week for many folk. There were plenty of big shops such as Mark Wells, Wareham and Arscott, Internationals and Liptons (with the smell of ground coffee beans wafting up the streets and biscuit tins stood on top of each other for display on the pavements, also the local lads loved to run along and see how many they could kick over!). There were also outfitters, namely Hicks, Harveys and Ashfords. Harveys were noted for the girls getting employment in the gloving trade. Materials were taken around the villages for the ladies to knit gloves at a very cheap rate, then returned and finished and packed for despatch mostly to Yeovil. Shops were open late on Saturdays, so the town was busy, as people did not get paid until the last minute. The town band played in the Market-place with Mr Read playing the cornet in one hand and beating time with the other – all good fun!

During those years we had the Silver Jubilee of King George V and Queen Mary. The Market-place was decorated with wooden poles set in wooden barrels decorated with paper chains in blue and white. The celebrations started with a parade of the Mayor, Aldermen and Councillors to a service in the Parish Church; afterwards a dinner was served to the elderly people of the town in the Corn Exchange. Sports took place on the Recreation Ground for the younger people. There was a parade of decorated vehicles, etc. in the evening, with a bonfire on the Ham. Boats were lit up coming down the river from Bryanston, and then the day closed with a confetti fight in the Market-place and dancing late into the night – plenty of good honest fun.

The coronation of King George was very much along the same lines with plenty of fun and games. In the sporting world, the Football Club won the Dorset

The Corn Exchange is hosting a 'Surprise Night' during the First World War. It is thought that this was an important gathering but no positive information can be found.

*The Market-place, 1940, with Reg Pike (top) and
Dennis Dart, Les Bellows and ? Rabbits (bottom).*

*Father Christmas at Hicks, 1957, with Leslie
Anne Bellows and a pram nearly as big as herself.*

Senior Cup – the only time in its history beating
Weymouth 2-1, the team being made up from all
corners of the town. The team ended up being pulled
round the town in their own bus, just like the FA
Cup, and there were cheering and clapping crowds
everywhere. It being the weekend of the Jubilee it
carried on over the weekend to Monday, so there were
many sore heads around Blandford!

The Second World War came, making the town a
very busy place in the early days. Blandford Camp
was built in 1939 for the intake of 21-year-old lads.
Before the camp was completed the lads were housed
in a tented area, the first weekend there was terrible
thunderstorm and the tents were washed away. The
first units on the camp were training units of the
Royal Artillery, with Ack-Ack Guns and search-
lights. The RASC moved into the town, any empty
houses being used for billets for the soldiers. Their
large trucks, etc. were kept in Bryanston Drive.
About this time the Rifle Brigade moved into the
area, disappearing overnight to take part in the relief
of Dunkirk. For days, Blandford Station became very
busy as train after train arrived with the tired and
weary troops, the townspeople came to the station
with jugs of tea, etc. to cheer them up [and it was]
a very sad sight.

After the reforming of the Army the British 3rd
Division took over the area using the Corn Exchange
as dining rooms and cookhouses. The Market-place
was turned into a parade ground and many disused
shops were used as billets. Later this Division was
replaced by the 38th Welsh Division and the
Americans took over in 1942. The town was lucky
not to be hit by enemy bombs, although plenty were
dropped around the area, including on the camp
where some lives were lost. The Crown Hotel had
damage to the roof by a bomb and caught fire; this can
still be seen to this day. A visit was paid to the town
by King George VI and Queen Elizabeth who slept
the night on the royal train in the station yard and
then visited a field being harvested at Bryanston
before visiting the Army units.

I was called up in the Army at the age of 18 in
1942 and served five years in Burma. When
demobbed I joined the British Legion for a while and
re-joined in 1968. In the early days the Legion was
run from the Odd Fellows Hall in The Plocks.
Cooper House (now the RBL headquarters) was
purchased in 1945 by a group of members including
the late Mr Fred Woods, Ernie Bastable, Harold
England, Mr McNally, Major Beckett and other
members. Alterations were carried out by voluntary
helpers. Extensions have been built on as the club
grew larger. I have served on the Royal British
Legion Branch Committee for a number of years
and now I am the President, a fact of which I am
very proud.

Mrs M.E. Hoskings' Memories

Born in Edward Street in 1913, Mrs Hoskings lived in the Railway Cottages and vividly remembers that the road was compressed stone and chalk; tarmac had not reached this part of town. Behind the station was a warehouse owned by the railway, and one night a fire destroyed the building leaving only the walls and some internal beams. This became a playground for the children.

At the end of Edward Street on Salisbury Road was the Police Station and although children got up to high jinks the mere mention of Sergeant Otter would ensure they would behave themselves.

The weekly fair took place on the fields opposite (Fairfield Road) when the livestock would be brought to be sold. The boys would assume the role of herdsmen running around with their sticks, and at times tormented the animals. After the fair the water cart would arrive and the children would have great fun watching the road being washed down.

Blandford was a very busy town with plenty to do. Children played outside all day with the favourite areas being the Milldown, Campdown and the Water Meadows. Campdown was off Shaftesbury Lane close to Tin Pot Lane and memories of picking wild raspberries with her parents are vivid in the mind of Mrs Hoskings. The Water Meadows, known in later years as the Hatches, were also a favourite area, where many a happy sunny afternoon was spent jumping across the stream; this was to continue for many a year until development claimed the area. The Marsh and Ham saw the children paddling in the stream with jam jars looking for tiddlers, and those who wanted a swim would cool off in the waters above the weir. Boats were a regular sight on the river and could be hired for 2s.6d. an hour.

Left: *Celia Foot and Sheila Stevens boating on the Stour, 1950.*

Below: *Boating on the river heading up to Bryanston, c.1940.*

At the end of the harvest the farmers would bring their grain to the Corn Exchange to be graded and then sold. Blandford had a flourishing market – with vendors trading their goods. Anyone could take goods to be sold and Senior and Godwin would auction them to the highest bidder. Rabbits, hares and pheasants would be on sale along with the dairy produce. Those who bought rabbits took them home and skinned them. Later in the day the 'rabbit woman' would walk the town and pay 3d. for each skin.

Many shows were staged in the Corn Exchange, and among the favourites were productions by Gilbert and Sullivan. They were very well supported and the townspeople would spend a happy evening sitting on wooden benches – the only ones to have backs on were the raised ones at the back to save you from falling backwards.

Deer Park in Whitecliff Mill Street was another favourite area. It was fenced off with iron railings and the deer and peacocks would roam freely. The deer would come to greet the children although they were

Fairfield Road, 1924. Bessie Bellows with daughter Winnie.

Rita McPhillamy and Dorothy Portsmouth holding the toddler on the Ham, 1947.

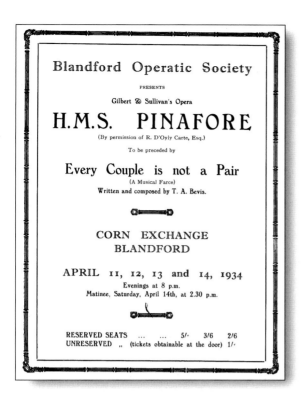

A programme advertising a Gilbert and Sullivan production in the Corn Exchange, 1934.

more interested in the walnut trees which would provide them with their treat for the day.

Opposite the hospital on Milldown Road were wooden buildings built in the shape of an aeroplane and Mrs Hoskings remembers her mother going there to pay her insurance.

The Recreation Ground was another source of entertainment where the tennis courts were available for hire. For those who could not afford such luxury time was spent on the field.

Blandford Grammar School

Mrs Hoskings was a pupil at the school from 1924 to 1930 and recalls the following:

The school had six year groups, with the Sixth Form only having from two to five pupils (we were not called students). The school week was Monday, Tuesday, Wednesday morning, Thursday, Friday and Saturday morning. The day started with morning assembly and we were lined up in year groups the youngest being on the front row. All the staff attended assembly, and hymns were sung and school notices were read out. At the end of assembly a pupil played the piano as we marched out across the playground in all weathers to start our lessons. The Sixth Form did not have a classroom of their own, all our books and pens were kept in the chemistry lab desks, and we used an empty classroom when other years were not using them, as they were having PE, chemistry or singing lessons.

The uniforms for the girls were navy gymslips, white blouses, navy cardigans, navy bloomers (with a pocket for a handkerchief) and black stockings. In the summer we wore pale-blue 'tootal' frocks with a fawn collar and short sleeves with fawn cuffs. Hats were always worn – black velour in winter and Panamas in summer with the school hatband. For the boys the uniforms were grey pullovers and trousers, shorts for the junior boys, black and red striped blazers, and always a school cap. In the winter both boys and girls would wear navy-blue gabardine macs.

Pupils who did not live in town came on the train. The cane was frequently used on the boys and the girls had lines or had to write out the theorem of Pythagoras. The house system was in force with St Andrew's (blue), St David's (yellow), St Patrick's (green) and St George's (red).

Scholarship places were awarded and in my year– 1924 – they were Joe Hunt, George Ingram, Ted Miller, Kay Beaton, Winnie Berry, and myself.

Sports day was in June, usually on Derby day, and the trophy was awarded to the house winning most points in the events. An arts festival was for a time held annually and again all houses competed, events being piano playing, solo singing, recitation, and a short French play. Again the trophy was awarded to the house with the most points. Some time between 1924 and 1929 a memorial gate was erected across the entrance to the school in memory of those pupils who had died during the First World War.

Staff I remember include the headmaster Mr W. Greenhalgh (more feared than loved I think) and Mr Hughes who taught geography, botany and RE and for whom any inattentive pupil was the target of a piece of chalk. Then there was Miss Phillips who taught French, a dedicated, painstaking and excellent teacher, but any misbehaviour earned from her the penalty of 20 or more sums. These were long multiplication, three figures by three figures, and each successive sum increased by one number; for example, 375 x 288 and 376 x 288 and so on. Needless to say we only worked out the first couple of sums and filled in the rest with approximations. I doubt if Miss Phillips ever checked any one of them. Other staff included Miss Potts who taught English, later Mr Walkins and Mr Toft who taught maths.

One of the highlights of the year would be to listen to the Oxford and Cambridge boat race. The headmaster arranged for a wireless set to be set up in the assembly hall and the boys mostly supported Oxford while the girls favoured Cambridge.

For the Christmas party in 1928 six of us performed a charade as entertainment. One of the five scenes was of a film studio with 'Gloria Swanson' starring, and another one was a sketch on Hughey's geography lesson, complete with chalk throwing and all. (We'd asked and obtained permission to 'use a geography lesson.') Mr Hughes became headmaster when Mr Greenhalgh retired.

Memories from the 1920s
(The late) Muriel Clark

We lived in Fairfield Road and opposite there was a little corner shop belonging to Mr Loader, surrounded by an orchard where the garage is at present. Over the road from the old site of the Badger Inn was Jeans Nurseries whose busiest time was providing the flowers for funerals.

One of my daily jobs was to purchase the meat because we did not have refrigerators in those days. Colliers was in Salisbury Street then opposite Earley's. For a family of eight, 4½d. would buy a neck of lamb. My dog would always come with me and one day he rushed out of the shop with a chain of sausages swinging from his mouth – needless to say we had a good dinner that night.

Mr Cleal of Salisbury Street was well known for his delicious ice-cream, which tasted like custard. Mr Loader's corner shop sold packets of tea containing coupons, and when you had collected the required amount you could choose a wooden pencil box with a sliding lid decorated with flowers. I chose one with lily of the valley on it and kept it for years.

Once a year, in a mushroom field near the cemetery, the Daily Express organised aeroplane flights, costing 5 shillings a trip. The mushrooms were particularly good in that field and not too far away in Whitecliff Mill Street from a fish shop owned by the Brooks, fish and chips cost 3d. – a real feast.

In the winter we used to wait for the man who came round selling crumpets from his handcart. He did a good trade, and we used to toast these in front of the open fire on long toasting forks.

As it grew dark the lamplighter would come along on his bicycle carrying his long pole. The lamps were gas, lit from a pilot light inside. Two chains with loops hung down on either side of the lamp. The lamplighter inserted a hook attached to his pole into the loop on one of the chains and lit the lamps. To extinguish the lamp the next morning, the other chain would be pulled. All the lamps had fancy ironwork which was very much prettier than today's concrete stalks. Although now electric, the lamp on the bridge over the river is one of the originals. We used to play under these lamps on fine evenings. There were no cars and by the time the lamps were lit, the horses were stabled and the carts put away, making the road quite safe.

Many people remain vivid in my mind. There was Miss Denn who lived where Wessex Court is now. Her garden reached down to the Dental Practice in Salisbury Street. She was always dressed very smartly and wore a lace handkerchief over her head. My uncle worked in the milk factory in Damory Street, and on Sunday mornings, myself and my five brothers and sisters would visit him and be given a tall glass of cold, frothy milk. There was Mrs Pike who sold faggots and peas, and lived in Orchard Street. You took your own dish and she would serve you from the door. In Dorset Street, the Reeds sold groceries and confectionery. In Orchard Street Mrs Bowden and her daughter took in bags of rags and bought rabbit skins; a halfpenny for wild and a penny for tame, the fur of the tame rabbits being of better quality. They also sold bundles of salt fish and with the aroma of fish, rags and rabbit skins there was a very pungent smell in the shop, but this did not stop anyone gathering there for a good gossip.

Before the 1939 war, the Fire Station was at the top of Orchard Street in North Place. After the war it moved to the bottom of Damory Street. The firemen were part time, and would have to rush from their place of work to attend the fire.

Mr Stickley was a photographer in Damory Street. He only had two backdrops, which meant that everyone who had their photograph taken appeared to be in the same place. It was many years before he changed them. Twisty Turner made beehives and regularly fought as an amateur boxer, which was arranged by Mr George Wilson. Twisty couldn't take his drink. Very little sent him over the top. Once, after a moderate drinking session he began fighting a lamppost near the Star Inn. Along comes a policeman and Twisty, attacking another part of the lamppost, said 'It's a good thing you've come along Constable, otherwise there would have been a massacre'. Other boxers who regularly fought were Con Fenn, Harry Rebbeck, Harry Hoarder and George Haskett, all against well-known boxers, Freddy Mills, Ted Sherwood and Teddy Packham. After the matches, star turns of the show would be Slimmer Holloway who fought the fighting farmer from Stickland, neither very good boxers but very entertaining. It was 6d. (old pence) to enter and there were never ever any empty seats. A hat used to be handed round to pay the boxers.

Whitecliff Mill Street, 1920. **Left to right:** *Rose Bellows, Tom Melmouth and his wife. Tom was a porter at the chicken auction which used to be held behind what is now Loaders and the Pine Shop in East Street.*

An Overview of Blandford

Lynn Lindsay (née Bourne)

1960–68

Born in Blandford in 1952, I have vivid memories of the town. My mother, grandmother and great grandmother were also local, so I have many relatives that live, and have lived, in the town. My first memories are of school, Blandford Infants School being the first. The school has now been converted into houses behind Wessex Court. The most vivid memory of the school was the smell; the Gas Works were just outside and you could see the large tanks disappearing into the skyline. The fun of the day was not to walk up the path to school but to climb over the railings on the edge of the pavement, and then walk up the path. I guess kids love to climb. We didn't wear uniform and we stayed at this school until we were seven years old.

The next school was Archbishop Wake. The school had a wall going down through the middle, and this was to separate the boys from the girls. The school was on Park Road and was known to the locals (amusingly) as Park Road Academy for Girls/Boys. The staff at the school in 1963 were: Year 1: Miss Tuffin, Year 2: Miss Musselwhite, Year 3: Miss Crissell (headmistress), Year 4: Mrs Laws.

The school day always started with tables, when we all had to stand and recite them parrot fashion. All children knew their tables even if they did not understand sums. Reading aloud was also an everyday lesson, and you learnt very quickly about pronunciation of words, for a wrong-sounding word would send the rest of the class into peals of laughter. PE lessons would sometimes be on the Recreation Ground, but high-jump lessons were always in the schoolyard. Miss Crissell would put the frame up, and put a couple of mats down for the landing area, and off we would go.

Blandford Infants School, 1957. Puzzles are the order of the day. Left to right: David Tompkins in the background, Lynn Bourne, Sylvannia Allen and Leslie Anne Bellows.

Blandford Infants School, 1958. Left to right: Judy Neale, Sheridan Pitman, Sandra Ansell, Lesley Ware.

Blandford Infants School, 1960. Left to right, back: Ceilia Williams, Johnny Vincent, Penny Johnson, Jonathan Taylor, Sarah Brickell, David Heard, Sheila Hiscock, Malcolm Cross, Virginia Ingram, Edward Lane, Jennifer Moody, Malcolm Munday, ?, Robert Hall; front: Janet Ovens, Michael Barham, June Bellows, Brian Manson, Christine Bourne, Dereck Smith, Anne Moses, Denzil Tapper, Wendy Clarke, David O'Donnel, Helen Hardy, Jeremy Adams.

Blandford Infants School, 1959.

Blandford Girls School, 1962. Left to right, back: Pauline Crook, ?, Gina Johnson, Marion Hiscock, Janice Masters, Lesley Ware, Susan West, Felicity Brown; middle: Sandra Ansell, Elaine Tuck, Susan Upward, Diane ?, Georgina Lowe, Jill Stevens, ?, Gail Grief, ?, Fiona Axtell, Jill Mason, Diane Gee; front: Veronica Mathews, Sheridan Pitman, Alison Green, Elizabeth Hoskings, Judy Neale, Pauline Upward, Leslie Anne Bellows, Judith Parker, Leslie James, Shirley Whitlock.

School Photograph, 1961, at Archbishop Wake Junior School. Left to right, back: Kenneth West, Dale Grief, John Bellows, Stephen James, Trevor James, Nigel Chard, John Willie, Stuart Montgomery; middle: Miss Powis, ?, Anne Pitman, ?, Heather Miller, Felicity Dawson, Jill Dacombe, Stella Edwards, Stuart Greenfield; front: Marion Williams, ?, Jean Tuck, Geraldine Mulvey, Wendy Belbin, Pat James, Linda Ironside, Wendy Whiteley, ?, Elizabeth Lorimer.

Arch-bishop Wake Junior School, 1962. Left to right, back: ? Holman, Jimmy Rimmer, Gordon Tuck, Stuart Montgomery, Stephen Lucas, ? Stickley, Stuart Greenfield; middle: John Bellows, Mark Peach, Pat James, Felicity Dawson, Garry Phillips, Jackie Chant, Anna Hunt, David Stringer, Stephen Turner; front: Helen Wort, Marion Williams, Janet Adams, Teresa Pearce, ?, Gaynor Bailey, Helen Terapin, Shirley Grief, Janet Moody, Judith Heaney.

North Dorset Secondary Schools Relay Champions, 1969. Left to right, back: Chris Copeland, Mike Dove, June Bellows, Christine Bourne, ?; front: Anne Pitman, Wendy Starks. Christine Bourne also won the 80yd hurdles.

Blandford Secondary Modern Senior Netball Team, 1967. Left to right, back: Veronica Mathews, Dianne Skipper, Amanda Ward, Jackie White; front: Val Read, Janet Ricketts, Lynn Bourne.

The school did not have indoor toilets; these were at the top of the yard and in the winter not the most desirable. The school was warm with big boilers in the rooms, and in the winter the bottles of milk that all children had at morning break were put by the side of them to take the chill off. I remember that well – ugh warm milk! At break times both schools would congregate on either side of their wall and talk; but this was discouraged and you were soon sent packing to the middle of the playground. Most of our games centred around the skipping rope. The whole school used to take part, with two children holding the long rope. We used to sing along as we jumped through the rope and if you stopped the rope, then you would have to take the end and start turning it. This was very tiring and the aim was never to get caught, although the girls turning the rope knew who to turn it faster for.

School dinners were in the canteen and dinner money had to be taken to school on Mondays for the whole week. The cost was 2s.6d., not a princely sum but for some children Mondays was not a good day for their parents, so they would pay on Fridays, the day after pay day. No fuss was ever made and the children never felt intimidated. Although uniform was not compulsory there was a school blazer which was only worn by those girls from a more affluent background.

Next was either the Grammar School for those who passed their 11-plus, or the Secondary Modern for the rest. The modern school was dubbed the 'Palace', not only for its size but also for the amenities. The school boasted its own swimming pool, albeit quite small, a separate dining room and a large hall where indoor games took place. The grounds were extensive with tennis courts, which doubled up as the netball courts, hockey and football pitches, and a full athletics track with high-jump and long-jump areas. Sport played a major part in the education system at that time, and was fiercely competitive.

School colours were awarded to those who excelled and I remember the pride of wearing the green and silver tie that was presented with your colours. The uniform was grey and green, the school tie being bottle green, so those who had colours felt very important. PE teachers then were Chris Copeland and Mike Dove, who also ran school clubs out of school hours, which were heavily supported. The school had very good teams and won many North Dorset and county titles.

The school also had an extensive arts department, which included a pottery room.

I remember Mike Suffield well; although not very arty his classes were well received. Mike still lives in the town and owns the Hambledon Gallery. Another teacher, Mr Edmonds of the woodwork/metalwork department, used to live in the town. He had a huge garden with fruit trees, a haven for the children brave enough to climb the wall and scrump the apples. You had to be quick to elude him, but many a fine day was spent trying to dodge him. Other staff who remain vivid in my memory are Jean Joyce, Haydn White, and 'Taffy' Grenville. They lived in the school houses on Salisbury Road, and I am sure this promoted good behaviour at home for those of us that lived on the estates.

In September 1968 the comprehensive system of education came to Blandford. The Grammar School and Secondary Modern became one school, the new Blandford Upper School, and the Grammar School finally got their palace.

Outside Play

The Ham in the summer was the only place to go, with the river and the swimming pool in one place. The weir held the greatest fascination for those who were brave. The challenge would be to walk across to the other side with the river in full flow; this was achieved by many, but for those who didn't succeed a ducking was the order of the day. Again the smell was a vivid memory, on hopping days at the brewery the smell would drift over the whole area and as children this was not very pleasant. We would also paddle down the river to catch minnows with our nets and put them into jam jars secured with a string handle, carrying home our spoils at the end of the day to show off to our parents, only to be sent back the next day to put them back.

The swimming pool was the highlight of the day if you had enough pennies in your pocket, and what fun

Susan Fenn sitting on the river bank, 1962.

Opening of Blandford Swimming Baths, c.1924.

An early photo of Blandford's pool with boards and slide. They were eventually removed because the pool was not deep enough.

*Marianne Bourne, manager of
Blandford's open-air pool 1966–86.*

*Blandford Swimming Pool, 1966, with group of
swimmers in the middle of the pool.* Left to right, back:
Colin Guy, Angela Riggs, ?; front: Richard Kevern.

*Michael Brighton and Kelly Pitt
enjoying the toddler pool, 1984.*

we had. When the water was green and you couldn't see the bottom was best as this meant that the water was warm but of course this was not safe. Marianne Bourne ran the pool at this time and when the pool was dirty (no filter systems then) she would open the outlet and empty the water, scrub the bottom with a brush and then refill from the inlet at the shallow end with cold mains water. Although the pool looked lovely it was so cold. This didn't deter the children and it wasn't long before it warmed up again. The pool did eventually have a chlorination system, which was gas, and the large cylinders were housed in a locked cupboard outside facing the Ham. In the late 1970s a toddler pool was built on the side of the main pool and remained in full use until the new pool was built on the site of Blandford School. The pool was finally demolished in the late 1990s but still remains in the hearts of many as an important part of their childhood.

Water again, but this time at Pulley's Field which was opposite the lower part of Langton Road, where again you had to be quick. The shortcut was through Mr Pulley's garden and this would take you right down to the river's edge. Mr Pulley kept his cows on this area and you would have to dodge the cowpats, which went right down to the water's edge because the cows used the river as their drinking hole. Mr Pulley had an old caravan on the field and the children would use this as a den.

Walking down Langton Road to Langton Church is another memory – again not on the road but through the woods alongside the river. There was a bridge and again walking and jumping from it was the dare. A few left that bridge not through their own choice. There was the Hatches on Camp Road for those who lived on the estates at the top of town and you could walk through either the Buttercup Fields, now Larksmead area, or through the woods which are now the back of Tudor Gardens. This is where those with an aptitude for long jump came into their own. When the grass was long it was very slippery and when launching yourselves off, many a time you would slip into the stream. Picnics were taken and I remember spending many a pleasant day there.

Recreation Ground

The grandstand seemed so big. After football matches we would climb under the seats and see how many pennies we could find and then would go to either Godwins (the garage opposite the Bus Station) or Jolly's on the corner of Damory Street to buy sweeties. Jolly's was also the official tuck shop for the Grammar School. The Recreation Ground also had swings and a huge slide. The slide was particularly good; the more that went down it, the faster it became, but many a child went home with a bruised backside.

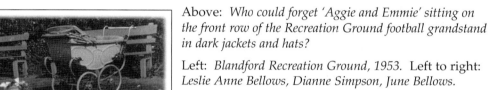

Above: *Who could forget 'Aggie and Emmie' sitting on the front row of the Recreation Ground football grandstand in dark jackets and hats?*

Left: *Blandford Recreation Ground, 1953. Left to right: Leslie Anne Bellows, Dianne Simpson, June Bellows.*

Below: *Blandford Recreation Ground, 1953. Winnie Simpson with niece June and daughter Dianne in the background.*

Blandford Institute Football Club, 1920–21. Left to right, back: *S. Neale, T. Tanswell, D. Cutler;* middle: *L. Jay, J. Neale, W. Pitman, W. Newman, F. Bellows, S. Moss, A. Blandford;* front: *W. Lucas, C. Knight, H. Tapper, T. Neale, S. Cox.*

This picture shows that gymnastics was clearly another popular sport in Blandford at one time. Blandford Gymnasts, c.1905.

Blandford Football Team, 1933, with Miss Castleman-Smith (the first lady to become Mayor in the same year).

More Fun and Games

Another favourite haunt, walking along Shaftesbury Lane and going down Tin Pot Lane, was the Milldown which you reach without going into town. The best time to go was when the blackberries came out, and children were sent up to pick the fruit for a pie or a crumble. Needless to say by the time they got home they had eaten too many and didn't want any tea.

At the end of the harvest when the bales were being stored for the winter fodder there was a mass exodus from town. Again the play centred around sport with climbing and jumping over the bales at Pimperne Hay Barns. This was another full day out and you would go out after breakfast and come back at teatime.

Outside play was enjoyed by all, after all the only thing to keep you inside the house was either to do homework or help your mother with the daily chores. We all preferred to play outside. Other games played included hopscotch and the pavements were well chalked, although we did have to clean them ourselves. Marbles was an art and if you had ball bearings then you could soon fill up your marble bags. Holes were made in the pavements and the girls would soon be

happily at play. Leapfrog was played in Hunt Road where on the island there were four posts. Great fun was had here. It was not so good for the girls in dresses and many a rip in your party frock earned a dressing down from your mother.

Children seemed to be happy when I was a child and with close community groups it was like one big happy family. There were arguments of course and occasional friction, but generally we all looked out for each other and neighbours were more like extended family and became 'aunties' and 'uncles'.

Blandford Youth Club was situated in The Plocks and was extensively used. For those who just wanted to chat or drink coffee there was a room downstairs. For those a little more energetic there was the trampoline upstairs – a health-and-safety issue today but great fun; you were in danger of hitting the roof if you bounced too high but catching the open beams was the aim.

In the Corn Exchange was to be found another evening's entertainment in the form of roller skating which was well supported. Chairs formed the rink for formal competitions and the whole area was used for the general skateabout. We even skated to music and tried to perform moves, not to the high standard of today's skaters but with the same enthusiasm.

Above: *Blandford Carnival, c.1892. Children,* left to right: *Lily M. Gross, Lynda Percy, Gladys Wareham, Percy Hare, May Hole, Daisy Dyke (at back). Mr Parsons is standing with the horse.*

The cinema was a favourite. Mr Green with his smart suit, collar and tie would be in the foyer as the doors opened. Half way through the film the ladies would come in with their ice creams and drinks and stand in front of the screen and the film wouldn't start again until the queues were finished. Upstairs was for the courting couples because the back row had double seats. The cinema eventually closed down and became the Bingo Hall for many years. It was always hoped that this would be the new indoor swimming pool but was eventually to become a supermarket.

Situated in East Street, the Snack Bar was a favourite with the locals. It had a juke box and a huge seating area and was always full. It was also a meeting place for the mods and rockers, so many disagreements would be settled outside.

Blandford Forum Carnival was when the whole of the town came out to play. It was probably the largest gathering of townspeople during the year. It was a major event and both the children's and evening parades were well supported. Preparation for the events would start early in the year and elaborate costumes were made. Vehicles were sponsored by local businesses who would also provide the drivers. There were many bands and the evening parade seemed to last forever as the bands stopped the procession while they played. After the procession

the town was alive with people. The fair was held in the Market-place, and Church Lane, The Plocks and Sheep Market Hill would have all the side shows. It was certainly a fun-filled evening and a late, late night for the children.

Blandford Carnival, early 1960s. Jean Tattersall with her family – a milking we will go.

Blandford Carnival, 1939–1977

Blandford Carnival, 1959. Hilda Fenn with daughter Susanne and her granddaughter Christine Bourne.

Above: *The 1946 Carnival and the Bats float. Dick Sibley is peering from behind the bike, middle row 3rd from the right.*

Left: *Dot Joyce and Lucy Foot receive their prize from Wimborne Carnival Queen, 1959.*

Carnival parade at Recreation Ground, date unknown.

Blandford Carnival, 1939–1977

*Christine Bourne, 1961,
Carnival attendant in an
outfit made by Betty Penny
who went on to create
the very successful
'Cavalcade of Costume'.*

*Celia O'Donnel, Win Fry and Myrtle
Leak ready to perform a Pow-Wow,
1972.*

*Lizzie Kinnear on the right leading
the group with Key Markets
(now Somerfields) clearly visible
in the background.*

Above: *Blandford Carnival Princess, attendants and
pages, 1961. Left to right, back: Sandra Ansell,
Yvonne Lomax, Zöe O'Brian, Christine Bourne,
Maureen Brennan; front: Peter O'Brian,
Denzil Tapper.*

Right: *Carnival stalwarts
Peggy Robbins and Vi Street.*

Blandford Carnival, 1939–1977

Linda Hall as Blandford Junior Princess, 1976.

Hunt Road Vikings, 1973. Jane O'Donnel, Sean O'Donnel, Kevin O'Donnel, Sharon Hardy, Pat O'Donnel, Doug Leak, Ann Hardy.

London Pride, Barnes Close entry, 1977. Left to right: Victoria Lindsay, Beverley Downes, Kate Downes, Sharon Lawton, Corinne Fenn, Michael Roscoe, Claire Lawton, Samantha Fenn, Sallyanne Fenn. All the outfits were tailor made by local dressmaker Dawn Lawton.

Friends and families at the Carnival. Cissy Oliver, Win Fry, Dot Joyce, Lucy Foot, Vi Street, Sue Green, Linda Green.

Blandford Carnival, 1939–1977

Blandford Carnival Queen, 1973 – Renira Chard seated on the far left competing in the Dorset Carnival Queen Competition.

Dawn Caines as Blandford Junior Princess, 1977.

Lisa Gosney as Blandford Junior Princess in 1978, with attendants Nicola Bell on the right and Michelle Street on the left.

Windsor Davies inspecting the parade looking as if he is still on the set of 'It ain't half hot'. Harold Galpin, member of the Carnival Committee, is standing behind.

Carnival Queen Susan Bye with her princesses, Nicky Kirby and Caroline Ware.

Blandford Carnival, 1939–1977

This must have been a wet year as judging is taking place in the Corn Exchange. The tiles on the walls were a main feature of the Corn Exchange and are green. They are still behind the refurbished walls.

September 1977, raising money for Blandford Museum, with a vehicle sponsored by Hospital Metalcraft.

Nicola Bell as Carnival Queen, 1983. Nicola was presented with a gold clock by the Carnival Committee for her achievements. Nicola won all the titles. She was attendant in 1978, Princess in 1980, Miss Teenager in 1982, and Queen in 1983.

Snow White and the Seven Dwarfs. Dawn Caines as Snow White looks to have her hands full. Esme Butler with her daughter dressed as a duck can be seen on the left of the picture.

Blandford Swimming Club

Formed well over 50 years ago the club was the idea of Daphne Alner. Daphne was at this time running the swimming pool and could not officially set up a club. Mr Carter, who went on to become Alderman Carter, set the wheels in motion and Blandford Swimming Club was formed. Daphne with her husband Ken were to become 'The Club'. Club nights were Thursday evenings after the pool shut to the public, and Sunday afternoons again when the pool was closed.

The club was very successful in County and South West competitions with many championships being won by local Blandford children. Daphne and Ken's commitment to the club went much further than coaching on club nights. Obviously in the winter the town did not have the facilities to train the children, so Daphne and Ken would take the swimmers either to Bournemouth or any other available indoor pool to continue their training. This was at their own cost and many children in Blandford owe them a great deal of gratitude.

When Bovington Camp was built an indoor pool was built and for many years the club used this facility for their winter training. Ken died in 1997 but is fondly remembered, and still Daphne continues. She is now in her 70s and still runs the club, teaching swimming at the pool in Blandford School. Daphne was also actively involved in the South West ASA. Daphne was Dorset ASA President and Western Counties ASA President and her proudest moments were when her swimmers would be part of these teams. One of her greatest pleasures was when Blandford swimmers brought the medals home, and these were abundant in the 1960s when Blandford Swimming Club held the most county titles – but perhaps the biggest medal should be given to her. On behalf of all those that were part of 'The Club' I would personally like to thank Daphne for her dedication to the children of Blandford. I would like to add that this has been a lifetime of unpaid voluntary work to the town.

Blandford Swimming Club Gala, c.1966. Daphne Alner presenting a trophy to Phil Brown. Others in the photograph include: Stephen Christopher, Jackie Pike and Jackie Chant. Note in the background the pipework which fed the pool with clean water from the mains, hence the low temperature as there was no heating in those days.

Photo Gallery Spanning the Years 1908–1982

Views of Blandford

View of the church from the Marsh and Ham. Note the lack of buildings, date unknown.

Blandford Bridge photographed from Blandford St Mary, with a bus crossing over, date unknown.

Views of Blandford

Barnes Homes, Salisbury Road. Note the ornate lamps on the front gate. This appears to be the original building without subsequent extensions. The present warden is Mrs Jean Wells who is also Blandford's Town Crier.

Approaching Blandford from Durweston, with the River Stour on the left.

Isolation Hospital & Workhouse

The old Isolation Hospital located on Shaftesbury Lane, next to U Drive. The nurse was Miss Lucas and the ambulance driver was her brother Bill. The hospital had several wards. When it closed it became a toy factory, and though it had many employees lead soldiers were distributed to out-workers for painting.

Nurses' home for the Isolation Hospital on Shaftesbury Lane.

Right: Left to right: Les, Velma and Winnie Bellows. Les is wearing the uniform of the Bluecoats. He lived with his parents and sisters in the Workhouse from 1928 to 1939.

Below: Old Castleman House which was the old Workhouse on the Fair Field.

Snow, Storm & Flood

The Crown Meadows during the floods of December 1979 before the erection of the Blandford flood defences.

Above and opposite page: *Pictures dated 31 May 1979 showing the last great flood of Blandford and the effect it had in the town.*

Snow, Storm & Flood

Snow, Storm & Flood

Sue James taking a well-earned rest on the hedgerow in Shaftesbury Lane during the snows of February of 1963. Pat James and David O'Donnel are having great fun with their toboggans.

Snow in Hunt Road, 19 February 1978.

Snow in Newman Close, 19 February 1978.

School

Infants School, Blandford, 1908. Arthur Foot and Harry Blandford are in the picture although it has not yet been discovered which they are.

Archbishop Wake First School, 1982. Left to right, back: Sue Gatehouse, ?, Barry Mason, Michael Harris, ?, Nicholas Brine, Sultan Wilmington, Andrew Gover, David Nicolson, Mrs Davies; middle: Marcus Mato, ?, ?, Tracy Lindsay, Sarah Hurley, Sallyanne Fenn, Sharon Pitman, Victoria Lindsay, Katy Jackson, Laura Cowley, ?, Kevin Valentine; front: Jeanette Parker, ?, ?, Louise Pridmore, ?, Tracey Mason, Sarah Ballard, ?.

Sporting Life

Blandford Football Team, 1938. Left to right, back: *P. Saunder, R. Perry, ? Lee, ?;*
3rd row: *L. Matthews, Fred Pitman, Alan Read;* 2nd row: *Benny Miles, L. Ryals, Ray Pitman,*
A. Upward, Ray Stretch; front: *Ken Joyce, Jimmy Freak, Leslie Bellows.*

Blandford Girls School Hockey Team, 1945.
The games mistress was Miss Edmondson and the picture was taken on the Grammar
School playing field, now the fields of Blandford School. Left to right, back row
includes: *Mary Read, Kathleen Hallet, Eleanor Card, Sheila Marsh, Jeanette Seaford;*
front: *Joyce Matthews, Sylvia Pike, Betty Boltash, Marianne Fenn, Brenda Scott.*

Sporting Life

The Bats Cycling Club, 1946. The track that they used was behind Rosebank Laundry in Salisbury Road.
In the back row 2nd from the left is Derek Rayment and 3rd from the right is Leonard Harris.
In the front row 3rd from the left is Reg Joyce, far right is Sparrow Amey, and 2nd from the right is Roy Harris.

The Bats ready for the off, 1946.

Young Liberals

Young Liberals dance, 1950.

Liberal Club outing, 1950s.

Special Events

Coronation Street Party, 1953. Visible are Flats Nos 1 and 3 Barnes Close, with King's Road in the background.

Collingwood Corner Commemoration at Blandford Camp, 1949.

Special Events

The Silver Thread Christmas Dinner, 1969, held at the British Legion Club, Blandford.

Queen Mother's 100th birthday, 4 August 2000. It was also a very special day for Jim and Win Woolley of 59 Barnes Close, as they celebrated their 60th wedding anniversary. Behind Win is a card from Her Majesty the Queen.

Celebrations in the Kings Arms Hotel on the anniversary of the great fire of Blandford. David O'Donnel with a lady on each arm.

PART THREE:
A Millennium Portrait

*No.2 Albert Place. Albert Place was originally a
terrace of 12 cottages back to back, built in the 1860s,
but the two cottages nearest the street fell down in
the 1950s, hence the red-brick end elevation to
the existing terrace. Eight of the cottages were
redeveloped in 1974–5 to form four cottages, with
the last of these being converted in the 1980s. It is
thought that the original buildings were for railway
workers. Nigel Port has lived at No.2 since 1984.*

Residents of Blandford

No.30 Albert Street.

No.21 Albert Street.

No.2 Alexandra Street. The house
was originally two railway cottages
which were converted in 1975.
The Piper family has lived here
since 1994.

No.1 Andrew Close – the only white bungalow in the
close. It is just a few minutes from our beautiful town.

Thyme Cottage, 8 Alfred Street. Ramon Stone,
a Blandford clock-maker, has worked from
these premises since 1986.

No.1 Angus Close. The Cakir family have lived here since April 1990.

No.12 Andrew Close.

No.5 Angus Close. Alan and Cindy Nobles with sons Gary and Christopher – the second generation to live in the house which was built c.1971 for Alan's parents, Gordon and Betty Nobles.

No.10 Anne Close. Carol and Phil Williams and youngest son Craig have lived at Anne Close since February 1998. They have two other children, Ian and Tanya.

No.9 Ashmore Close. Pictured are the present owners the Kellaways. (The previous owners were the Kellaway-Moores!)

No.6 Ashmore Close. Blandford paramedic Bob Harrison, his wife Jenny and her daughter Bec, a pupil at Blandford School and member of Forum Marching Brass.

No.21 Ashmore Close. The Downes Family – Brent, Susan, Angela and Emily – occupants since 1984.

No.9 Badbury Drive.

No.31 Barnes Close. Cliff and Lynn Lindsay have lived here since 1976 and with daughter Victoria have been very happy in the property. The view from the balcony is superb – open fields and green, green grass.

42 Barnes Close. Harold and Doris Pullman, 'Happy Gardeners', moved here in August 1951. The property was rented from the Council until 1981 and the couple then purchased the house in January of that year. They are the longest-term tenants still living on the estate.

No.24 Bayfran Way – Peter, Hazel and David Warrington.

No.1 Bryanston Street. Gillian Williams and son Anthony recently moved to 1 Bryanston Street from Albert Street.

No.13 Bryanston Street.

No.27 Bryanston Street – and when you have finished that job... !

No.24 Cadley Close. Mrs Julie Stimpson shown outside the house where she has lived with her husband Dave and three sons, Michael, Gary and Jonathan, since 1995.

No.9 Cadley Close. Tina, Ted, Mike and Matt Langford plus Zöe the dog.

No.23 Castleman-Smith Close.

No.17 Chapel Gardens,
The Warren household.

No.1 Charles Street. The Symmons family have owned 1 Charles
Street for 18 years. The house is one of a terrace of six built by
the Somerset & Dorset Railway Company for its employees.

No.4 Dairy Field. Steve and Carole Humphrey with their son Freddy outside the house where they have lived for the past five years.

No.1 Dorset Place. Lynn and Peter Jacobs have lived at 1 Dorset Place since 1978.

No.63 Damory Street – Councillor Mike Owen and kids – the mastermind of Portrait 2000.

No.11 Damory Street. Mr and Mrs David Aitken have lived here since 1953 when they purchased the property for the sum of £600.

No.49 Eastleaze Road.

No.55 Eastleaze Road.

No.12 Elizabeth Road.

No.10 Edward Street. Dave, Nickie,
Sam (11) and Joseph (8) Griffiths.

No.56 Elizabeth Road. Mr and Mrs Pitman have
lived in this house for nine years. Mr Pitman was
born in Blandford 35 years ago and Mrs Pitman
has lived in Blandford for 25 years.

No.35 Elizabeth Road. Alan and Mary
Woodland have lived in this house for 47 years.

No.19 Fields Oak. The Ali family have lived in this house for over 15 years and think that it is a great neighbourhood.

No.2 Fishers Close.

No.2 Field View. Mr Roy Wort has lived in the property for 76 years. He is the fourth generation of his family to have lived here.

No.28 Fishers Close. Mummy, Liam and baby Darryl Garbutt with mate Ben Kimber from next door (No.27). Mr Garbutt, Station Commander of Blandford Fire Station, was not able to have his photo taken with the family as he was over the road at the Fire Station on drill night.

No.4 Froxfield. The Heaney family have lived in Froxfield Road for 16 years.

No.8 Greenhill. The Smith family of Greenhill 2000; seven years at No.8!

No.8 Hambledon Gardens. David Melbourne with his wife Maureen and children Natalie and Oliver. David came to Blandford in 1986 to teach at Blandford Upper School.

No.30 Hambledon Gardens. Tony and Amanda Mitchell have raised their family from infancy to manhood at their home in Hambledon Gardens since moving there in 1981.

No.21 Hanover Court, Whitecliff Mill Street.

No.48 Harewood Place.

No.12 Holland Way. Terry and Kay Everett with Lawrence. The house was built in 1972, and has been a happy family home for the Everetts since that time.

No.22 Hunt Road. Nigel and Pam Towning have lived in this house for 31 years.

No.8 Jubilee Way. Lucy and Colin Sims with daughter Amelia.

Left: *Ashley Reach, 40 Kings Road. Garry and Hazel Barker with daughters Jennifer and Denise. The family have lived at the property since 1988, which was built in 1970 for Mrs Newman.*

Below: *No.2 Lady Baden Powell Way. Mrs Caroline Francis has lived here since 1996 with her two children, Richard (aged 15) and Rebecca (aged 8).*

Above: *No.28 Kingston Close. Steven, Charmaine, Kelly (aged nine), Jake (aged five) and Dominic (aged 18 months) in the house which the family has lived in for 3½ years. Charmaine comes from Blandford and Steven from Nottingham and they decided to move back to Blandford after Charmaine had been away for 14 years. Charmaine's maiden name was Milner.*

No.10 Lane Close.

*Left: Kildare, Langton Road.
The Samways family. The girls
are in the school uniforms of
St Leonards Middle School and
Arch-bishop Wake First School.*

*Below: Southlea,
40 Larksmead.
The Laws family
has been resident
since August 1999.*

Above: *No.38 Langton Crescent.
The Mariner family.*

Right: *No.37 Lockeridge Close.*

Right: *No.10 Marston Close. Karen, Jamie, Justin and Hannah Hall have lived here for eight years.*

Below: *No.56 Marston Close. The Majury family have lived at the property since 15 February 1991.*

Above: *No.48 Medbourne Close.*

Left: *Pets Corner, 32 Mary Cossins Close. The houses in Mary Cossins Close were built in 1993. Paul, Maxine, Curtis and Jordan Young are outside their house with pets Faye, Kieren and Lottie.*

No.1 Milldown Road. The Curl family. This house was built in 1922 and owned, until 1985, by the John Illes Barnes Charity for farmers and their widows.

'Coppers', 2, The Orchard, Milldown Road. The Fergusons and their dog, Holly, at home.

Beachcroft, Milldown Road. The house has been occupied by the Haywood family since 1979.

Railway Cottage, Milldown Road. The Railway Children!!

No.30 Mortain Close. Stephen, Tracy, Naomi and Aaron. The house was built 13 years ago and was the last house built on the Damory Down. Stephen and Tracy were born in Blandford and have lived in the house for 13 years.

Left: *No.42 Old Farm Gardens. Roger, Deborah and baby Alfie Sims have always lived in Blandford.*

Below: *No.2 Orchard Street. Alison and Nick (parents), Ellanor, Richard and John – residents for six years.*

Above: *No.21 Orchard Street. Anita Oliver with her three sons Steve, Harry and George.*

Above: *No.12 Park Lands.*

Right: *No.3 Peel Close. Blandford is the perfect place to bring up a family. David and Susan Randles with sons Oliver, Nicky, Thomas and Jonathan.*

Left: *No.9 Percy Gardens – a quiet corner.*

Below: *No.33 Philip Road. David, Amenda, Joanna and Martin Bealing with Martin's friend Daniel Symes.*

No.9 Philip Road. Robert and Wendy Hill with their dog Pebbles outside 9 Philip Road where they have lived since August 1998.

No.68 Preetz Way. The Filkins family – occupiers since April 1996.

No.26 Preetz Way. Ian (local vet), Susie and Hanna Patton (Kieran on the way!!) purchased the house new in December 1994.

No.25 Queens Road. Mr John McGowan Hayes,
Mrs Jackie McGowan Hayes, Callum, Holly,
Poppy and Finbar – they have been in the property
for seven years and moved in a week after
Poppy was born.

50 Queens Road. Maryrose Macdonald and
Dennis Wardleworth, at 50 Queens Road
for over 20 years; four grown-up children.
She a retired teacher; he a retired scientist;
active members of Blandford Labour Party.

Aga-Dale, Rosebank Lane, Golden Anniversary.
The house was built in 1950 for the owner's
grandfather and the Domoney family picture
shows the third and fourth generations
outside the family home.

No.15 Ramsbury Close. The Kerby family – Mandy,
Andy, Emily and Gavin have lived in Ramsbury Close
since May 1991. Emily and Gavin have attended
Milldown First School, Milldown Middle School and
the Blandford School. Andy works as an engineer at
Flight Refuelling, Wimborne, and Mandy works
at the Council Offices at Nordon. Andy was
brought up in Winterborne Stickland and Mandy
moved to Dorset in 1979 from Felixstowe in Suffolk.

Right: *No.59 Salisbury Road. Anthony, Debra, Francesca and Gianluca Reed. The family has occupied the property for seven years.*

Above: *No.20 Salisbury Crescent. Colin moved into No.20 when the houses were built in 1947 and has enjoyed living here ever since.*

No.79 Salisbury Road. Councillor Haydn White (3 times Mayor of Blandford) with his wife Glenda.

No.103 Salisbury Road. The Witt family – Bill, Maureen with sons Robin and Stephen and their partners Vanya Murray and Beth Burnley.

No.109 Salisbury Road. This might be the only Plymouth Rock in Blandford.

No.3 Forum Mews, Shorts Lane. Diana O'Rourke has lived in the property for five years.

No.8 Tudor Gardens. Ian Taft, Amanda, Christopher and David Wileman.

No.3 Victoria Road – Peter Collington.

Victoria House, Victoria Road.

No.1 Wilson Park.

No.3 Whitecliff Gardens. Stephen and Lesley Wright, both born at Letton, with their son Gary. Lesley is the granddaughter of George Davis whose bakery shop was on the corner of Damory Street and East Street.

Business & Shop Premises

ACL Structures Limited, Holland Way Industrial Estate,
was one of the first occupiers of the estate in 1963
when it was surrounded by farmland.

Blandford Tyre & Battery Service,
Unit 9b Sunrise Business Park.
The 'tyred' lady!!

R & H Crew & Son Ltd,
Wimborne Road – Ford dealers since 1956.

CLP Computer and Office Supplies,
Unit 7, Uplands Industrial Park.

Right: Hospital Metalcraft Limited,
Blandford Heights Industrial Estate
– manufacturers of the 'Bristol
Maid' range of medical equipment.
Established in 1953, they moved
to Blandford 25 years ago.
The founder of Hospital Metalcraft
was Jack Davis and the photograph
shows his grandson Andrew
with some of the office staff.

Right: *Iracroft Limited, Blandford Heights Industrial Estate – bending tubes on Blandford Heights for over 25 years.*

Below: *Sarum Electronics Limited, Clump Farm Industrial Estate – manufacturers of heating and air-conditioning controls. The company moved from Sixpenny Handley to Blandford in April 1997.*

Above: *Wyvern Innleisure Limited, Clump Farm Industrial Estate.*

Left: *Stanley Pond Limited, Blandford Heights Industrial Estate – employees and directors of Stanley Pond Limited. The family began trading in Blandford in 1753.*

Left: *Lesley's Hair Centre, Barnack Walk – established in 1986.*

Below: *John Bilsland, Market Place.*

Above: *Blandford Saddlery, East Street.*

Right: *Gemini, Salisbury Street. Blandford's general drapers from 1987–2002.*

*Arthur Conyers, West Street.
Arthur Conyers established his
gunsmiths business in East Street
in 1886. In Kelly's Directory of 1895
he is shown as having a second shop in
East Street which dealt in bicycles.
He was also shown at this date as being
Captain of the Blandford Fire Brigade.
In early 1900 he acquired the present
premises in West Street and built a
motor garage at the rear where Safeways
now stands. The business was operated
by the Conyers family until November
1981 when the gunsmithing and
fishing-tackle side of the concern was
acquired by the present partners, R.W.
Stagg and C.J. Gordon. The garage was
demolished to make way for Safeways.*

*Greyhound House,
Market Place.*

*Halifax and Douglas
King, East Street.*

*Hairtique,
Salisbury Street.*

*Hardings, West Street – one of
the few shops in Blandford that
has been under the same ownership for more than 30 years.*

*Home décor and DIY, Salisbury
Street – Trevor Knight and Peter
Kellock at the opening of the new
shop in the refurbished Cherry's
building in Salisbury Street.*

*Humberts Chartered
Surveyors, Market Place.*

*Lloyds Bank,
Market Place.*

*Ottoman Restaurant,
East Street.*

Left: *Rowena Ellis –
Patchworkers Paradise,
East Street.*

Below: *Taylors Chemist, Salisbury
Street. Formerly a department
store, the shop has been completely
refurbished inside and is now a
pharmacy. The exterior has been
restored and the original shop
frontage maintained.*

Above: *The Crown Hotel,
West Street. James Mayo
and some of the hard-working
Crown Hotel staff.*

Right: *The Gorge
Café, East Street.*

Public/Advisory Services

*Blandford Community Hospital –
'the heart of a healthy community'.*

*Blandford Fire Station. The officers and fire-fighters of
Blandford Fire Station enjoying a rare break from duty.*

*Eagle House Surgery.
Some of the partners and
staff. Eagle House was
rescued from dereliction
in 1993 – prior to that the
surgery had been at the
Old Bank House.*

Job Centre.

*Tread, Blandford's young people's advice and informa-
tion centre, opened in Salisbury Street in October 1994.
The Centre provides both a social meeting place for
young people and advice and information on a wide
range of issues as well as access to statutory agencies
and specialist organisations.*

Clubs & Groups

Abseiling.

Abseiling.

'The Bells!'

Air Training Corps.

Blandford Rugby Club, Under 11s.

Blandford Rugby Club.

Blandford Scout Group.

Stour Valley Canoe Club.

Stour Valley Canoe Club.

Blandford Carnival

It's spring but we can still put our Carnival Queen on Santa's sledge.

She is either collecting for the Carnival or trying to hitch a lift.

Sometimes they move – sometimes they stop, why?

Blandford Festival

Amazing what you can find on the banks of the Stour during the Festival.

The Town Crier, Mrs Jean Wells, 'Crying' in front of the Fire Monument which was erected in 1760 by John Bastard.

The rear view of the Old House.

Miscellaneous

The eclipse in 1999 wasn't brilliant in Blandford as it was too cloudy although it felt very eerie.

The Mayor of Blandford, Councillor Haydn White, shown with Mr Cyril Hill who has just received the Freedom of Blandford Forum (1999).

Mayor Making Ceremony (1999).

It won't be long before this street furniture looks quaint and old-fashioned!!

Market Day at Blandford Forum.

A selection of the photos from Portrait 2000 which was screened during Christmas 1999.

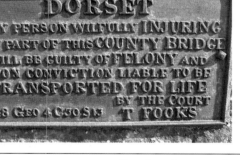

Penal notice erected on Blandford Bridge in the 1830s.

Churches & Halls

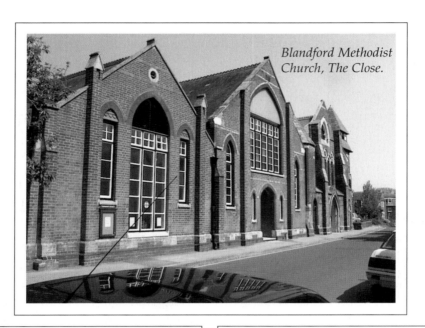

Blandford Methodist Church, The Close.

Blandford Cemetery, Salisbury Road.

Blandford Methodist Church Congregation, The Close.

Town Hall, Market Place.

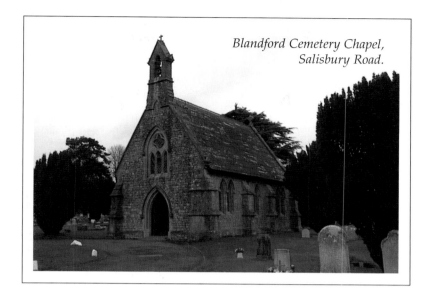

*Blandford Cemetery Chapel,
Salisbury Road.*

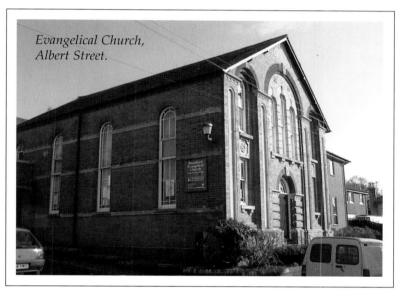

*Evangelical Church,
Albert Street.*

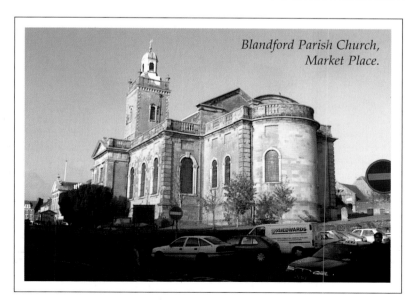

*Blandford Parish Church,
Market Place.*

Subscribers

George Adams, Blandford Forum, Dorset, 1923–2001
G. E. Adams, Poole, Dorset
Dave and Hilary Adlem, Blandford Forum, Dorset
Mr Ernie F. C. Amey
Rosemary A. Amey, Blandford Forum, Dorset
Martin Amey, Orchard Street, Blandford, Dorset
Les Andrews, Blandford Forum, Dorset
Rosemary Angell, Blandford, Dorset
C. F. Ashmore, Redfield, Bristol
James Atkins, Blandford Forum, Dorset
S. Atwell and A. Bealey, Blandford Forum, Dorset
Rita A. Austin, Blandford
William E. F. Avery, Blandford Forum, Dorset
Jill Barber, Fulham, London
Jim Barber, Swinscoe, North Staffordshire
Mike Barber, Terrington, North Yorkshire
Peter Barber, Blandford Forum, Dorset
Denny Barr, Blandford Forum, Dorset
Michael and Lorraine Baskott, Blandford Forum, Dorset
Anthony T. Bastable B.E.M.
Alan and June Bennett, Gillingham, Dorset
Sara Bennett (née Holland), Wimborne, Dorset
Mary D. Berry, Newport, Gwent
Trevor Betts, Brockham, Surrey
Diane Beynon, Blandford Forum, Dorset
The Bignold family, Blandford Forum, Dorset
Roy Biles, Pimperne, Blandford Forum, Dorset
James Bishop, Blandford Grammer School 1954–58
S. Bishopp, Sarum Electronics Ltd.
Joy Thora Blakemore, Blandford Forum, Dorset
Hilton G. Blandford I.Eng. AMRAes., Windsor, Berkshire
Blandford Methodist Church
Mr and Mrs S. Bollatsh, Blandford Forum, Dorset
Lauren A. Brewer, Blandford Forum, Dorset
Martin J. Brickell, Fern Cottage, Blandford Forum, Dorset
Tony and Chris Brighton, Blandford St Mary, Dorset
David L. Brine
Dora M. Bugg, Blandford Forum, Dorset
The Burnley family, Blandford Forum, Dorset
John Burtt, ex Durweston, Dorset
Mr Arthur Bush, Blandford Forum, Dorset
George R. Campion, Blandford Forum, Dorset
Raymond P. and Winifred R. Carter, Blandford Forum, Dorset
Garry C. Cave, Blandford Forum, Dorset
Ann and Arthur Chant, Blandford Forum, Dorset
Mr Nigel C. A. Chard, Blandford St Mary, Dorset
Mrs Ellen Cheeseman, Blandford Forum, Dorset
Mr and Mrs W. J. Christopher, Blandford Forum, Dorset
Patrick A. Collier, Blandford Forum, Dorset
Roy W. Collier, Tiverton, Devon
H. Collis (Blacksmith), Star Yard, Blandford Forum, Dorset
Penny Copland-Griffiths
Susan P. Corp, Reading, Herts.
Matthew G. Cowlard, Blandford Forum, Dorset
Matthew W. and Katrin Cowley, Blandford Forum, Dorset
Gordon R. Cox, Blandford Forum, Dorset
Gaynor C. Cromwell (née Bailey), Salisbury, Wilts.
Tony Cross, Alton, Hants.
Tom Cuff, Blandford Forum, Dorset
Richard H. Cuff, Blandford Forum, Dorset
Fran and Alan Cuff (née Bennett), Wells, Somerset
Pamela Cuff-Urquhart, Perth, Western Australia
Allan R. Cutler, Blandford Forum, Dorset
Mr John Davies, Blandford Forum, Dorset
Mel Davies, Blandford Forum, Dorset
Dulcie Dennis, Blandford Forum, Dorset
Philip Dennis, Witney, Oxon
Brian Dennis, Roskilde, Denmark
William John and Eileen Dennis, Blandford Forum, Dorset

R. and A. Dickinson, Blandford Forum, Dorset
Neil Ditch, Blandford Forum, Dorset
Tom Ditch, Blandford Forum, Dorset
Roger J. Downes, Colchester, Essex
Francis E. R. Downes, Blandford, Dorset
B. E. and S. C. Downes, Blandford, Dorset
Mr R. W. Downes, Blandford, Dorset
Sylvia Dunford, Dover, Kent
Michael D. Edmonds, Jo'burg, R.S. Africa
Dr T. E. Edmonds, Morton, Leics.
David S. G. Edmonds, Blandford Forum, Dorset
Clint R. Ellis, Blandford Forum, Dorset
Simon J. Evans, Blandford Forum, Dorset
Mr A. F. Evetts, Blandford Forum, Dorset
Mr Terrence C. Fenn, Blandford Forum, Dorset
Thersea Field, Eythorne, Kent
Mrs B. Fisher (née Bollatsh), Robertsbridge, Sussex
Mrs M. Fitzgerald, Blandford Forum, Dorset
Georgina Fletcher (née Adams), Sutton, Surrey
Barry E. Foot, Holbury, Hants.
Guy Foot, Lascelles Court, Bournemouth
Celia Foot, Blandford, Dorset
Raymond B. Foot, Blandford St Mary, Dorset
Brian Foot, Blandford Forum, Dorset
Leslie R. J. Foot, Glastonbury, Somerset
Mrs P. Foster-Bazin, Blandford Forum, Dorset
Paul Francis, Blandford, Dorset
N. Fry, Weymouth, Dorset
L. Fry, Blandford Forum, Dorset
Lewis W. Fry
Brian and Anita Fry, Okeford Fitzpaine, Blandford, Dorset
J. and J. Fulluck, Blandford Forum, Dorset
Jennifer C. Galuschka, Blandford Forum, Dorset
Mrs Linda J. Garbutt, Blandford Forum, Dorset
Maureen V. George, Blanford Forum, Dorset
Betty Gillingham, Blandford Forum, Dorset
Rose and Dave Goddard, Blandford Forum, Dorset
Joan Goldsbrough, Blandford Forum, Dorset
Mrs C. E. Guest (née Hardy), Blandford Forum, Dorset
Ruth M. Hallett, Blandford Forum, Dorset
P. and A. Hancock, Blandford Forum, Dorset
Richard J. Hardy, Blandford Forum, Dorset
Peter G. Hardy, Blandford, Dorset
Brian Harris, Blandford Forum, Dorset
Colin G. Harvey, Toronto, Canada
Haskell, Blandford Forum, Dorset
Colin and Maureen Haskett, Melbourne, Australia
Mrs Samantha J. Hawkins, Blandford Forum, Dorset
Peter J. Hawkins, Blandford St Mary, Dorset
Jennifer Haywood
Roger K. G. and Patricia E. Healing, Blandford Forum, Dorset
The Heaney family
Bethany Hendry, Blandford Forum, Dorset
Lt Col. and Mrs D. P. Herring, Blandford Forum, Dorset
Cyril E. Hill, Blandford Forum, Dorset
R. A. and W. J. Hill
Mr Philip D., Mrs Violet M., and Miss Angela R. Hiscock, Blandford Forum
Mrs G. Hobbs (née Foot), Blandford, Dorset
Mr Matthew J. Holland, Blandford, Dorset
Owen and Marlene Holland, Blandford, Dorset
Harry Horlock-Stringer, Lopen, South Somerset
Marjorie E. Hosking, Blandford Forum, Dorset
Eleanor Howard, Blandford Forum, Dorset
Nigel and Jackie Hudson, Blandford Forum, Dorset
Mr and Mrs Martin G. Hunt, Blandford Forum, Dorset
Val Ingram, Blandford Grammar School 1953–60
Simon Jacobson, Blandford Forum, Dorset
Phyl James, Blandford Forum, Dorset
Geoffrey G. James, Blandford Forum, Dorset
Sam and David Jardine
Gerald F. Jones, Blandford Forum, Dorset
Nigel P. Jones, Blandford Forum, Dorset

Anne C. Jones, Blandford Forum, Dorset
Rachael Joseph (née Holland), Blandford, Dorset
Thelma and Reg Joyce and family, Blandford Forum, Dorset
Mrs Sylvia B. Kelly (née Stickley), Liphook, Hampshire
A. M. and A. B. Kerby, Blandford, Dorset
Zena M. and John D. Kerley
Mrs B. M. Killer, Blandford Forum, Dorset
Adrian, Louise and Emma Knight, Blandford Forum, Dorset
Hazel J. Knight, Blandford Forum, Dorset
Anthea Lancaster, Marnhull, Dorset
Michael Lane, Blandford Forum, Dorset
Tina and Ted Langford, Blandford Forum, Dorset
Mr J. G. (Jim) Langridge, Blandford Forum, Dorset
David and Ruth Law (née Barnes), Queensland, Australia
Mr and Mrs J. Laws, Blandford Forum, Dorset
Doug and Myrtle Leak (née Thorne), Blandford Forum, Dorset
Kenneth R. Lillington, Blandford Forum, Dorset
Sheila M. Lockyer, Bournemouth, Dorset
Duncan MacIntyre, Braco, Perthshire
The Madill family
Bridget Maidment, Blandford, Dorset
Brian and Ann Manson, Blandford Forum, Dorset
Dudley T. J. Manson
Barry Mason, Vancouver, Canada
Peter and Susan McCahy, Blandford Forum, Dorset
Geoffrey H. McEwen, Blandford Forum, Dorset
Betty M. McGill, Blandford Forum, Dorset
Heather McIntosh, Blandford Forum, Dorset
Robert W. McLaren, Blandford Forum, Dorset
Stuart Alexander McLean
Myra McSherry (née Bailey), Messingham, N. Lincs.
Maureen Melbourne, Blandford Forum, Dorset
Ann Miles, Blandford Forum, Dorset
Sue and Vic Miles (née Bennett), Pimperne, Dorset
Mr and Mrs S. Miles and family, Blandford Forum, Dorset
Sarah Mitchell, Blandford Forum, Dorset
Jacqueline Mockford, Damory Down, Blandford Forum, Dorset
Lily May Morgan (née Foot)
Barbara Morris (née Legge), Sutton Coldfield/formerly of Pimperne
Gerald and Susan Mosney, Blandford Forum, Dorset
Joop Mous and Will Vlaskamp, Breda, Nederland
Mrs Valerie B. Nankervis, Blandford Forum, Dorset
Mr Kenneth Neale, Winterbourne Houghton, Blandford, Dorset
Margaret Lucy and Michael Neill Neill, Blandford Forum, Dorset
Gordon S. Nobles, Blandford Forum, Dorset
Alan S. Nobles, Blandford Forum, Dorset
Kevin O'Donnell, Blandford Forum, Dorset
Shaun P. O'Donnell, Blandford Forum, Dorset
Carol G. Oliver
Tom Ormerod, Lower Bryanston, Dorset
Peter G. Oxford, Blandford Forum, Dorset
Edwin C. Parker, Blandford Forum, Dorset
David Parry, Bryanston Street, Blandford Forum, Dorset
Major John Paton (Ret'd) Ex Reme, Inverurie, Aberdeenshire
Pat and Jan Patrick, Navan, Second Street, Blandford, Dorset
Barry Payne, Gauteng, R. South Africa
Mrs Doris E. Payne (née Steel), Blandford Forum, Dorset
Kitty Peverley (née Clark), Blandford Forum, Dorset
Eric Pike, Blandford Forum, Dorset
Andrew John Pike, Blandford Forum, Dorset
Richard Pilcher, Cerne Abbas, Dorset
Frederick H. Pitman, Blandford Forum, Dorset
A. H. A. and B. A. Pluthero, Blandford Forum, Dorset
Tim Pond, Blandford Forum, Dorset
Andrew and Sally Porter, Blandford Forum, Dorset
Dorothy E. Powell, Blandford Forum, Dorset
L. W. Prill, Blandford Forum, Dorset
Mr Harold and Mrs Doris Pullman, Blandford Forum, Dorset
David and Susan Randles and family, Blandford Forum, Dorset
Ian J. Read, Larksmead, Blandford Forum, Dorset
John and Pam Rees, Blandford Forum, Dorset
Miss Ann Rice, Hill View, Alfred Street, Blandford Forum, Dorset

Sandra Richards, Blandford Forum, Dorset
Ian R. Ricketts, Blandford Forum, Dorset
Richard T. Riding
Regan W. Rimmer, Blandford Forum, Dorset
Paul A. Rimmer, Blandford Forum, Dorset
Mr Andrew Robertson, Blandford Forum, Dorset
Judith A. Robertson, Tarrant Keyneston, Dorset
Mr and Mrs B. Rodgers, Blandford Forum, Dorset
Dorothy Samways, Admirals Walk, Bournemouth
Betty Scott, Blandford Forum, Dorset
Jacky and Brian Scott, Iwerne Minster, Blandford, Dorset
Gillian M. Sibley, Blandford Forum, Dorset
Sue Simpson, Blandford Forum, Dorset
Georgina Skeats, Blandford Forum, Dorset
Peter Slocombe, Pimperne, Dorset
John M. Smith, Blandford Forum, Dorset
Mr and Mrs R. J. Spreadbury, Pimperne, Blandford Forum, Dorset
Mr and Mrs R. R. Spreadbury, Blandford Forum, Dorset
Patricia V. Squibb, Blandford Forum, Dorset
 St. Leonard's School, Blandford Forum, Dorset
Mrs E. G. Stacey (née Hardy), Bromley, Kent
Mark Stanley, Blandford Forum, Dorset
Vi M. Stapenhill, Blandford Forum, Dorset
Graeme G. Stapenhill, Ferndown, Dorset
Anita Starkey, Blandford Forum, Dorset
Paul, Tracy, Natalie, Georgia and Victoria Starr, Blandford Forum, Dorset
P. A. Stephens, Blandford Forum, Dorset
Suzette Street (née Holland), Wimborne, Dorset
Pamela Sturmey, Blandford, Dorset
Mr C. Sturmey, Blandford, Dorset
Stanley, Margaret and Michelle Tapper, Blandford Forum, Dorset
Mr G. J. and Mrs K. Y. Tapper, Pimperne, Dorset
Ian and Norma Taylor, Blandford Forum, Dorset
Jonathan D. Taylor, Blandford Forum, Dorset
Philip G. Thorne, Blandford Forum, Dorset
J. P. L. Tory, Durweston
Nigel and Pam Towning, Blandford Forum, Dorset
J. O. R. Tupper, Blandford Forum, Dorset
Mr Dave Upton, Blandford Forum, Dorset
Norman and Carol Vatcher, Bryanston, Dorset
Karen White and Stephen Vaughan, Blandford Forum, Dorset
Andrew, Trudi, and Jessica Vick, Blandford Forum, Dorset
Mrs Renee Wallace, (née Wells), Blandford Forum, Dorset
John F. W. Walling, Newton Abbot, Devon
Mr M. Arnold Wallis, Blandford, Dorset
Gordon 'Jim' Wareham, Blandford Forum, Dorset
Leslie George Warren
Mr and Mrs A. Warwick, Pimperne, Blandford, Dorset
Fred Waterman, Pimperne, Dorset
Dennis E. Waterman, Blandford Forum, Dorset
Janet and Stephen Webb, Blandford Forum, Dorset
Miss Doreen Wells, Blandford Forum, Dorset
Western Design Architects
Kingsley A. C. White, Blandford Forum, Dorset
H. R. and G. White, Blandford Forum, Dorset
Heather and Brian White, Blandford Forum, Dorset
Amanda, Christopher and David Wileman and Ian Taft,
    Blandford Forum
Sally Williams, Blandford Forum, Dorset
Jean and David Williams, Blandford Forum, Dorset
Ellie Wills 16.11.99 and Connor Wills 22.10.96, Blandford Forum, Dorset
Dr Ian Wilson, Blandford
Steve Witt, Fleetwood, Lancs.
Robin Witt, Oxford
Bill Witt, Blandford Forum, Dorset
Mr Gerald Witt
Mary and Alan Woodland, Elizabeth Road, Blandford Forum, Dorset
Mr and Mrs H. Woolley, Blandford Forum, Dorset
Stephen, Lesley and Gary Wright, Blandford
Robin M. Wyatt, Blandford Forum, Dorset
Wyvern Inn Leisure Ltd., Clump Farm Industrial Estate
Margaret E. Yeatman, Blandford Forum, Dorset

ALSO AVAILABLE IN THE SERIES

SOME OF THE MANY FORTHCOMING TITLES

For details of any of the above titles or if you are
interested in writing your own community history, please
contact: Community Histories Editor, Halsgrove House,
Lower Moor Way, Tiverton Business Park, Tiverton,
Devon EX16 6SS, England, e-mail: sales@halsgrove.com
If you are particularly interested in any of the images in
this volume, it may be possible to supply a copy.
Please telephone 01884 243242 for details.

*In order to include as many historic photographs as
possible in this volume, a printed index is not
included. However, the Community Histories are
currently being indexed by Genuki. For further
information and indexes to volumes in the
series, please visit:
http://www.cs.ncl.ac.uk/genuki/DEV/indexingproject.html*